CIVIL WAR
101

CIVIL WAR

101

Donald Cartmell

GRAMERCY BOOKS
NEW YORK

This 2003 edition is published by Gramercy Books, an imprint of
Random House Value Publishing, a division of Random House, Inc.,
New York, by arrangement with Career Press.

Gramercy is a registered trademark and the colophon
is a trademark of Random House, Inc.

Random House
New York • Toronto • London • Sydney • Auckland
www.randomhouse.com

Edited by Dianna Walsh
Typesetting and Interior Design by John J. O'Sullivan

Printed and bound in the United States

A catalog record for this title is available from the Library of Congress.

ISBN 0-517-22308-2

10 9 8 7 6 5 4 3 2 1

Dedication

This book is dedicated to my son Seamus,
and to all my friends and family
who rallied around the flag
when the cause seemed lost.

*"War on paper and war in the field are as different as darkness from light,
fire from water, or heaven from earth."*

—William Faulkner

Acknowledgments

I would like to thank Robert Cartmell and Jere Berger for keeping my Web site *This Week in the Civil War* up and running while I was otherwise occupied working on this book.

Also, thanks to Tom Hornback for his assistance with list ideas and for his help in procuring many of the pictures featured in this book, especially those from the National Archives.

A special nod also goes to Peter Trumbull for helping to edit the book and for going over many of the extremely rough early drafts.

Finally, thank you to Michael Lewis and all the people at New Page Books for their encouragement and assistance throughout this project.

Contents

Introduction

INTEREST IN THE CIVIL War has ebbed and flowed ever since the old veterans began passing away. The first great outpouring of attention in the 20th century was driven by the creativity of a wave of Southern writers like William Faulkner and Robert Penn Warren. These authors were part of the last generation who were able to see an old Rebel veteran in person and to experience life in a rural-based economy, yet they also were the first to witness the beginnings of large-scale commercial growth in the South. It was this dichotomy that spurred their exploration into the meaning of the war and its impact on American culture.

The next great wave of interest occurred during the Civil War centennial in 1961-1965. Much like the celebration of the American bicentennial in 1976, this national experience was driven by commerce. Kicked off in Montgomery, Alabama, by the reenactment of the inauguration of Jefferson Davis, 46 states set up centennial commissions to organize and sponsor various events. As is usually the case, this type of overexposure led to a glut of inferior products and a general malaise in the public's attitude toward the Civil War that lasted far longer than the

The battle of Bentonville, North Carolina, the last major battle of the war. (Library of Congress)

original celebration. It is painfully apparent at many Civil War battlefields that the visiting room maps and displays have not been updated since the centennial. Park attendance has also suffered when compared to competing recreational activities. As an example, the Stones River battlefield, located in Murfreesboro, Tennessee, drew only 138,000 visitors in 1977; by contrast, Opryland, U.S.A, a country music-related theme park only 30 miles away drew more than two million paying customers.

The tide began to turn again when Michael Shaara's book *The Killer Angels* was published in 1975. Despite the fact that the book received mixed reviews and sold poorly, Shaara was awarded the Pulitzer Prize for his fictional portrayal of Gettysburg. *The Killer Angels* might have languished as just another good Civil War novel if Ted Turner hadn't chosen to film it as the inaugural offering of historical movies he planned to broadcast on television. Renamed *Gettysburg*, the film turned out so well that Turner decided to release it as a full-fledged movie. However, before Ted Turner brought *The Killer Angels* to life, Shaara's novel had had an even greater impact on the resurrection of the Civil War. It was on Christmas Day in 1984 that filmmaker Ken Burns finished reading *The Killer Angels*. The book gave Burns the "courage" he needed to take on the challenge of turning the Civil War into a documentary.

More than anything else, Burns' documentary shook the cobwebs off the Civil War by focusing on ordinary people and how they were affected by, and sometimes changed, history. Burns described the Civil War as "the American Iliad, as relevant today as at any time in our history," and as "more defining of us as a nation than any other event before or after." It is a measure of the war's enduring hold on the imagination of Americans that we as a nation keep coming back to the Civil War. Perhaps the phenomenon was best described by social philosopher Lewis Mumford, who said that each generation rediscovers and re-examines that part of their past that brings the present new meaning and new possibilities. For Americans, that part of the past is the Civil War.

The vast scope of the war and the vibrant personalities who rose to greatness during this country's harshest trial by fire have left behind a rich tapestry of facts, figures, quotes, enigmas, and stories. This book touches on some of them, it is hoped, in an interesting and informative way. It is easy for the casual reader, or even for someone who studies the war in depth, to get lost in the minutiae and vast array of details that are available. By including a variety of loosely related topics, I hope to add some flavor to the war and to bring some perspective to this, the greatest American tragedy.

CHAPTER 1

Looking Back, Looking Forward

T HE ONLY THING THAT both the North and South could agree on in the 1860s was that each side was fighting for freedom. One of the songs that typified the era and that was extremely popular on both sides of the lines, albeit with slightly different lyrics, was *The Battle Cry of Freedom*. This song was originally written by George F. Root for a rally at Court House Square in Chicago. While Northern soldiers sang the original lyrics: "Down with the traitors, up with the star," their Southern counterparts responded with: "Down with the eagle, up with the cross." However, both sides agreed when it came time to shout "the battle cry of freedom." When he traveled to Gettysburg to dedicate the National Cemetery in November 1863, Abraham Lincoln declared that the North was fighting for a "new birth of freedom." Never able to match Old Abe's flair with the pen, Jefferson Davis, nevertheless, was equally adamant about the cause he represented. According to Davis, the South was forced to take up arms "to vindicate the political rights, the freedom, equality, and State sovereignty which were...purchased by the blood of our revolutionary sires."

The ruins of Columbia, South Carolina.
(Library of Congress)

While they could agree that freedom was the issue at stake, finding a suitable name for the conflict remained elusive. Many Southerners heralded the revolutionary aspects of the cause, but unfortunately the title "Revolutionary War" had already been taken. After the war was long over and work was begun compiling all the documents of the war into an official record, a suitable name had to be found that would be acceptable to both sides. After much discussion, "The War of the Rebellion" was chosen and seemed to settle the matter. However, 20 years after the *Official Records* were published, Congress decided to give its opinion on the proper name for the conflict. On March 2, 1928, in Senate Joint Resolution No. 41, Congress recognized the name "War Between the States" as the official name because, they argued, 22 non-seceding states made war upon 11 seceding states to force them back into the Union of States. Over the years, however, this controversy fell into obscurity because most Americans simply began to refer to it as "The Civil War."

The term *civil war* was originally used by Julius Caesar in his memoirs to describe the struggle between his forces and those of his rival Gnaeus Pompeius for control of the Roman state. Since that time, the designation has been used almost exclusively to describe wars between factions within a state for control over that entire state. The following is a list of some of the wars that fit that classical definition:

8 Classic Examples of Civil Wars

1. The War of the Roses in England (1455-1485)
2. The War of Three Henries in France (1587-1589)
3. The English Civil War (1642-1650)
4. The Carlist Wars in Spain (1833-1839 and 1872-1876)
5. The Taiping Rebellion in China (1850-1864)
6. The Chilean Civil War (1891)
7. The Russian Civil War (1918-1920)
8. The Spanish Civil War (1936-1939)

4 STATES STILL FLYING THE CONFEDERATE FLAG

1. Georgia: Based on the Stars and Bars, the battle flag was added to the fly.
2. Florida: Red saltire cross to recall the battle flag added in 1900.
3. Alabama: White with red saltire cross to salute the Confederate battle flag.
4. Mississippi: The canton is the battle flag, and three horizontal stripes recall the Stars and Bars.

☆☆☆

The name "Civil War" is not really an accurate description of the American conflict of 1861-1865. First, the United States of America never officially recognized the existence of the Confederate States of America. To do so would have paved the way for European intervention in the conflict. Lincoln always maintained that secession was illegal, and he even disavowed the "presidency" of Jefferson Davis. On the other hand, the Confederate States passed an act "recognizing the existence of a war between the United States and the Confederate States" on May 6, 1861. More importantly, it was never the goal of the Confederacy to displace or supplant the Federal government in Washington. Legally speaking, secession entailed only the right to withdraw from the United States. With all this confusion, it is no wonder that the war has been given numerous titles throughout the years. The following is a list of some of the other names used to describe this great conflict:

28 Alternate Names for the Civil War

1. The War for Constitutional Liberty
2. The War for Nationality
3. The War for Southern Nationality
4. The Second American Revolution
5. The War for Southern Independence
6. The War for States' Rights
7. Mr. Lincoln's War
8. The Southern Rebellion
9. The War for Southern Rights
10. The War Against Northern Aggression
11. The Yankee Invasion
12. The War for Separation
13. The War for Southern Freedom
14. The Lost Cause
15. The Late Unpleasantness
16. The War to Suppress Yankee Arrogance
17. The War of the Southern Planters
18. America's Civil War
19. The War Between the States
20. The Civil War Between the States
21. The War for Abolition
22. The War for the Union
23. The Confederate War
24. The War of the Southerners
25. The War of the North and South
26. The War Against Slavery
27. The War of the Rebellion
28. The Brothers' War

The reason many of these names have a certain Southern flair is because the war means different things and is learned about in different ways in the South than in other parts of the country. Southern author Robert Penn Warren described it this way: "I…picked up a vaguely soaked-in popular notion of the Civil War, the wickedness of Yankees, [and] the justice of the Southern cause….The impression of the Civil War certainly did not come from my own household ….I got it from the air around me."

Novelist and historian Shelby Foote put it even more bluntly: "Southerners are in close touch with some things that the rest of the country doesn't know much about, and one of them is military defeat." The following is a list of statistics that describe the devastating effects that the war had on the Southern people:

20 Confederate Statistics of Defeat

1. 25 percent of all white men of military age in the South were killed.
2. 4 percent of the total population of the South was killed during the war.
3. 1 of every 19 white Southerners perished during the war.
4. 25 percent of all participants (including blacks) were left incapacitated by the war.
5. 25 percent of the South's general officers were killed during the war.
6. The population of the Confederate states dropped by 500,000 during the war years.
7. More than 10,000 former slave holders abandoned their homes and left the South after the war.
8. $2 billion worth of property (meaning slaves) was lost as a result of the war.
9. $34 million worth of war property was claimed by treasury agents.
10. 66 percent of all assessed wealth, including the market value of slaves, was lost.
11. The public debt in 1866 in North Carolina and South Carolina combined was $23 million.
12. Land was valued at $3 to $5 an acre after the war, 17 percent of its value in 1860.
13. The real value of all property dropped 30 percent.
14. The Freedman's Bureau controlled more than 850,000 acres of abandoned land.
15. 500,000 farms and plantations in the South were bankrupt, insolvent, or destroyed.
16. The price of cotton fell from $1.25 per pound to less than $0.20 per pound.
17. In Columbia, South Carolina, alone, 1,386 buildings were burned or in ruins.
18. More than 60 percent of Southern-based railroad companies were bankrupt and most rail lines were inoperable.
19. All states that seceded were subject to martial law by a Federal occupation force.
20. 20 percent of the total revenue of Mississippi in 1866 was allotted for buying artificial arms and legs.

☆☆☆

The major reason for the economic devastation of the South after the war was very simple: Most of the time, the armies were marching, fighting, and foraging on Southern soil. One can only imagine the impact that an army of 100,000 or so hungry soldiers can have on a neighborhood. The four most devastated sections of the South were the 100-mile corridor between Richmond and Washington, the scene

Battle debris on Henry House Hill after first battle of Bull Run.
(Library of Congress)

of most of the battles between the Army of the Potomac and the Army of Northern Virginia; the path of General Sherman's army during his march through Georgia; the Shenandoah Valley, burned by Phil Sheridan's men in the autumn of 1864; and Middle Tennessee, the scene for major campaigns in every year of the war. The following is a list of the states that saw the most fighting during the war:

14 States That Had the Most Engagements

	State	*Number of Engagements*
1.	Virginia	519
2.	Tennessee	298
3.	Missouri	244
4.	Georgia	108
5.	Mississippi	186
6.	Arkansas	167
7.	Kentucky	138
8.	Louisiana	118
9.	North Carolina	85
10.	West Virginia	80
11.	Alabama	78
12.	South Carolina	60
13.	Florida	32
14.	Maryland	30

☆☆☆

Given the fact that neither side could agree on a single name for the entire war, it should not be surprising that many of the 2,255 officially recognized engagements also have multiple names. One of the reasons for this was the Union command's obsession with rivers and streams. When a major battle was fought, the Union commanding general usually sought to name it after the nearest body of water. Daniel Harvey Hill, the acerbic-tongued Confederate general, explained it this way: "The troops of the North came mainly from cities, towns, and villages, and were, therefore, impressed by some natural object near the scene of the conflict and named the battle from it. The soldiers from the South were chiefly from the country and were, therefore, impressed by some artificial object near the field of action....Thus, the first passage of arms is called the battle of Bull Run in the North, [from] the name of a little stream. In the South it takes the name of Manassas, from a railroad station." The following is a list of some of the major battles with multiple names:

15 Battles with Two Names

	Union Name	*Confederate Name*
1.	Bull Run	Manassas
2.	Wilson's Creek	Oak Hills
3.	Logan's Cross Roads	Mill Springs
4.	Pea Ridge	Elkhorn Tavern
5.	Pittsburg Landing	Shiloh
6.	Fair Oaks	Seven Pines
7.	Second Bull Run	Second Manassas
8.	South Mountain	Boonsboro
9.	Antietam	Sharpsburg
10.	Chaplin Hills	Perryville
11.	Stones River	Murfreesboro
12.	Elk Creek	Honey Springs
13.	Olustee	Ocean Pond
14.	Sabine Cross Roads	Mansfield
15.	Opequan Creek	Winchester

☆☆☆

The term *Lost Cause* was popularized by Richmond journalist Edward Pollard in 1866 when he published the first comprehensive history of the war under that title. Since that time, thousands of books and articles have been published about the Civil War. It is a measure of the war's persisting popularity that it was also featured in many of the early moving pictures. When the veterans of Gettysburg gathered for the 50th anniversary of the battle in 1913, Thomas Ince's *The Battle of Gettysburg* was showing in movie theaters around the country. The movie premiered at New York's Grand Opera House to a capacity crowd that went wild. Perhaps the most important and groundbreaking movie released in the 20th century was D.W. Griffith's *The Birth of a Nation,* and the films most spectacular scenes were the battle sequences that were filmed at night and made to resemble Mathew Brady photographs. Another popular movie that featured the "Lost Cause" and the Civil War was *Gone with the Wind*. Although not as historically flawed as *The Birth of a Nation*, this film also suffers from racial stereotyping and a romanticization of plantation life.

The focus shifted the next time the Civil War was resurrected for mass consumption. The production by the ABC television network was called *Roots*, and it marked the emergence of a new television format called the miniseries. Thirteen years later, Ken Burns tapped into America's love affair with the Civil War to bring attention to yet another television format—the documentary. The success and popularity of Burns' *The Civil War* is perhaps the most surprising and revealing. Not only did 40 million people tune into PBS to watch the documentary, but they stayed for 11 hours of stark black-and-white photographs. The following is a list of films that have used the Civil War as a theme or as a backdrop:

50 Civil War-Related Films

1. *The Birth of a Nation* (1915)
2. *The General* (1926)
3. *Jezebel* (1938)
4. *General Spanky* (1936)
5. *Gone with the Wind* (1939)
6. *Jesse James* (1939)
7. *Abe Lincoln in Illinois* (1940)
8. *Dark Command* (1940)
9. *Santa Fe Trail* (1940)
10. *Virginia City* (1940)
11. *Young Mr. Lincoln* (1940)
12. *They Died with Their Boots on* (1942)
13. *A Southern Yankee* (1948)
14. *She Wore a Yellow Ribbon* (1949)
15. *The Red Badge of Courage* (1951)
16. *Yellow Neck* (1955)
17. *Friendly Persuasion* (1956)
18. *The Searchers* (1956)
19. *Raintree County* (1957)
20. *The Proud Rebel* (1958)
21. *The Horse Soldiers* (1959)
22. *The Jayhawkers* (1959)
23. *An Occurrence at Owl Creek Bridge* (1962)

22 Popular Songs of the Civil War

1. "Dixie"
2. "Old Black Joe"
3. "'Tis But a Little Faded Flower"
4. "John Brown's Body"
5. "Maryland, My Maryland"
6. "The Vacant Chair"
7. "Battle Hymn of the Republic"
8. "The Bonnie Blue Flag"
9. "Drafted into the Army"
10. "We Are Coming, Father Abraham, 300,000 More"
11. "Babylon Is Fallen"
12. "The Battle Cry of Freedom"
13. "Just Before the Battle, Mother"
14. "When Johnnie Comes Marching Home"
15. "All Quiet Along the Potomac Tonight"
16. "Beautiful Dreamer"
17. "Come Home, Father"
18. "Sherman's March to the Sea"
19. "Tenting on the Old Camp Ground"
20. "Where, Oh Where, Has My Little Dog Gone"
21. "Ellie Rhee"
22. "Marching Through Georgia"

24. *Johnny Shiloh* (1963)
25. *Rio Conchos* (1964)
26. *Major Dundee* (1965)
27. *Shenandoah* (1965)
28. *Alvarez Kelly* (1966)
29. *The Desperados through Texas* (1968)
30. *The Undefeated* (1969)
31. *The Beguiled* (1970)
32. *Rio Lobo* (1970)
33. *The Outlaw Josey Wales* (1976)
34. *Roots* (1977)
35. *The Private History of a Campaign that Failed* (1981)
36. *The Blue and the Gray* (1982)
37. *Uncle Tom's Cabin* (1987)
38. *Glory* (1989)
39. *Civil War Diary* (1990)
40. *The Civil War* (1989)
41. *Dances with Wolves* (1990)
42. *The Last of Mrs. Lincoln* (1991)
43. *The Killing Box* (1993)
44. *Gettysburg* (1993)
45. *Guns of Honor* (1994)
46. *Rewriting History* (1995)
47. *Andersonville* (1996)
48. *The Night Lincoln Was Shot* (1998)
49. *The Hunley* (1999)
50. *Ride with the Devil* (1999)

☆☆☆

In addition to being reflected in movies and films, the Civil War also holds the roots of many prominent and powerful people. A quick look at these relationships shows numerous ties to the great conflict and may also reveal something about the character of these men. For example, while Jimmy Carter and Dwight Eisenhower could each boast of having two grandfathers who fought in the war, neither Theodore Roosevelt nor Franklin Delano Roosevelt could make such a claim. In fact, Teddy's father hired a substitute to avoid being drafted and Franklin's grandfather concerned himself with business ventures during the war. Poor Warren G. Harding's father tried to enlist twice in the Union Army, only to be rejected both times after contracting typhoid fever. The following is a list of five modern politicians or generals whose lives were touched by the war:

5 20th-Century Figures Touched by the War

1. **Woodrow Wilson:** Surprisingly, Wilson, who would later be president of Princeton University and Governor of New Jersey, spent the war years as a small boy in Augusta, Georgia. His first memory as a 4-year-old was standing in his father's gateway and hearing someone pass by and say that Mr. Lincoln was elected and there was to be a war. Wilson was not old enough to fight for the South, but he was old enough to help make cartridges in his living room for the embattled Confederate army in Georgia. Later in life, Wilson would freely admit that he believed that the South was fully justified in seceding from the Union, and he also held a private screening of *Birth of a Nation* in the White House and proclaimed that the film was "all too true."

2. **Richard Nixon:** On July 3, 1863, musician (drummer) Richard Enderlin of Company B, 73rd Ohio Volunteer Infantry Regiment, risked his own life to crawl between the lines to save a desperately wounded man who was crying in such pain that Enderlin could stand it no longer. The wounded soldier was Private George Nixon. Ignoring the constant firing around him, Enderlin reached Nixon, who was lying only a short distance in front of the Confederate picket line, and dragged him to the safety of the Union lines. Unfortunately, Nixon's wound was mortal; he died and was buried in the Gettysburg National Cemetery. For his bravery, Enderlin was promoted to sergeant by his company commander. George Nixon left behind an infant son who would later become the father of President Richard Nixon.

3. **Harry Truman:** Truman's grandparents, Solomon and Harriet Young, lived in Liberty, Missouri, and were visited five times by foraging Union soldiers. On the most memorable occasion, Jim Lane, an ardent abolitionist and future senator from Kansas, personally directed the plundering. After William Quantrill sacked Lawrence, Kansas, the Youngs, along with 20,000 fellow Missourians, were forced into exile for allegedly supporting Rebel guerrillas. Truman's great-uncle, Jim "Crow" Chiles, rode with William Quantrill and "Bloody Bill" Anderson and by all accounts was a hearty participant in their murderous activities during the war. He survived the war and was killed in a gunfight with the Deputy Marshall of Independence, Missouri. Harry's father, John Truman, was too young to fight in the war, but was forced to flee the house and hide in a cornfield one night when Rebel cavalrymen came looking for recruits.

4. **General Douglas MacArthur:** As an 18-year-old lieutenant in the 24th Wisconsin at the battle of Chattanooga, Tennessee, Arthur MacArthur grabbed the regimental colors during the charge up Missionary Ridge. Although he was a conspicuous target, MacArthur received only a scratch

while succeeding in leading the rush to the top of the ridge; he was awarded the Congressional Medal of Honor for his heroics. Before the war was over, Arthur would rise to the rank of lieutenant-colonel and see action in numerous battles in the West. Seventy-nine years later, his son Douglas would also win the Medal of Honor for his tenacious defense of the Philippine Islands and the island of Corregidor during World War II. They are the only father and son to win the prestigious award.

World War II hero General George Patton being greeted in Los Angeles, California.
(National Archives)

5. **General George S. Patton:**
Like his father, grandfather, and three great-uncles, George attended the Virginia Military Institute. (George lasted only one year before transferring to West Point.) While George earned his fame as a tank commander during World War II, his grandfather served as an infantry commander in the Confederate army during the Civil War. George Smith Patton served as colonel of the 22nd Virginia Infantry and was killed in the third battle of Winchester, Virginia, in September 1864. Great-uncle Waller Tazewall Patton served as colonel of the 7th Virginia Infantry, and was mortally wounded at Gettysburg. Great-uncle John May Patton served as colonel of the 21st Virginia Regiment. Finally, great-uncle William McFarland Patton fought as a cadet sergeant in Company B of the Corps of Cadets at the battle of New Market, Virginia, and participated in the victorious charge that ended the battle. His family heritage had such a strong influence on George Patton that throughout his life he believed in reincarnation and felt that he had lived as a warrior in previous times and places.

32 FAMOUS CIVIL WAR HORSES

1. Ajax: Ridden by Robert E. Lee early in the Civil War; was too big and returned to the farm.
2. Baldy: Belonged to George Meade. Shot several times but always recovered.
3. Bayard: Union General Philip Kearny's black horse. Kearny was killed while riding him.
4. Beauregard: Belonged to Wade Hampton; bold-spirited horse was killed in battle in 1863.
5. Beppo: Charger belonged to Union General Judson Kilpatrick, killed in battle at Aldie, Virginia.
6. Billy: Belonged to General George Thomas; a big powerful bay named after General Sherman.
7. Billy: Owned by Union General James Penfield. His name is on a monument in New York.
8. Billy: Belonged to Union Lt. Frank Haskell. Shot in the lung but carried Haskell to safety.
9. Black Bess: Confederate General John Hunt Morgan's black mare.
10. Brown Roan: Ridden by Robert E. Lee early in the Civil War; not up to the strain of battle.
11. Bullet: A bay horse used by General Jeb Stuart.
12. Burns: General George McClellan's tall black horse. It would head to the stable at dinner time.
13. Butler: Ridden by General Wade Hampton. Won a jumping contest after the war.
14. Chancellor: Ridden by Jeb Stuart; killed at Chancellorsville.
15. Charlie: Belonged to General Nathaniel Banks. Known as the only horse to unseat Ulysses S. Grant.
16. Cincinnati: Given to Grant by dying man in Cincinnati; he refused 10,000 in gold for him.
17. Comet: Owned by Confederate Colonel Blackford; dark mahogany bay with a white star.
18. Custis Lee: George A. Custer's horse. Killed accidentally in a buffalo hunt after the war.
19. Daniel Webster: George McClellan's dark bay thoroughbred.
20. Decatur: Union General Philip Kearny's horse; he died in battle.
21. Dolly: Belonged to William T. Sherman until stolen.
22. Don Juan: General Custer rode him in the Grand Review.
23. Fannie: Belonged to General Joseph Johnston; a bay thoroughbred; survived the war and retired.
24. General: A gray ridden by Jeb Stuart at Battle of Yellow Tavern in 1864.
25. Hero: James Longstreet's favorite bay charger; name pronounced as Haro.
26. Sam: General Sherman's bay, a fast walker, wounded several times. He died in 1884.
27. Skylark: Belonged to Jeb Stuart, a gift from a female admirer.
28. Traveler: Favorite of Robert E. Lee. Buried on campus of Washington and Lee University.
29. Napoleon: Winfield Scott's favorite, died at 30 in 1870.
30. Nellie Gray: Confederate General Fitzhugh Lee's horse; killed at battle of Winchester.
31. Old Sorrel: Stonewall Jackson's favorite; skeleton preserved at VMI museum in Lexington
32. Virginia: A bay thoroughbred ridden by Jeb Stuart at Gettysburg.

CHAPTER 2

Timeline to Secession

THERE HAVE BEEN MILLIONS of words written about the various causes of the Civil War. However, whether the reasons cited are states' rights, the pressures of westward expansion, or the growing industrial and political power of the North, slavery is always lurking just below the surface. Not only did slavery divide the country politically, it also divided the nation geographically, and these were the two primary ingredients necessary for civil war. The way the economies of the North and the South developed in the 17th and 18th centuries exacerbated the differences that existed naturally in such a geographically large and diverse area. The match that ignited this powder keg was the strong pull each state held on its citizens. Robert E. Lee was one of many Southern-born officers who reluctantly resigned his commission out of loyalty to his home state. Several weeks before Virginia seceded, Lee told a friend, "If Virginia stands by the old Union, so will I. But if she secedes, then I will follow my native state with my sword, and, if need be, with my life."

Tragic Prelude from a mural drawn by John Steurt Curry. (National Archives)

After he made his fateful decision to resign his commission and end his 32-year career in the United States Army, Lee explained his reasons in a letter to his sister Ann Marshall: "With all my devotion to the Union, and the feeling of loyalty and duty of an American citizen, I have not been able to make up my mind to raise my hand against my relatives, my children, my home." The timeline in this chapter will trace the evolution of slavery in North America, especially its growth in the South, as well as the delicate political balance that developed between the states north and south of the Mason-Dixon Line.

Early exploration of the New World was driven by a search for foreign trade. The prices people were willing to pay for spices and other goods from India and Asia made sailors willing to risk the dangers of a quest for a direct sea route. It wasn't until John Rolfe tried planting tobacco in 1612 that the early colonists in Virginia stumbled upon a way to make money. Within five years, 20,000 pounds of this precious commodity had been shipped to England, spurring a reform in land policies that was designed to entice more investors, more planters, and more ser-vants to come to the New World. Even at this early stage, when very few African slaves had been brought to North America, the economies of the North and South were on divergent paths. By 1660, Virginia and Maryland were exporting more than seven million pounds of tobacco a year, and a key component of this trade was African slaves. By the beginning of the 18th century the Atlantic slave trade was bringing between 10,000 and 25,000 new slaves to the Americas every year. For plantation owners, slavery not only offered a permanent solution to the labor problem, but the slaves themselves appreciated in value by the simple process of human reproduction.

The Early Slave Trade and the Rise of Sectionalism in America, 1600-1750

1. 20 blacks were brought to Jamestown on a Dutch ship as indentured servants (1619).
2. The French entered the slave trade (1624).
3. 11 male slaves were brought to New York City (1626).
4. The first slaves were brought to Maryland and Massachusetts (1634).
5. The first slaves entered New Hampshire (1645).
6. Due to the dwindling supply of indentured servants, the Virginia legislature recognized slavery (1661).
7. Settlers were offered 20 acres for every black male and 10 acres for every female brought into the Carolina colony (1663).
8. Boston traders began to import slaves directly from Africa (1664).
9. The Royal African Company was founded and given the English monopoly on slave trade (1672).
10. Slave trade was opened to any ship flying the British flag (1698).
11. Total slave population in the colonies reached 28,000; 23,000 were in the South (1700).

12. Slave population reached 236,000; over 206,000 were living south of the Mason-Dixon Line (1750).

☆☆☆

It was not so much the content of its character as it was the content of its soil that brought the bulk of the slaves to the South. However, by the time of the Revolutionary War, every colony had slaves, and there were more than 500,000 on the North American continent. The geographic disparity was clear, however: There were 300,000 slaves in Virginia and South Carolina alone, while the states of New York, New Jersey, Pennsylvania, Connecticut, Massachusetts, and Rhode Island combined for fewer than 30,000.

The spirit of the revolution was felt in all the colonies. One of the first actions of the Continental Congress of 1774 was to decree the end of the trans-Atlantic slave trade. Every state, even Virginia and South Carolina, took measures to slow or halt the importation of slaves in the 1770s and 1780s. The

Auction house on Whitehall Street Atlanta, Georgia.
(Library of Congress)

framers of the Constitution were well aware of the double standard implied in a country where "all men are created equal," yet had one-sixth of the population held in slavery. The framers went to great linguistic lengths to insure that the Constitution would not recognize, in the words of James Madison, that there could be "property in men," and creative language was used to avoid any literal sanction of slavery. Even in Article IV, Section 2, in what is known as the fugitive slave clause, the Constitution only refers to "person(s) held to service of labour."

One of the most overlooked elements of the Revolutionary War period is that it brought about an end to slavery in the Northern states. In addition, Thomas Jefferson was very nearly able to preclude slavery from entering what was known as the Northwest Territory—the region west of Pennsylvania, north of the Ohio River, east of the Mississippi River, and south of the Great Lakes. However, his provision failed in Congress by a vote that was changed at the last minute by the illness of a delegate. Jefferson's consolation prize was the passage, three years later, of the Northwest Ordinance, which excluded slavery from territory north of the Ohio River.

Birth of a Nation: Slavery in Revolutionary War America, 1760-1810

1. Population of South Carolina was 90,000 blacks and only 40,000 whites (1765).
2. Pennsylvania slave trade hampered by 20-pound tax on every imported slave (1773).
3. Continental Congress banned the importation of slaves (1774).
4. New York granted freedom to slaves who served three years as soldiers (1774).
5. Connecticut banned the importation and sale of slaves (1774).
6. The Declaration of Independence was signed (1776).
7. Vermont became an independent republic and abolished slavery in its constitution (1777).
8. Gradual emancipation was granted in Pennsylvania (1780).
9. The Massachusetts constitution abolished slavery (1780).
10. Congress rejected Thomas Jefferson's proposal to exclude slavery from all western territories (1784).
11. The importation of new slaves was ended in all states except South Carolina and Georgia (1786).
12. The U.S. Constitution was approved; 1 slave = 3/5's of a person (1787).
13. Vermont became the 14th state to enter the Union (1791).
14. Kentucky entered the Union as a slave state (1792).
15. The cotton gin was invented; cotton became the number-one cash crop in the South (1793).
16. The Louisiana Purchase added 827,000 square miles to the United States for a price of $15 million (1803).
17. The slave trade was abolished by Congress; slaves already in the United States could still be bought and sold (1808).

☆☆☆

The United States of America was enjoying the Era of Good Feelings and beginning to flex its muscles in the international arena through the Monroe Doctrine when Missouri submitted its petition to join the Union in 1819. Slavery was legal in Missouri, and most people expected the state to join the Union as a slave state, as Alabama and Mississippi had done in the previous two years. However, Missouri was the first territory west of the Mississippi River, made up of land secured by the Louisiana Purchase, to request statehood. The Ohio River and the Mason-Dixon Line had always been understood to be the boundary between slave and free states, and there were no such guidelines for the territories lying to the west. Senator James Tallmadge of New York struck the first blow of the great slavery debate by introducing legislation prohibiting the importation of any additional slaves into Missouri and granting freedom to the children of slaves already in the state when they reach the age of 25. The Tallmadge Amendment was passed by the House of Representatives, which was dominated by free states, but defeated in the Senate. Senator Henry Clay crafted a compromise that temporarily ended the debate and allowed Missouri entry into the Union

Henry Clay presents his famous compromise while Millard Fillmore, John C. Calhoun, and Daniel Webster look on. (National Archives)

as a slave state. In exchange, Maine was allowed to enter the Union, keeping the precarious balance between slave and free states, and slavery was forever banished from all other land north of Missouri's southern borderline.

John C. Calhoun struck the next blow in 1829 by anonymously publishing the *South Carolina Exposition and Protest* as a response to the Tariff of 1828, also known as the Tariff of Abominations. According to Calhoun's nullification theory, states were not obligated to obey Federal laws unless they were made into amendments to the Constitution. South Carolina adopted his Ordinance of Nullification in 1832, but Calhoun was unable to get any other Southern states to join the crusade. President Andrew Jackson responded with his own *Proclamation to the People of South Carolina,* which asserted that "disunion by armed force is treason," and Congress passed the Force Bill authorizing the president to use the military to collect Federal tariffs. Once again, the dispute was quelled by a compromise bill, which lowered the hated tariff and convinced South Carolina to rescind the Ordinance of Nullification. This was the dry run of secession and Calhoun, in addition to providing a blueprint for the South should slavery ever be seriously threatened, would spend the remaining 20 years of his life trying to unite the South against radical Northern abolitionists.

The next great slavery dispute erupted as a result of the good old-fashioned American policy of Manifest Destiny. By the time the Mexican-American War ended and the Treaty of Guadalupe Hidalgo was signed, the Texas border was set at the Rio Grande River, and the territories of California and New Mexico, more than 500,000 square miles of territory, were in American hands. It was up to the "great compromiser," Senator Henry Clay, to produce yet another agreement that could settle the differences that erupted from this great land expansion. Working with Stephen Douglas and Daniel Webster, Clay pushed through an omnibus bill that granted the admission of California as a free state, organized the new territories of New Mexico and Utah, and prohibited the slave trade in the District of Columbia. In addition, to appease the slave states, a new stringent Fugitive Slave Act was enacted. Although Clay's Compromise of

Battle of Molina Del Rey, copy of lithograph by James Bailie.
(National Archives)

1850 was heralded by moderates from all sections of the country, it also sowed the seeds of future discord by setting the precedent of popular sovereignty to determine if the new territories would be slave or free.

Expansionism and the Rise of Abolitionism, 1815-1850

1. Under the Missouri Compromise, Maine was admitted as a free state and Missouri as a slave state (1820).
2. Congress declared that foreign slave trade was to be recognized as piracy and punishable by death (1820).
3. Slavery was officially abolished in New York State; 10,000 blacks were freed (1827).
4. Nat Turner led an uprising in which 57 whites were killed in Southampton County, Virginia (1821).
5. South Carolina challenged Federal authority by "nullifying" the tariffs of 1829 and 1832.
6. The American Anti-Slavery Society was organized in Philadelphia, Pennsylvania (1832).
7. Oberlin Collegiate Institute was founded as the first integrated, co-educational college (1832).
8. The House of Representatives voted not to receive any antislavery petitions (1840).
9. Nine years after American settlers staged a revolt and won independence, Texas was granted statehood (1845).
10. England ceded the Oregon Country to the United States (1846).
11. The treaty of Guadalupe Hidalgo ended the Mexican War, giving the United States control of a vast stretch of land between Texas and the Pacific Ocean (1840).

12.   The Compromise of 1850 brought California into the Union, as well as the territories of New Mexico and Utah (1850).

☆☆☆

The house of cards constructed by Henry Clay and his merry band of compromisers began to crumble when Clay succumbed to tuberculosis in 1852. Stephen Douglas attempted to fill Clay's shoes, but suffered from a fatal flaw—a belief in the concept of squatter sovereignty. Originally introduced as part of the Compromise of 1850, squatter sovereignty gave the residents of New Mexico and Utah the opportunity to choose their own destiny, slave or free, through the ballot box. Douglas used this concept as the centerpiece of the Kansas-Nebraska Act in the hope that it would solve the slavery question once and for all. However, before the resultant furor could subside, Chief Justice Roger Taney, using his own brand of nullification, released the Dred Scott Decision and, at least in theory, rendered all further Congressional debate on the subject of slavery in the territories moot. After Taney's decision there was no going back or compromising about the slavery issue. The subsequent collapse of the Whigs and Democrats as national political parties paved the way for the Republicans to become the only political party capable of garnering enough electoral votes to win the presidency.

Prelude to War, 1851-1860

1.   Kansas-Nebraska Act repealed the Missouri Compromise (1854).
2.   Northern or 'Conscious' Whigs joined the Free Soilers to form the abolitionist Republican Party (1854).
3.   David Christy published *Cotton Is King,* which proclaimed the supremacy of cotton at home and abroad (1855).
4.   Abraham Lincoln left the Whig Party to join the newly formed Republican Party (1856).
5.   Pro-slavery forces raided and sacked Lawrence, Kansas, the abolitionist center of the state (1856).
6.   Three days after the sacking of Lawrence, Kansas, John Brown retaliated in the Pottawatomie Massacre (1856).

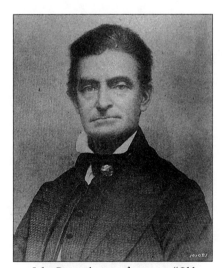

John Brown became famous as "Old Osawatomie Brown" in 1856.
(National Archives)

7. The Supreme Court, in *Dred Scott v. Sanford*, ruled against citizenship for blacks (1857).
8. Abraham Lincoln and Stephen Douglas held a series of debates during the Illinois primary (1858).
9. The pro-slavery Lecompton Constitution was rejected in a territorial vote in Kansas (1858).
10. John Brown led a raid on the Federal armory at Harper's Ferry; Brown was defeated and hung (1859).
11. The Republican party nominated Abraham Lincoln for president (1860).
12. The (northern) Democratic party nominated Stephen Douglas for president (1860).
13. The (southern) Democratic party nominated John C. Breckinridge for president (1860).
14. The Constitutional Union party nominated John Bell for president (1860).
15. Lincoln won presidential election; South Carolina seceded from the United States (1860).

CHAPTER 3

Dividing
the Union

WHEN ABRAHAM LINCOLN WAS elected as the 16th President of the United States, the Union was composed of 34 states, and the delicate balance between slave and free states had been irrevocably broken. There were now 19 free states and only 15 slave states. In addition, seven states, all from the Deep South, had already seceded from the Union before Lincoln was able to deliver his inaugural address in Washington, DC, on March 4, 1861. Although Lincoln at first tried very hard not to alienate the remaining slave states, his call for 75,000 militia to put down the rebellion after Fort Sumter quickly brought an additional four states—including Virginia the most vital of the remaining states—into the Confederacy.

The speed and efficiency in which the seceding states were able to establish themselves as the Confederate States of America was impressive. Within three months of Lincoln's election, the government of the Confederate States of America, residing in Montgomery, Alabama, had drafted a constitution, established a provisional congress, and elected a provisional president—Jefferson Davis. It would be 1870 before the last of the seceding states were readmitted into the Union.

11 Confederate States (Secession – Readmission)

		Secession	*Readmission*
1.	South Carolina	December 20, 1860	June 25, 1868
2.	Mississippi	January 9, 1861	July 1870
3.	Florida	January 10, 1861	June 25, 1868
4.	Alabama	January 11, 1861	July 13, 1868
5.	Georgia	January 19, 1861	July 15, 1870
6.	Louisiana	January 26, 1861	May 29, 1865
7.	Texas	February 1, 1861	March 30, 1870
8.	Virginia	April 17, 1861	January 27, 1870
9.	Arkansas	May 6, 1861	June 22, 1868
10.	North Carolina	May 20, 1861	June 25, 1868
11.	Tennessee	June 8, 1861	July 24, 1866

☆☆☆

The goal for Lincoln early in his presidency was to retain the loyalty and the resources of the volatile border states. Those were states that allowed slavery but did not officially participate in secession. On this subject, Lincoln quipped: "While I hope to have God on my side, I must have Kentucky." Lincoln showed restraint by respecting Governor Beriah Magoffin's declaration of neutrality and keeping Union troops out of the state until Confederate forces under Leonidas Polk entered the state. The Kentucky legislature responded by voting, by a three-to-one margin, that "the invaders must be expelled." Despite Lincoln's success in securing Federal political and military control over the border states, both Missouri and Kentucky elected governments-in-exile that were recognized by the Confederacy, and thousands of men left these states to enlist in the Confederate army.

4 Border States: Undecided in 1861

1. Delaware: State legislature rejected offers by several Confederate states to leave the Union.
2. Maryland: Immediate occupation by Union troops rendered the question of secession moot.
3. Missouri: Secession convention adopted resolutions favoring peace and compromise.
4. Kentucky: State legislature adopted a resolution of neutrality.

Unlike the South, which was relatively homogenous, the states that remained loyal to the Union were made up of five separate and disparate regions. To win the war, Lincoln's administration had to draw upon the strengths of each region, while at the same time being sensitive to their inherent differences. However, the great strength that Lincoln could rely on was that the loyal states, including the four border states, contained 22 million people who controlled 75 percent of the nation's wealth and 81 percent of its industrial capacity.

19 Loyal States in 1861 by Region

	State	Region
1.	Maine	New England
2.	Connecticut	New England
3.	New Hampshire	New England
4.	Vermont	New England
5.	Rhode Island	New England
6.	Massachusetts	New England
7.	New York	Mid-Atlantic
8.	Pennsylvania	Mid-Atlantic
9.	New Jersey	Mid-Atlantic
10.	Ohio	Old Northwest
11	Illinois	Old Northwest
12.	Indiana	Old Northwest
13.	Wisconsin	Old Northwest
14.	Michigan	Old Northwest
15.	Iowa	Great Plains
16.	Minnesota	Great Plains
17.	Kansas	Great Plains
18.	California	Far West
19.	Oregon	Far West

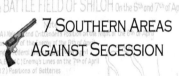

7 SOUTHERN AREAS AGAINST SECESSION

1. East Tennessee
2. Winston County in northern Alabama
3. Rabun County in the mountains of Georgia
4. Ozark Mountains of northern Arkansas
5. Hill counties (Jones County) of Mississippi
6. Western and central North Carolina
7. Western counties of Virginia

For most of the participants of the Civil War, choosing sides was as easy as figuring out one's own home state. However, there were some men who decided to take up the cause of an adopted state. The reasons were as varied as the individuals involved, but often included the feelings of a spouse. An example can be found in the case of General George Thomas, a Virginian who fought for the North largely because his wife was from Troy, New York. He paid a high price for his decision. Not only was he mistrusted by many in Lincoln's administration for being Southern, but Thomas was also forever scorned by his relatives in Virginia. Other examples can be found with Northerners who married into Southern families. Men like Samuel Cooper, Roswell Ripley, Walter Stevens, and Martin L. Smith married into Southern families and, when the time came, gave up their Northern heritage to fight for the South.

What is most surprising, when considering the depth of animosity that had developed between the North and the South, was the large number of Northerners who ended up in important positions in the Confederacy. By the summer of 1863, the Confederacy held only two forts along the Mississippi River—Vicksburg and Port Hudson. At a time when losing control of the river meant splitting the country in two, both forts were commanded by men who were born in the North. Franklin Gardner, who commanded at Port Hudson, was born in New York City and was raised in Iowa. When his command was forced to surrender, Gardner, unlike most of the rest of the garrison, was kept in a prison camp for more than a year.

Northern-born John Slidell, Confederate diplomat arrested en route to France.
(*Battles and Leaders*)

The stigma attached to Vicksburg commander John Pemberton, a native of Philadelphia, after he surrendered was even greater. Given a high command despite his Northern birth, Pemberton was surrounded by rumors that he secretly planned to surrender the river fortress to the Federals. Pemberton's decision to surrender on July 4, 1863, in order to get the best terms available from the patriotic Yankees, forever stamped him as a traitor in the eyes of many Southerners. After Vicksburg, there was no place in the army for General Pemberton who, unable to secure a new command, voluntarily resigned his commission and served the remainder of the war as a lieutenant-colonel.

In addition, the only Southern general to desert from the army was also a Northerner from birth. Daniel Frost, a brigadier-general and inspector general for the Army of the West, left the army after his wife was banished from her home in St. Louis. Frost, who never submitted his resignation to the War Department, brought his family to Canada and was dropped from the army rolls in December 1863.

33 Rebel Officers Born in the North

Name	Title/Rank	Birthplace
1. Samuel Cooper	General	Hackensack, N.J.
2. John C. Pemberton	Lieutenant-General	Philadelphia, Pa.
3. Lunsford Lomax	Major-General	R.I.

Name	Title/Rank	Birthplace
4. Bushrod Johnson	Major-General	Belmont City, Ohio
5. Franklin Gardner	Major-General	New York, N.Y.
6. Otto Strahl	Major-General	McConnelsville, Ohio
7. Samuel French	Major-General	Gloucester City, N.J.
8. William Allen	Brigadier-General	New York, N.Y.
9. Johnson Duncan	Brigadier-General	York, Pa.
10. William Miller	Brigadier-General	Ithaca, N.Y.
11. Edward Perry	Brigadier-General	Richmond, Mass.
12. William McComb	Brigadier-General	Mercer City, Pa.
13. Daniel Ruggles	Brigadier-General	Barre, Mass.
14.. Roswell Ripley	Brigadier-General	Worthington, Ohio
15. Chaudius Sears	Brigadier-General	Peru, Mass.
16. Albert Blanchard	Brigadier-General	Charleston, Mass.
17. William Steele	Brigadier-General	Albany, N.Y.
18. Archibald Gracie	Brigadier-General	New York, N.Y.
19. Josiah Gorgas	Chief of Ordnance Bureau	Running Pumps, Pa.
20. John Slidell	Ambassador to France	New York, N.Y.
21. Frances Shoup	Chief of Artillery Army of Tenn.	Laurel, Ind.
22. Daniel Leadbetter	Chief Engineer Army of Tenn.	Leeds, Maine
23. Walter Stevens	Chief Engineer Army of N. Va.	Penn Yan, N.Y.
24. Martin L. Smith	Chief Engineer Army of N. Va.	Danbury, N.Y.
25. Jedediah Hotchkiss	Topographical Engineer	Windsor, N.Y.
26. Lloyd J. Beall	Commandant Marine Corps	R.I.
27. William Gilham	Commandant V.M.I.	Ind.
28. William Parker	Superintendent Naval Academy	New York, N.Y.
29. Albert Pike	Commander Indian Territory	Mass.
30. Caleb Huse	European Purchasing Agent	Newburyport, Mass.
31. Daniel Frost	Inspector Gen. Army of the West	Schenectady, N.Y.
32. David Bridgeford	Provost Martial Army of N. Va.	New York, N.Y.
33. William Quantrill	Captain	Dover, Ohio

☆☆☆

There were also 38 men who were born in Southern states, but who remained loyal and served as generals in the Union army. The only Confederate states that did not produce a Northern general-officer were Arkansas, Texas, and Mississippi. Even Charleston, South Carolina, the birthplace of the Confederacy, provided the Union with a general. Stephen Hurlbut was born and raised in Charleston, joined the South Carolina Bar, and even served as an adjutant of a South Carolina regiment during the Seminole wars in Florida. He moved to Belvidere, Illinois, in 1845 and was appointed by President Lincoln as a brigadier-general of volunteers when the war broke out.

However, Hurlbut proved to be a poor officer who used his position to make money, and a special commission recommended his arrest and trial for his actions as the garrison commander of Memphis, Tennessee, in 1864. The case was allowed to die, and Hurlbut was "honorably mustered out" of service. He rebounded after the war and was elected as a congressmen in Illinois in 1872, and he became the minister to Peru in 1891. However, he was again charged with lining his own pockets during the war fought between Chile and the allied nations of Peru and Bolivia.

The following is a list of Union generals who were born in Southern states:

38 Union Generals Born in the South

Name	State
1. David Bell Birney	Alabama
2. William Birney	Alabama
3. Edward Davis	Florida
4. John McIntosh	Florida
5. Lewis Watkins	Florida
6. John C. Fremont	Georgia
7. Montgomery Meigs	Georgia
8. Joseph Rodman West	Louisiana
9. T.T. Crittenden	Maryland
10. Andrew Hamilton	Maryland
11. Joseph Hawley	North Carolina
12. Andrew Johnson	North Carolina
13. Solomon Meredith	North Carolina
14. Stephen Hurlbut	South Carolina
15. William Campbell	Tennessee
16. Samuel Carter	Tennessee
17. Alvan Gillem	Tennessee
18. William Harney	Tennessee
19. Isham Haynie	Tennessee
20. James Spears	Tennessee
21. Jacob Ammen	Virginia
22. Philip St. George Cooke	Virginia
23. John Davidson	Virginia
24. James Denver	Virginia
25. Isaac Dubal	Virginia
26. Alexander Dyer	Virginia
27. Lawrence Graham	Virginia
28. Thomas Harris	Virginia
29. William Hays	Virginia
30. John Newton	Virginia
31. Benjamin Prentiss	Virginia
32. George Ramsay	Virginia
33. Jesse Reno	Virginia

Name	State
34. Winfield Scott	Virginia
35. John Stevenson	Virginia
36. William Terrill	Virginia
37. George Thomas	Virginia
38. William Ward	Virginia

CHAPTER 4

Family Ties

THE POWERFUL FORCES THAT split the country also divided many prominent families, including the family of President Abraham Lincoln. Mary Todd Lincoln, a native of Kentucky, had one full brother, three half-brothers, and three brothers-in-law who served in the Confederate army; in addition, her half-sister Emilie, the widow of Confederate General Benjamin Hardin Helm, came to stay at the White House during the winter of 1863-64. Mary's own loyalty was also called into question by several members of the Committee on the Conduct of the War and some spoke of Mrs. Lincoln as being "two-thirds pro-slavery and the other third Secesh."

Union Brigadier-General Phillip St. George Cooke, whose only son became a Confederate general, had three daughters who married men who also went on to become generals during the war; one for the Union and two for the Confederacy. However, it was his son-in-law, Confederate General J. E. B. Stuart, who wrecked his military career by riding around, through, and over Cooke's cavalry division early in the war. While Stuart went on to become the premier cavalier of the war, St. George Cooke saw no further field service after being embarrassed. Stuart's aide-de-camp, Major H.B. McClellan, also came from a family divided by the war. His cousin was Major-General George McClellan, two-time commander

Union General Philip St. George Cooke, his three daughters all married men who became generals during the Civil War. (*Battles and Leaders*)

Union General George McClellan with staff, Generals McMahon, Meade, and Sweitzer; Colonel Coburn; and Captains Prince de Joinville and Count de Paris. (National Archives)

of the Army of the Potomac. Major McClellan proved his worth during the great cavalry battle at Brandy Station by commanding a battery that held off a Union charge that would have captured Stuart's headquarters.

Franklin Buchanan, ex-commander of the Washington Naval Yard and veteran of Commodore Perry's expedition to China, faced his own brother during his first engagement as captain of the powerful Confederate ironclad *C.S.S. Virginia*. In the engagement, Franklin was wounded, but his brother McKean Buchanan was killed. Another set of brothers who ended up on opposite sides of the war were James and William Terrill. Virginia natives, both men secured military educations—James at the Virginia Military Institute and William at West Point—before the war. While they ended up on different sides, both men rose to the rank of brigadier-general. Unfortunately, they also share the distinction of being the only set of brothers, serving as generals on opposing sides, who were killed in combat.

Other notables who felt the divisive pull of the war on their families include Federal Postmaster-General Montgomery Blair and Confederate Secretary of War John C. Breckinridge. Blair's niece, Louisa P. Buckner, was captured while smuggling quinine through the lines and thrown in Old Capitol Prison. Breckinridge, the former vice president, had two cousins, both Presbyterian ministers, who remained loyal to the Union. One of these cousins had two sons in the Confederate army and one in the Union army. Incredibly, a Yankee Breckinridge captured a Confederate Breckinridge during the fighting outside Atlanta in 1864.

16 Military Families Divided by the War

Union Army	Relationship	Confederate Army
1. President Lincoln	brother-in-law	General Benjamin H. Helm
2. Generals William Birney and David Bell Birney	cousins	General Humphrey Marshal
3. General George McClellan	cousin	Major H. B. McClellan
4. General George Meade	brother-in-law	General Henry Wise
5. General Thomas L. Crittenden	brother	General George B. Crittenden
6. General Thomas T. Crittenden	cousin	General George B. Crittenden
7. General Edwin Sumner	son-in-law	General Armistead L. Long
8. Generals Napoleon Buford and John Buford	cousins	General Abraham Buford
9. General Edmund Kirby	cousin	General Edmund Kirby Smith
10. General John B. McIntosh	brother	General James M. McIntosh
11. General James Ripley	uncle	General Roswell Ripley
12. General Henry Hastings Sibley	cousin	General Henry Hopkins Sibley
13. General John Wood	second cousin	General Benjamin H. Helm
14. General William Terrill	brother	General James Terrill
15. General Philip St. George Cooke	son	General John Rogers Cooke
	son-in-law	General J.E.B. Stuart
16. Lieutenant McKean Buchanan	brother	Admiral Franklin Buchanan

☆☆☆

When the Civil War erupted, the United States army could count only 1,098 officers and 15,304 enlisted men. The vast majority of the officers, who would be needed to lead the armies of the North and South, were graduates of the West Point Military Academy. Located along a bend in the Hudson River in New York State, West Point had been training military leaders since 1802. In the words of historian James McPherson, West Point "created a band of brothers more tightly bonded by mutual hardship and danger in war than biological brothers." However, the strains of war severed many of those bonds as most of the Southern-born graduates resigned from the army to follow the fortunes of their native

Thomas Jonathan Jackson, ranked 17th in the West Point Class of 1846. (National Archives)

states. In the end, more than one-third of the officers in the United States army resigned their commissions to serve in the Confederate army. Of the 60 major battles fought in the Civil War, 55 saw West Point graduates commanding on both sides, and a West Point graduate commanded on at least one of the sides in the remaining five battles.

The most prolific West Point class, in terms of producing Civil War generals, was the class of 1846. Almost immediately after graduating, the vast majority of the class, 53 out of 59 members, were detailed for service in the Mexican War. During the war, 37 of these newly minted West Pointers were breveted for gallantry, including Thomas J. Jackson, who was breveted three times for bravery. The battle of Antietam was their high-water mark as classmates George McClellan led the Army of the Potomac, while Stonewall Jackson commanded half of General Lee's Army of Northern Virginia. In all, eight former members of the Class of 1846 fought in the battle, five as Union generals and three as Confederate generals.

23 Classmates Who Fought in the War: The Class of 1846

	Name	Rank	Military rank during war
1.	Charles Stewart	1	Colonel of Engineers (Union)
2.	George McClellan	2	Major-General (Union)
3.	John Foster	4	Major-General (Union)
4.	*Jesse Reno	8	Major-General (Union)
5.	Darius Couch	13	Major-General (Union)
6.	*Thomas J. Jackson	17	Lieutenant-General (Confederate)
7.	Truman Seymour	19	Major-General (Union)
8.	*John Adams	25	Brigadier-General (Confederate)
9.	Samuel Sturgis	32	Major-General (Union)
10.	George Stoneman	33	Major-General (Union)
11.	James Oakes	34	Brigadier-General (Union)
12.	Dabney Maurey	37	Major-General (Confederate)
13.	Innis Palmer	38	Major-General (Union)
14.	David R. Jones	41	Major-General (Confederate)
15.	George Gordon	43	Major-General (Union)
16.	Alfred Gibbs	42	Major-General (Union)
17.	Cadmus Wilcox	54	Major-General (Confederate)
18.	William Gardner	55	Brigadier-General (Confederate)
19.	Samuel Bell Maxey	58	Major-General (Confederate)
20.	George Pickett	59	Major-General (Confederate)
21.	*A. P. Hill(a)	NA	Lieutenant-General (Confederate)
22.	John Gibbon(a)	NA	Major-General (Union)
23.	Birkett Fry(b)	NA	Brigadier-General (Confederate)

*   Killed in action

(a) - Graduated with Class of 1847

(b) - Did not graduate/dismissed from West Point

☆☆☆

There were many families that sent multiple members off to fight in the war. Even George Armstrong Custer, one of the most dashing and charismatic figures to emerge from the conflict, found himself upstaged by his younger brother Tom. At the battle of Namozine Church, Virginia, Tom captured the regimental flag of the 2nd North Carolina, and at Sailor's Creek, he charged across the lines to capture the flag of the 2nd Virginia Reserve Battalion. For his exploits, Tom Custer became the first man to be awarded two Medals of Honor, a feat his famous brother was unable to match.

Union General Alexander McDowell McCook, one of the 14 fighting McCooks. (National Archives)

The family that holds the title of contributing the most members to the war was the famous "Fighting McCooks of Ohio." The two patriarchs of this family, Daniel and his brother John, fathered 14 men who fought in the Union army. In addition, both men, despite their advanced ages, found ways to serve on the battlefield: John, as a volunteer surgeon, and Daniel, a former law partner of Secretary of War Edwin Stanton, as a paymaster and volunteer aide. The war ended tragically for Daniel when he was killed while riding with the advance guard that was chasing John Hunt Morgan's raiders. Daniel was convinced that Morgan's men had been involved in the murder of his son Robert earlier in the war, and he was out for revenge. Instead, the 65- year-old was shot and only lived long enough to have all his personal effects stolen. In all, six members of the McCook family rose to the rank of general: Robert, Alexander, Daniel, Edwin, Edward, and Anson. Four members lost their lives fighting for the Union.

14 Fighting McCooks

Name	*Service*
Tribe of Dan	
1. Major Daniel	Killed during Morgan's Ohio raid
2. George Wythe	Recruited and trained troops in Ohio
3. General Robert Latimer	Killed by guerrillas near Dechard, Tennessee
4. General Alexander McDowell	Breveted for bravery four times
5. General Daniel	Killed leading an assault on Kenesaw Mountain, Georgia

Name	*Service*
6. General Edwin Stanton	Wounded three times during war
7. Private Charles Morris	Killed at First Bull Run while serving in 2nd Ohio
8. Captain John James	Wounded at Shady Grove, Virginia

Tribe of John

9. John	Volunteer surgeon
10. General Edward Moody	Breveted five times for bravery
11. General Anson George	Commanded a brigade in the 14th Corps
12. Lieutenant Henry Christopher	Served as chaplain for nine months
13. Roderick Sheldon assault	Naval officer severely injured during on Fort Fisher
14. Lieutenant John James	Served in 1st Virginia (Union)

CHAPTER 5

This Month in 1861

POLITICAL AFFAIRS DOMINATED MOST of 1861: the secession of 13 Southern states, the election of President Abraham Lincoln, and the Trent Affair. In the Trent Affair, two Southern diplomats, John Slidell and James Mason, were captured en route to Europe by a Union warship. The resulting furor, which almost drove England to declare war, ended with the release of the diplomats, complete with a cryptic apology written by Secretary of State William Seward. On the battlefield, the Confederacy scored major victories in Virginia at Bull Run and in Missouri at Wilson's Creek.

In July, Union General Irvin McDowell commanded the 30,000-man army that marched toward Manassas. Spurred on by political pressure, and against the wishes of General Winfield Scott, McDowell's force was winning the day until reinforcements under Joe Johnston reached the field and turned the tide. The retreat quickly turned into a rout, giving the Confederacy an impressive military and psychological

Confederate commissioners being brought aboard the San Jacinto as prisoners of the United States. (Library of Congress)

victory. General Nathaniel Lyon led the Union force that marched into Missouri. Confident that he could snuff out Rebel resistance in the state before it got too organized, Lyon overextended his lines and was defeated by a Rebel force commanded by Sterling Price. The following is a list of some of the important events that occurred during each month of 1861:

The stone wall ferociously defended by the Confederates during the battle of Fredericksburg, Virginia. (National Archives)

☆ **January:** Florida, Alabama, Georgia, and Louisiana secede from the Union.

☆ **February:** The Confederacy creates a constitution and elects Jefferson Davis as its provisional president.

☆ **March:** Abraham Lincoln is inaugurated as the 16th President of the United States.

☆ **April:** Confederate forces under General Beauregard fire upon Fort Sumter. President Lincoln calls for 75,000 volunteers and declares a blockade of Southern ports.

☆ **May:** Arkansas, Tennessee, North Carolina, and Virginia secede from the Union.

☆ **June:** France joins England in declaring neutrality.

☆ **July:** Battle of Bull Run. First major battle ends in a smashing Confederate victory.

General George Brinton McClellan, the Union's Young Napoleon. (National Archives)

☆ **August:** Battle of Wilson's Creek ends in another Confederate victory, opening the state of Missouri to four more years of strife.

☆ **September:** Andrew Sidney Johnston assumes command of all Confederate forces in the West.

☆ **October:** Generals George McClellan and Joe Johnston keep their respective armies inactive, to the great consternation of their respective presidents.

☆ **November:** Trent Affair explodes when two Confederate diplomats are captured, almost sparking a war between the United States and England.

☆ **December:** Kentucky is admitted as the 13th and last state to the Confederacy.

CHAPTER 6

You're in the Army Now

B Y THE TIME PRESIDENT Lincoln issued his call for 75,000 volunteers after the fall of Fort Sumter, more than 60,000 men had already been enrolled in the Confederate army. This quick mobilization occurred largely because many Southern militia units were already organized and ready for action. Most of the men who joined up were young, Protestant, and unmarried. In addition, less than one-quarter owned slaves or belonged to slave-holding families, and only about one in 20 were of foreign birth, the bulk of these being either Irish or German.

The men of Perry County, Alabama, were among the first to organize and join the Confederate army in the spring of 1861. While the vast majority of these men were farmers, the 125 members of what would become Company A of the 8th Alabama Volunteer Regiment also included a dentist, a horse dealer, a mason, a machinist, a peddler, a physician, a saddler, a teamster, and a trimmer. The 8th Alabama joined three other regiments from Alabama to form a brigade commanded by Cadmus Wilcox, and the unit fought in all the major battles of the Army of Northern Virginia before surrendering with General Lee at Appomattox Court House.

10 year old Johnny Clem of Newark, Ohio, also known as the Drummer Boy of Chickamauga. (Library of Congress)

Fort Sumter on April 14, 1861, after the Union surrender. (National Archives)

Vital Statistics: Company A, 8th Alabama Volunteers

Place of birth	Number	Percent
1. Alabama	93	74 %
2. Georgia	14	11 %
3. Ireland	4	3 %
4. Other	14	11 %

Marital Status	Number	Percent
1. Single	78	62 %
2. Married	43	34 %
3. Unknown	4	3 %

Occupation	Number	Percent
1. Farmer	92	74 %
2. Mechanic	7	6 %
3. Laborer	4	3 %
4. Clerk	3	2 %
5. Printer	2	1 %
6. Teacher	2	1 %
7. Other	10	8 %
8. Unknown	5	4 %

☆☆☆

The height of more than half of the volunteers from the state of Indiana was recorded upon enlistment. While the figures approximated the average of the army as a whole, one local doctor informed the adjutant-general of Indiana that these men were "the tallest of all natives of the United States." Although that was not the case, the tallest unit in the army did come from Indiana and was called the Monroe County Grenadiers. This unit, which became the 27th Indiana, did not allow anyone shorter than 5'10" to join, and included a lieutenant who earned the nickname as the "Biggest Yankee in the world." At 6'10", Lieutenant David van Buskirk towered over the average 5'6" soldier. After being captured and sent to Libby Prison, Buskirk was taken to town every night, given as much food as he wanted, and displayed to the public for a small fee. While his fellow prisoners were starving, Buskirk gained 25 pounds before being exchanged and sent back to the North.

While no one shorter than 5'3" was allowed to join the regular army, the volunteers were not so fussy. More than 1,000 men shorter than that prescribed height served during the war, with the shortest member of the Union army measuring in at 3'4".

Vital Statistics, Part II: Indiana Soldiers

	Height	Number	Percent
1.	> 5'1"	501	+0%
2.	5'1"	263	+0%
3.	5'2"	971	+0%
4.	5'3"	2,503	2%
5.	5'4"	5,387	4%
6.	5'5"	9,171	8%
7.	5'6"*	14,373	12%
8.	5'7"	15,328	13%
9.	5'8"	19,140	16%
10.	5'9"	15,472	13%
11.	5'10"	15,047	13%
12.	5'11"	8,706	7%
13.	6'	6,679	6%
14.	6'1"	2,614	2%
15.	6'2"	1,357	1%
16.	6'3"	406	+0%
17.	> 6'3"	336	+0%

Total: 118,254
*Mean height of a Civil War soldier

☆☆☆

Due to the rigors of 19th-century warfare, the Civil War was very much a young man's war. While the average age for a general during the war was a youthful 37, the typical fighting man was much younger. More than 60 percent of the enlisted men were younger than 25 years old, and almost half were between the ages of 18 and 21. While boys younger than the age of 17 were not officially allowed to join the army, many managed to attach themselves to various units as drummer boys and stretcher bearers until, by the end of the war, more than 12,000 young boys eventually became recognized as veterans of the Union army.

Boys in the Union Army

	Age	Number
1.	17	6,425
2.	16	2,758
3.	15	2,178
4.	14	773
5.	13	330
6.	12	127
Total:		12,591

☆☆☆

The most famous drummer boy of all was 10-year-old Johnny Clem of Newark, Ohio. Early in the war, Clem ran away from home and joined the 22nd Michigan; he was present at most of the major battles that occurred in the West. At Chickamauga, Clem earned his nickname as "The Drummer Boy of Chickamauga" by wounding a Confederate officer with his sawed-off shotgun. For his exploits, he was given sergeant's stripes and awarded a silver medal by the daughter of Treasury Secretary Salmon Chase.

However, Clem was not the only boy-soldier to be cited for bravery. Thirteen-year-old Willie Johnson from St. Johnsbury, Vermont, a drummer boy in Company D of the 3rd Vermont, was awarded a Medal of Honor for bravery under fire during the Seven Days' campaign. Although it is impossible to determine who was the youngest soldier in the Confederate army, after the war a good number of Rebels came forward to claim the honor. The following is a list of some of the men who claimed to be the youngest Rebel:

The 9 Youngest Rebels

	Name	Age	Unit
1.	George S. Lamkin	11	Stanford's Mississippi Battery
2.	John B. Tyler	12	1st Maryland Cavalry

	Name	Age	Unit
3.	T.D. Claiborne	13	18th Virginia
4.	E.G. Baxter	13	7th Kentucky Cavalry
5.	M.W. Jewett	13	59th Virginia
6.	W.D. Peak	14	26th Tennessee
7.	Matthew J. McDonald	14	1st Georgia Cavalry
8.	John T. Mason	14	17th Virginia
9.	T.G. Bean	15	University of Alabama Cadet Corps

By the beginning of 1863, both the North and South had used up all the men willing to enlist in the army for patriotic reasons. While the Confederacy employed semi-universal conscription to bolster its army, the Union relied upon generous bounties and a national draft. Before the war ended, four drafts were held in the North and almost a million men were sent notices to report to the local provost marshal's office.

However, receiving a draft notice in the 1860s was not the same as being inducted into the army. While many men simply refused to report, even those who passed the army physical were in little danger of ever having to face a Rebel bullet. After those who could pay the $300 commutation fee or who could afford to hire a substitute were weeded out, less than a quarter of the drafted men joined the ranks of the Union army, and many of those unwilling soldiers deserted at the first opportunity. The following is a list detailing the final effect of the 983,000 draft notices sent out by the Federal government:

The Tale of 4 Dismal Drafts

	Action	Total	Percent
1.	Exempted for physical or mental disability	311,000	32%
2.	Actually drafted	207,000	21%
3.	Failed to report after being drafted	161,000	16%
4.	Sent home because local quota filled	97,000	10%
5.	Paid $300 commutation fee	87,000	8%
6.	Furnished substitutes	74,000	7%
7.	Joined ranks	46,000	5%

The Confederate congress passed the first conscription law in American history on April 16, 1862. Under this law, every able-bodied white male citizen between the ages of 18 and 35 was liable for military service. This highly unpopular law added about 200,000 men to the Confederate ranks despite the fact that Southerners could still avoid military service by procuring a substitute or by qualifying for an occupational exemption. However, when the Confederate congress added a provision to exempt one white man on every plantation with 20 or more slaves, many people complained that it had become a rich man's war, but a poor man's fight. Mississippi Senator James Phelan had this to say about the exemption: "Never did a law meet with more universal odium....Its influence upon the poor is calamitous." Despite widespread protest, the law was never repealed.

There was also room for fraud with the occupational exemptions granted by the Confederate government. To take advantage of these exemptions, many new schools and apothecary shops suddenly sprang up. However, none could match the ingenuity of Governors Joseph Brown of Georgia and Zebulon Vance of North Carolina for manipulating this law. Together, these governors accounted for 92 percent of all Confederate state officials exempted from the draft because of their insistence that militia officers qualified for an occupational exemption. Eventually one Confederate general complained that militia regiments from Georgia and North Carolina consisted of "3 field officers, 4 staff officers, 10 captains, 30 lieutenants, and 1 private."

MILITARY UNIT SIZE

	Unit	Union Army	Confederate Army
1.	Company	34-40	35-40
2.	Regiment	350-400	350-400
3.	Brigade	800-1700	1400-2000
4.	Division	3,000-7,000	6,000-14,000
5.	Corps	12,000-14,000	24,000-28,000

9 'Other' Rebel Exemptions

1. Confederate and state civil servants
2. Railroad and river workers
3. Telegraph operators
4. Miners
5. Industrial laborers
6. Hospital personnel
7. Clergymen
8. Apothecaries
9. Teachers

☆☆☆

The easiest way to avoid being drafted into the Union army was to pay the $300 commutation fee. This policy infuriated many who could not afford to pay the fee and inspired newspaper headlines such as "$300 or Your Life." Eventually the tension grew until there were outbreaks of violence in many cities throughout the North. The issue came to a head in New York City in July 1863 during a riot that claimed the lives of about 120 people. For three days rioters controlled the streets of the city until 20,000 veteran troops were sent to keep the peace and enforce the draft.

The number of men who took advantage of the commutation varied greatly in the states of the North. For example, in Kansas only two men paid to avoid military service; in Illinois, a state that furnished almost 250,000 men to the Union army, only 55 men paid the commutation fee. States that were more industrialized or that had a strong Democratic Party organization took greatest advantage of the commutation fee. In addition, many localities appropriated funds from property taxes to pay the fee, and draft insurance societies were organized to pay the fee in exchange for a few dollars a month.

$300 Men: The Top 11 States

	State	Paid commutation
1.	Pennsylvania	28,171
2.	New York	18,197
3.	Ohio	6,479
4.	Massachusetts	5,318
5.	Wisconsin	5,097
6.	New Jersey	4,196
7.	Maryland	3,678
8.	Kentucky	3,265
9.	Michigan	2,008
10.	Maine	2,007
11.	Vermont	1,974

☆☆☆

In general, the physical requirements for joining the army were minimal. A person needed a couple of good teeth, a trigger finger, and the ability to march to be accepted into the army. Nevertheless, the enrollment board established an extensive list of physical infirmities that would exempt one from service. While the vast majority of physicals were cursory at best, thousands of potential soldiers were able to avoid military service due to their medical conditions. The following is a list of 50 medical conditions that precluded a person from joining the army:

50 Ways to Leave the Army

1. Manifest imbecility or insanity.
2. Epilepsy.
3. Paralysis, general or of one limb, or chorea.
4. Acute or organic diseases sufficient as to leave no reasonable doubt of the man's incapacity for military service.
5. Confirmed consumption, cancer, aneurysm of the large arteries.

6. Inveterate and extensive disease of the skin.
7. Decided feebleness of constitution, whether natural or acquired.
8. Scrofula or constitutional syphilis.
9. Habitual and confirmed intemperance sufficient to have materially enfeebled the constitution.
10. Chronic rheumatism.
11. Great injuries or diseases of the skull, epilepsy, or other manifest nervous or spasmodic symptoms.
12. Total loss of sight, loss of sight of right eye, cataract, loss of crystalline lens of right eye.
13. Other serious diseases of the eye affecting its integrity and use.
14. Loss of nose; deformity of nose so great as seriously to obstruct respiration.
15. Complete deafness.
16. Cleft palate; extensive loss of substance of the cheeks, or salivary fistula.
17. Dumbness; permanent loss of voice.
18. Total loss of tongue, or partial loss of tongue extensive enough to interfere with the use of the organ.
19. Hypertrophy or atrophy of the tongue, sufficient in degree to impair speech.
20. Stammering, if excessive and confirmed.
21. Loss of a sufficient number of teeth to prevent proper mastication of food and tearing the cartridge.

United States Navy recruiting poster.
(National Archives)

22. Incurable deformities or loss of part of either jaw, hindering biting of the cartridge.
23. Tumors of the neck, impeding respiration or deglutition.
24. Deformity of the chest sufficient to prevent the carrying of arms and military equipments.
25. Deficient amplitude and power of expansion of chest. A man 5'3" should not measure less than 30 inches in circumference immediately above the nipples and have an expansive mobility of not less than two inches.

26. Abdomen grossly protuberant; excessive obesity; hernia.
27. Artificial anus; stricture of the rectum.
28. Old and ulcerated internal hemorrhoids. External hemorrhoids are no cause for exemption.
29. Total loss or nearly total loss of penis.
30. Incurable permanent organic stricture of the urethra, in which the urine is passed drop by drop.
31. Stone in the bladder, ascertained by the introduction of the metallic catheter.
32. Loss or complete atrophy of both testicles from any cause.
33. Confirmed or malignant sarcocele; hydrocele, if complicated with organic disease of the testicle.
34. Excessive anterior or posterior curvature of the spine.
35. Loss of an arm, forearm, hand, thigh, leg, or foot.
36. Wounds, fractures, tumors, atrophy of a limb, or chronic diseases of the joints or bones, that would impede marching or prevent continuous muscular exertion.
37. Anchylosis or irreducible dislocation of the shoulder, elbow, wrist, hip, knee, or ankle joint.
38. Wounds or burns in degree sufficient to prevent useful motion of a limb.
39. Total loss of a thumb; loss of ungual phalanx of right thumb.
40. Total loss of any two fingers of same hand.
41. Total loss of index finger of right hand.
42. Loss of the first and second phalanges of the fingers of right hand.
43. Permanent extension or permanent contraction of any finger except the little finger.
44. Total loss of either great toe; loss of any three toes on the same foot.
45. The great toe crossing the other toes with great prominence.
46. Overriding or superposition of all the toes.
47. Permanent retraction of the last phalanx of one of the toes.
48. Club feet or splay feet; but ordinary large, ill-shaped, or flat feet do not exempt.
49. Varicose veins of inferior extremities, if large and numerous, having clusters of knots.
50. Chronic ulcers; extensive, deep, and adherent cicatrices of lower extremities.

☆☆☆

It was the duty of the provost marshal and his assistants to compile the lists of men eligible for the draft and to organize the procedure in which the men on the list were to be selected. Two deputy provost marshals were sent to each congressional district to organize the proceedings, and it was not very long before an entire bureaucracy was created to oversee this massive endeavor. As is usually the case with the Federal government, even back in the 1860s, specific instructions were given for almost any eventuality. The following is a list of just a portion of the forms that each provost marshal had at his disposal:

25 Forms of the Provost Marshal

1. Tri-monthly report of persons arrested.
2. Tri-monthly report of deserters arrested.
3. Monthly abstract of indebtedness.
4. Monthly report of persons and articles employed.
5. Monthly report of persons arrested.
6. Monthly returns of provost marshals' parties and deserters.
7. Monthly return of public property.
8. Traveling pay to drafted persons.
9. Transportation of deserters and so forth.
10. Purchases.
11. Postage and so forth.
12. Reimbursements of expenses paid.
13. Sub-voucher to claim for reimbursement.
14. Receipt roll of persons employed.
15. Exemption for son of widow, or aged or infirm parents.
16. Exemption for one of two sons of aged or infirm parents.
17. Exemption for only brother of dependent child or children.
18. Exemption on account of two members of family being in military service.
19. Exemption for father of dependent motherless children.
20. Exemption for unsuitableness of age.
21. Certificate of non-liability to military duty.
22. Certificate of disability.
23. Certificate of discharge.
24. Descriptive roll of drafted men.
25. Notification to persons of their having been drafted.

CHAPTER 7

A Soldier's Daily Life

I F THE OLD ADAGE that an army travels on its stomach is true, then the Union and Confederate armies should have become immobilized very early in the war. Neither army went into the field with a standardized manual for cooking, there was no thought given to the proper handling of food, and the whole idea of nutrition remained an unresolved mystery. To feed the huge and hungry armies in the field, both sides relied on hardtack and salt pork as standard rations. Hardtack, also known as "sheet-iron teeth dullers," or, when infested with vermin, as "worm castles," was the most indispensable feature of a soldier's diet. Also referred to as "army bread," hardtack was a biscuit about three inches square and a half-inch thick. In order to eat them, soldiers had to soak them in water or fry them in a thick layer of grease or pork fat. Dry as a bone and hard as a brick, the crackers all but disappeared from view in American society until very recently. However, the rise in popularity of Civil War reenactments has spurred a renewed interest in authentic hardtack. Now, G. H. Bent Co., a Boston-based bakery that supplied hardtack to the Union

Rebel soldier enjoying his rations from the stalk. (*Battles and Leaders*)

army during the 1860s, has renewed production and can barely keep it on the shelves.

Meat was also a dietary staple. Because food preservation had changed little in the previous century, meat either had to be freshly killed, pickled, smoked, or salted. To provide the soldiers with meat, especially when on the march or in the field, both armies relied upon salt pork. The following list describes the lengthy process that was necessary to prepare and preserve the pork:

5 Steps to Prepare Salt Pork

1. The meat is carefully sectioned as soon as possible after the pig is killed.
2. Saltpetre (rock salt) is then rubbed into the meat.
3. The meat is laid into a tub of salt.
4. The meat is left to season for about four weeks.
5. The meat is then put into a smokehouse until it lifts easily from the bone.

When the war began, the military regulations for proper rations for the soldiers were almost the same as those used during the Revolutionary War. While bread or hardtack and some sort of meat were included, fruit, fresh vegetables, and dairy products were not. To supplement this meager diet, it was up to the men to find what they could locally. Early in the war, many officers would not allow, or strictly punished, any soldier who foraged for additional food from nearby farms or villages. However, that slowly changed until, by 1864, General Sherman's "bummers" made a science out of scrounging anything and everything edible from the countryside while marching through Georgia and South Carolina. The Confederate government adopted the official United States Army ration early in the war, but was forced to periodically reduce their standard ration amounts because of chronic food shortages. As a result Southern soldiers, especially as the war dragged on, were forced to make do with much less until their ability to march and fight began to be seriously impaired. The following is a list of the rations issued to Union soldiers:

Daily Union Rations

(Per individual)

1. Three-quarters of a pound of pork or bacon, or one and one-quarter pound of fresh or salt pork
2. Eighteen ounces of flour or bread or 12 ounces of hardtack
3. One and one-quarter pound of corn meal

(Per each 100 man company)

1. Eight quarts of peas or beans, or 10 pounds of rice
2. Six to 10 pounds of coffee or one and one-half pounds of tea
3. Twelve to 15 pounds of sugar
4. Two quarts of salt

Well-stocked Union company kitchen. (National Archives)

The food issued to each soldier was usually pooled together and shared by squads of five or six men. This practice was officially discontinued in the Union army in March 1863, but continued for the most part unchecked until the end of the war. While soldiers on both sides of the line used creative means to supplement their rations, the Southern soldier had to be especially resourceful. Because food was generally scarce, and only the most basic ingredients were available, the soldiers would eat whatever was available. During the Vicksburg siege, rats, cats, dogs, and bullfrogs were used for food, with one soldier noting that "rat tasted like young squirrel." In addition, meals were often made from ingredients that were readily available. These included things such as artificial oysters, rabbit stew, hash, catfish stew, Indian pudding, and cornbread. The following is a list of the simple and easily attainable ingredients necessary for making artificial oysters. These ingredients were mixed together, separated into balls, flattened into oyster shapes, and fried on a skillet.

5 Ingredients for Artificial Oysters

1. Two eggs
2. Three-quarters of a cup of flour
3. A pinch of salt to taste
4. A pinch of pepper
5. Two cups of whole-kernel corn

☆☆☆

For many of the soldiers in the Union and Confederate armies, joining the army and going off to war was the first time they had been away from home. In addition to the bewildering array of army and camp regulations, the stress and strain of military life almost inevitably led to clashes between the enlisted men and the officers they were required to obey. The harshest punishment for breaking the rules, death by hanging, was almost always reserved for the most serious transgression—desertion in the face of the enemy. In order to make the strongest possible impression on the rest of the troops, commanding officers usually transformed a hanging into a well-staged spectacle, complete with hundreds of spectators and mournful music from the regimental band. Often several regiments would be arranged such that the condemned man could be marched into a hollow square of onlookers, with a grave already dug, and a coffin already waiting for its future occupant.

The second most serious crime—cowardice—was also treated very seriously. Usually, the unfortunate soldier would be stripped out of his uniform, have his head shaved, and have the letter "D" tattooed on his body with a red-hot iron. The soldier would then be physically expelled from camp and given a dishonorable discharge. The following is a list of some of the more frequent crimes and punishments that were meted out during the Civil War. In all cases involving an enlisted man, the punishment was set by the unit's commanding officer and not by any set of military standards or regulations.

13 Crimes and Punishments

Crime	*Probable punishment*
1. Drunkenness	Sent to the regimental guard
2. Talking back to an officer	Sent to the regimental guard
3. Not saluting a superior	Sent to the regimental guard
4. Missing roll call	Sent to the regimental guard
5. Not standing on guard duty	Sent to the regimental guard
6. Gambling	Sent to the regimental guard
7. Leaving camp	Bucking and gagging
8. Absent without leave	Mounting a wooden horse
9. Petty thievery	Time in a sweat box
10. Self mutilation	Hard labor in prison
11. Striking an officer	Solitary confinement
12. Cowardice in battle	Dishonorable discharge without pay
13. Desertion	Branding, drummed out of camp, tattooed, death by hanging

☆☆☆

Whenever the Union and Confederate lines stabilized in close proximity, informal "truces" would be arranged by opposing pickets and within a short time, items

Non-commissioned officers mess for Company D, 93rd New York Infantry. (Library of Congress)

would start to be exchanged by the men on the opposing sides. Newspapers were the most frequently requested item, and they became a staple source of information for the high command on both sides. On occasion, commanders would even send hand-picked soldiers out to solicit newspapers and innocently question enemy soldiers about recent troop movements. However, in most cases, this sort of fraternization was discouraged.

5 Popular Items Traded Between the Lines

1. Newspapers
2. Coffee
3. Tobacco
4. Peanuts
5. Whiskey

When a soldier was in camp, time was a much more persistent foe than the enemy. For most men, once the day's drilling was done and the meals cooked, there was little to be done. Along with music, the occasional theatrical performance, and impromptu social gatherings, playing sports was a popular pastime. Although still in its infancy as a national sport, baseball, especially the "Massachusetts rules" version of the game, was probably the most popular sporting activity for both the

Union and Confederate soldiers. In this updated version of the old game of "town-ball," teams of up to 15 players would defend a square infield, while batters would stand between fourth and first base and run around the basepaths in a counterclock-wise direction. The early version of football played during the war most closely resembled modern-day soccer. A rubber ball would be tossed among a large crowd of players who would attempt to kick it down the field.

The most dangerous of all sporting events were the improvised 10-pin bowling matches, because they sometimes included the use of explosive 12-pound spheri-cal case shells as bowling balls. On occasion, the shells would burst, emitting a huge flame and sending "flying bullets and fragments of the parting shell [hurtling] through the air." The following is a list of some of the more popular sporting activi-ties enjoyed by Civil War soldiers:

6 Favorite Pastimes

1. Baseball
2. Football
3. Boxing
4. Horse racing
5. Snowball fights
6. Bowling

Early in the war, the Union army relied extensively on militia companies that were already in existence prior to the start of the war. Because the standard-issue blue uniforms were not available in large enough numbers to accommodate this large influx of new recruits, these units wore their old militia uniforms and accou-terments in many of the early battles and skirmishes. This led to a bewildering array of colors and styles of uniforms, especially within the Army of the Potomac, and caused much confusion during the First Battle of Bull Run. As soon as possible after that battle, those units unfortunate enough to be wearing gray were issued standard blue Union uniforms.

10 Uniforms of the 6th Massachusetts Volunteer Militia

Company	Name	Uniform
1. A Company	Lawrence Cadets	Blue frock coats and pantaloons, white crossbelts
2. B Company	Groton Artillery	Dark blue frock coats and light blue trousers
3. C Company	Mechanic Phalanx	Gray uniforms with yellow trimming
4. D Company	City Guards	Gray uniforms with buff trimming

Company	Name	Uniform
5. E Company	Davis Guards	Dark blue frock coats and light blue trousers
6. F Company	Warren Guard	Dark blue frock coats and red trousers
7. G Company	Worchester Infantry	Full dress uniforms of blue
8. H Company	Watson Guards	Gray uniforms
9. I Company	Lawrence Infantry	Blue frock coats and red trousers
10. K Company	Washington Artillery	Gray uniforms

The Confederate army had no existing set of dress regulations when the war broke out, and the men in each volunteer company were required to dress themselves. Because many of the local volunteer and militia units featured gray uniforms, the Confederate War Department decided in September 1861, when it issued its set of dress regulations, to make gray the standard color for its army. Still, the Rebel volunteer companies retained their independence and personality by keeping the company names under which they were initially organized. The following is a list of some of the more unusual names used by Rebel units:

13 Rebel Company Names

1. Mississippi Yankee Haters
2. Mounted Wild Cats
3. New Garden Fearnoughts
4. Nickelsville Spartan Band
5. Pee Dee Wild Cats
6. Tyranny Unmasked Artillery
7. Hook and Ladder Guard
8. Clinch Mountain Boomers
9. Scuppernong Grays
10. Cherokee Stone Walls
11. Franklin Fire Eaters
12. Knights of the Border

CHAPTER 8

This Month in 1862

THE SHADOW OF ROBERT E. Lee loomed large over 1862. After being named to replace Joe Johnston (who was wounded at the battle of Seven Pines), Lee forced General McClellan's 100,000-man army to withdraw from the York River Peninsula, defeated John Pope's army at Second Manassas, and invaded the North for the first time. Unfortunately, General McClellan learned of the location of Lee's army in Maryland in time to force him to retreat after the bloodiest day of the war at the battle of Antietam.

In the West, little-known Ulysses S. Grant emerged as the most successful Federal commander. His victory at Fort Donelson opened up most of Tennessee for Union occupation, and only Henry Halleck's indecision slowed Grant's southern advance after the battle. After being surprised and nearly overwhelmed at Shiloh, Grant held on to achieve another victory and secure Federal control of the Tennessee and Cumberland Rivers. In the most overlooked event of the year, the gunboats of David Farragut ran past the forts protecting New Orleans and forced the city to surrender. At the time, the city, the largest in the Confederacy and of immense commercial and strategic importance, was almost completely unguarded in one of the biggest Confederate blunders of the war.

Confederate General Robert E. Lee, commander of the Army of Northern Virginia. (National Archives)

☆ **January:** The Union army wins a victory at the battle of Mill Springs, Kentucky, giving the Federal army control over the eastern part of the state.

☆ **February:** Ulysses S. Grant engineers twin victories at Forts Henry and Donelson, Tennessee.

☆ **March:** The first naval engagement between ironclads occurs between the *U.S.S. Monitor* and the *C.S.S. Virginia* near Hampton Roads and ends in a draw.

☆ **April:** Ulysses S. Grant's 37,000-man army is surprised and nearly routed by Albert Sidney Johnston's 42,000 Confederates. However, Grant holds on and counterattacks the next day to secure a victory at Shiloh, Tennessee.

Union ordnance ready for the Peninsular Campaign. (Library of Congress)

☆ **May:** Union naval forces under Flag Officer David Farragut capture New Orleans, Louisiana, the largest city in the Confederacy.

☆ **June:** Joe Johnston is wounded during fighting near Seven Pines, Virginia. Robert E. Lee is named the new commander of the Army of Northern Virginia.

☆ **July:** The Seven Days' battles end outside Richmond, Virginia, with the defeat and subsequent withdrawal of the Union army from the York Peninsula.

☆ **August:** The Second Battle of Bull Run ends in another overwhelming victory for General Robert E. Lee.

☆ **September:** Lee invades Maryland but is defeated at Antietam with great losses to his army.

☆ **October:** The Union victory at the battle of Perryville ends Braxton Bragg's invasion of Kentucky.

☆ **November:** General Grant begins his campaign to capture the Confederate fortress at Vicksburg, Mississippi.

☆ **December:** General Burnside's army is crushed by Lee's forces at Fredericksburg, Virginia. In Tennessee, the battle of Stones River ends with another withdrawal by General Bragg's army.

CHAPTER 9

The Battles

Confederate General Thomas J. "Stonewall" Jackson. (National Archives)

I N EARLY APRIL 1862, the battle of Shiloh was fought near Pittsburg Landing, Tennessee. Incredibly, during two bloody days of fighting, more men were killed than in all the previous battles in American history combined. The casualty figures stunned the nation. After the battle, according to one news correspondent from New Orleans, "the South never smiled again." What could not be known at the time was that there would be many more larger and bloodier battles.

These fantastically high casualty figures were the result of Napoleonic battle tactics being confronted by long-range infantry weapons. Napoleonic tactics emphasized the concentration of forces into an overpowering striking power, with the goal being the destruction of the enemy army. These shock tactics were moderately effective when armies were equipped with inaccurate muzzle-loading weapons, but that slim advantage disappeared with the introduction of the Minié ball in 1849. Instead of having a range of 75 yards at best, an individual infantryman could now fire accurately at targets 400 yards away. This development shifted the advantage greatly to the defending force and resulted in the failure of seven out of every eight attacks during the Civil War. While the armies of both the North and South adopted weapons that used a

Inside the 'Hornet's Nest,' Union lines during the battle of Shiloh. (Library of Congress)

.58-inch Minié-type bullet, most generals continued to rely exclusively upon Napoleonic tactics with disastrous consequences on the battlefield. The following is a list of the battle deaths suffered in all the United States' wars:

Battle Deaths from 10 American Conflicts

	Name of War	*Years*	*Battle Deaths*
1.	American Revolution	1775-1783	4,435
2.	War of 1812	1812-1815	2,260
3.	Mexican War	1846-1848	1,733
4.	Civil War*	1861-1865	214,938
5.	Spanish-American War	1898	385
6.	World War I	1917-1918	53,402
7.	World War II	1941-1945	291,557
8.	Korean Conflict	1950-1953	33,746
9.	Vietnam Conflict	1964-1973	47,355
10.	Desert Storm	1991	148

* Union army and Confederate army combined.

☆☆☆

When Robert E. Lee took over the Army of Northern Virginia in the spring of 1862, he commanded the largest army ever mustered by the Confederacy at a time when the capital city of Richmond, Virginia, was in desperate peril. He was successful in driving the Union army away after the Seven Days' campaign and, by the fall of that year, had embarked on his first invasion of the North. In the process, however, Lee's army suffered heavily and he would never again command such a force. Probably the largest army ever amassed by the North never saw action in a major battle. Shortly after the battle of Shiloh, General Henry Halleck consolidated three Federal armies for a drive on Corinth, Mississippi. Halleck's mighty force, more than 120,000 men strong, made such slow progress that the Rebels defending the city were able to slip away before the Union army could strike a blow. The following is a list of the 13 largest battles of the war in terms of men available for fighting:

Unlucky 13: The Largest Battles of the War

	Battle	Date	Union	Confederate	Total
1.	Seven Days	June 25-July 1, 1862	91,169	95,482	186,651
2.	Fredericksburg	December 13, 1862	106,007	72,497	178,504
3.	Chancellorsville	May 1-4, 1862	118,000	59,500	177,500
4.	Cold Harbor	June 3, 1864	108,000	59,000	167,000
5.	Wilderness	May 5-6, 1864	101,895	61,025	162,920
6.	Gettysburg	July 1-3, 1864	83,289	75,054	158,343
7.	Spotsylvania	May 9-18, 1864	83,000	50,000	133,000
8.	Chickamauga	September 19-20, 1863	58,222	66,236	124,458
9.	Antietam	September 17, 1862	75,316	40,000	115,316
10.	Second Bull Run	August 29-30, 1862	62,000	48,527	110,527
11.	Shiloh	April 6-7, 1862	62,682	40,335	103,017
12.	Petersburg	June 15-18, 1864	63,797	41,499	105,296
13.	Chattanooga	November 23-25, 1863	56,359	46,156	102,515

☆☆☆

While the North had the advantage in manpower and weaponry throughout the war, there were occasions when Rebel forces were superior on a particular battlefield. Despite being outnumbered and pursued by three separate Federal forces during his famous Valley campaign, Stonewall Jackson was able, on several occasions, to bring more forces to bear than his opponent. Most importantly, Jackson was able to secure victories with his advantage. Other Rebel commanders were not so fortunate. On two occasions early in his tenure as commander of the Army of Northern Virginia, Robert E. Lee held numerical superiority on the battlefield. In both instances, Lee proved unable to

Confederate General John Bell Hood, also known as Old Wooden Head.
(National Archives)

Despite being heavily outnumbered, the Union army was victorious at the battle of Jonesboro, Georgia. (Library of Congress)

take advantage of his good fortune and resorted to frontal attacks that severely weakened his army.

In July 1864, Joe Johnston was sacked as the commander of the Army of Tennessee. His replacement, John Bell Hood, immediately launched a series of attacks against Sherman's army. Several times Hood was able to succeed in attacking an isolated portion of Sherman's army, but his straight-ahead tactics cost him more than 25 percent of his army and he was eventually forced out of the city. The aggressive Hood, the youngest full general in the Confederate army, earned his nickname as "Old Wooden Head" for these unimaginative tactics.

9 Battles in Which the Confederate Army Had the Advantage and Still Lost

	Battle	Date	Commander	Advantage
1.	Jonesboro	August 31, 1864	John Bell Hood	+9,640
2.	Atlanta	July 22, 1864	John Bell Hood	+6,457
3.	Ezra Church	July 28, 1864	John Bell Hood	+5,224
4.	Malvern Hill	July 1, 1864	Robert E. Lee	+3,439
5.	Pea Ridge	March 7-8, 1862	Earl Van Dorn	+2,750
6.	Corinth	October 3-4, 1862	Earl Van Dorn	+853
7.	Bentonville	March 19-21, 1865	Joe Johnston	+768
8.	Mechanicsville	June 26, 1862	Robert E. Lee	+725
9.	Seven Pines	May 31-June 1, 1862	Joe Johnston	+19

☆☆☆

In 1897, Thomas Livermore presented a paper before the Military
History Committee of Massachusetts
in which he attempted to determine,
with as much accuracy as possible, the
number of men engaged, killed, and
wounded during the Civil War. In his
work, which eventually grew into
the book *Numbers and Losses in the
Civil War,* Livermore estimated the
number of hits (killed or wounded) per
1,000 men engaged for every major
battle and engagement during the war.
According to Livermore's calcula-
tions, the Union army suffered 112.09
hits per every 1,000 men engaged.
Surprisingly, the Confederate army
had a significantly higher figure of
150.47 hits per 1,000, despite inflict-
ing greater overall casualties on the

Confederate General Joseph Eggleston
Johnston. (National Archives)

Union army. Livermore speculated on the cause of this phenomenon: "An army
inferior in numbers...may lose as many men as a larger one opposing it, by
keeping its individuals longer under fire. Without the bravery and resolution to
do this to an extraordinary extent, the Confederates could not have prolonged
the Civil War for four years."

What is not surprising is the list of battles identified by Livermore as the most
deadly of the war. In almost every case, an attacking force was ordered to charge
an entrenched foe. The only time in the war that an attacking force suffered
more than 30 percent casualties in a single battle was the Confederates at Gettysburg. Punctuated by Pickett's charge, Robert E. Lee flung his troops against
strong Union defensive positions for three days and, in the process, wrecked his
army.

The ferocity of the fighting that took place away from the main theater of
operations in the East is exemplified by the fact that more than 60 percent of the
bloodiest battles took place outside the Richmond-Washington corridor. These
include some of the most desperate charges of the war, like the 54th Massachusetts against Battery Wagner, South Carolina and John Bell Hood's "forlorn
hope" assault on Franklin, Tennessee, late in the war.

View of Gettysburg, Pennsylvania, shortly after the battle. (National Archives)

14 Battles with More Than 200 Hits per 1,000

	Battle	Date	Attacker	Hits/1,000	Outcome
1.	Gettysburg	July 1-3, 1863	Confederate	301	Lost
2.	Wilderness/Spotsylvania	May 5-19, 1864	Union	296	Stalemate
3.	Port Hudson	May 27-July 9, 1863	Union	267	Lost
4.	Stones River	Dec. 31-Jan. 1, 1863	Confederate	266	Lost
5.	Olustee	February 20, 1864	Union	265	Lost
6.	Chickamauga	September 19-20, 1863	Confederate	259	Won
7.	Shiloh	April 6-7, 1862	Confederate	241	Lost
8.	Antietam	September 17, 1862	Confederate	226	Lost
9.	Atlanta	July 22, 1864	Confederate	222	Lost
10.	Cedar Mountain	August 9, 1862	Union	219	Lost
11.	Battery Wagner	July 18, 1863	Union	214	Lost
12.	Seven Days	June 25-July 1, 1862	Confederate	207	Won
13.	Franklin	November 30, 1864	Confederate	206	Lost
14.	Tupelo	July 13-15, 1864	Union	206	Lost

CHAPTER 10

The Leaders

Union General Ulysses S. Grant,
taken early in the war.
(*Battles and Leaders*)

PERSONAL BRAVERY UNDER FIRE was an essential ingredient for every officer who commanded troops in battle. The Civil War is replete with instances of generals calmly riding along the lines in the midst of a fight. Such evidence of personal bravery was deemed necessary, in part to gain the confidence of the men, but also to inspire them to stand up to the awful carnage that swirled around them. On two separate occasions in 1864, Robert E. Lee had to be forced to leave a battlefield by chants of "Lee to the rear," the men apparently realizing more so than Lee that his life was too valuable to risk while leading a charge.

General George Pickett has received a generous amount of criticism over the years for not personally leading his famous charge at Gettysburg even though, according to Confederate military regulations, he was exactly where he was supposed to be: safely in the rear directing the assault. General William Tecumseh Sherman explained it this way in a letter to his wife: "Soldiers have a right to see and know that the man who guides them is near enough to see with his own eyes, and…he cannot see without being seen." Even Abraham Lincoln, the Federal Commander-in-Chief, fell prey to this phenomenon by exposing himself to enemy fire while observing a Confederate attack at Fort Stevens outside Washington in July 1864. It is not surprising, given their propensity for getting close to the action, that many generals were injured or killed during the war. The following is a list of generals who risked their lives by exposing themselves to the guns of the enemy and lived to tell the tale:

20 Generals Exposed to Enemy Fire

Name	Battle
1. *Joe Johnston (C)	First Manassas, Virginia
2. *Chatham "Rob" Wheat (C)	First Manassas, Virginia
3. *A.P. Hill (C)	Williamsburg, Virginia
4. William T. Sherman (U)	Shiloh, Tennessee
5. Ulysses S. Grant (U)	Belmont, Kentucky
6. *Stonewall Jackson (C)	Winchester, Virginia
7. George McClellan (U)	Oak Grove, Virginia
8. John Breckinridge (C)	Baton Rouge, Louisiana
9. *Daniel Butterfield (U)	Gaines's Mills, Virginia
10. *Patrick Cleburne (C)	Richmond, Kentucky
11. *Leonidas Polk (C)	Perryville, Kentucky
12. Daniel H. Hill (C)	Antietam, Maryland
13. *James Longstreet (C)	Antietam, Maryland
14. *Winfield Hancock (U)	Antietam, Maryland
15. *Richard Ewell (C)	Groveton, Virginia
16. William Rosecrans (U)	Stones River, Tennessee
17. *J.E.B. Stuart (C)	Chancellorsville, Virginia
18. *Robert Rodes (C)	Chancellorsville, Virginia
19. George Thomas (U)	Tunnel Hill, Georgia
20. *Oliver O. Howard (U)	Dallas, Georgia

(U) = Union army
(C) = Confederate army
*Killed or wounded at some other point in the war.

There were also many instances when a general got close to the action and suffered either a severe injury or a mortal one. During the war, 160 generals were killed in battle (80 on each side), and numerous others were put out of action for long periods of time. The high casualty rate for general officers was especially unbearable for the Confederacy because, as the war dragged on, they did not have suitable replacements for the men lost. The Army of Northern Virginia alone lost three of its best corps commanders (Stonewall Jackson, A.P. Hill, and James Longstreet) to death or severe injury, leaving Robert E. Lee with markedly less talented men in these key positions while he struggled to hold off General Grant's onslaught in 1864 and 1865. To put this into perspective, both the Union and the Confederacy lost more generals individually in four years than the United States has in all other wars.

General Sherman (4) and staff, Generals Howard (1), Logan (2), Hazen (3), Davis (5), Slocum (6), Mower (7), and Blair (8). (National Archives)

American General/Officer Battle Deaths

	War	Dead generals
1.	Civil War (Confederacy)	80
2.	Civil War (Union)	80
3.	World War II	23
4.	Revolutionary War	12
5.	Vietnam Conflict	8
6.	Indian Wars	4
7.	Philippine war (1899-1902)	3
8.	War of 1812	2
9.	World War I	2
10.	All others	0

☆☆☆

Robert E. Lee firmly believed that his army, "if properly led," could go almost anywhere and win almost every battle. For most of 1862 and 1863, he backed up this belief by repeatedly defeating larger and better equipped Federal armies. However, Lee's victories took a steady toll on the officer corps he relied upon to lead his army. Time and again, Lee had to find replacement officers for men who were killed or wounded in battle. After his victory at Chancellorsville, Lee was forced to restructure his entire command. With two new corps commanders and an assortment of untested brigade and regimental leaders, Lee brought his army across the Potomac River and to the fateful showdown at Gettysburg. Many of the failures that eventually resulted in his defeat can be traced to the failures of these newly promoted officers.

After Gettysburg, the situation became even worse, because more than 27 percent of Lee's officers ended up being killed or wounded. In fact, four divisional and 14 brigade commanders were killed, wounded, or captured in the battle.

If the infantry regiment was the backbone of the army, the regimental commander, usually a colonel, was one of the most vital men on a the battlefield. Regiments led by well-trained and battle-tested colonels could be counted on to spearhead assaults, as well as to suffer extensive casualties without breaking. In addition, regimental commanders who excelled in the field were looked upon as future replacements for generals killed or wounded in battle. The following is a list of the 17 colonels lost to the

Confederate General Ambrose Powell Hill, commanded a corps at Gettysburg. (National Archives)

Confederacy during the Gettysburg campaign. While not well known, this group includes many men who probably would have been promoted to positions of greater responsibility had they not fallen in battle.

17 Confederate Colonel Casualties of Gettysburg

Name	Injury
1. R. C. Allen	Killed
2. I. E. Avery	Killed
3. D. H. Christie	Killed
4. W. D. DeSaussure	Killed
5. E. C. Edmunds	Killed
6. James Hodges	Killed
7. John Bowie Magruder	Killed
8. Waller T. Patton	Killed
9. W. D. Stuart	Killed
10. Joseph Wasden	Killed
11. Lewis Williams	Killed

Name	Injury
12. Birkett D. Fry	Captured
13. P. S. Evans	Captured
14. William Forney	Captured
15. William Gibson	Captured
16. J. K. Marshall	Captured
17. R. M. Powell	Captured

☆☆☆

The Union army was much better equipped to handle the loss of officers simply because the North had a much greater talent pool to draw from. However, there were Union regiments that suffered such dramatic losses in officers that it could not help but affect their combat effectiveness. An example can be found with the 1st Maine Heavy Artillery. Despite their name, most heavy artillery regiments were called upon to serve as ordinary infantry units. As an untested unit, the men of the 1st Maine Heavy Artillery were called to the front in May 1864 and did not hesitate when they were ordered to assault Confederate fortifications at Petersburg, Virginia. At a time when most Union veterans had ceased to make foolish charges, the 900 men from Maine plunged ahead into a devastating fire. When it was all over, 635 men were killed or wounded, and 13 officers were killed or mortally wounded.

The infantry regiment that lost the most officers during the entire war was the 61st Pennsylvania. Organized in Pittsburgh in September 1861, the 61st Pennsylvania saw action early and often, and, despite suffering heavy losses, continued to be an effective fighting force throughout the war. The resiliency of units such as the 61st Pennsylvania served as a testament to the men who fought in the ranks as well as to the officers who stepped forward to lead them. The following is a list of the regiments that suffered the most officers killed during the war.

14 Union Regiments With the Most Officers Killed

Regiment	Number of Officers Killed
1. 1st Maine Heavy Artillery	23
2. 8th New York Heavy Artillery	19
3. 61st Pennsylvania	19
4. 5th New Hampshire	18
5. 12th Massachusetts	18
6. 48th New York	18
7. 73rd New York	18
8. 81st Pennsylvania	18
9. 145th Pennsylvania	18
10. 31st Maine	18
11. 20th Massachusetts	17

Regiment	Number of Officers Killed
12. 14th Connecticut	17
13. 62nd Pennsylvania	17
14. 63rd Pennsylvania	17

☆☆☆

Losing a commanding officer to enemy fire was difficult, but losing an officer to what we now refer to as "friendly fire" was so devastating that it was often covered up by those involved. Late in the afternoon of September 14, 1862, Major-General Jesse Reno, a divisional commander in the 9th Corps, launched an attack through Fox's Gap in South Mountain. In the confusion of battle, the inexperienced men of the 35th Massachusetts fired a volley at a group of riders that they could barely see. Unfortunately, the riders were General Reno and his staff, and the only man hit was Reno himself. With a bullet lodged near his heart, Reno spoke his last words: "I am killed. Shot by our own men." The manner in which Reno died was kept a secret for 20 years.

Confederate General James Longstreet, severely wounded by friendly fire during the battle of the Wilderness in 1864.
(*Battles and Leaders*)

On May 5, 1864, General Robert E. Lee's "Old Warhorse," James Longstreet, was seriously wounded by friendly fire while preparing to launch an attack that could have given the Confederates a smashing victory during the Wilderness battle. In the fusillade that hit Longstreet, fellow General Micah Jenkins was shot in the head and mortally wounded. The irony of losing Longstreet to friendly fire, almost a year to the date and in almost the exact same place that Stonewall Jackson was also shot by his own men, could not have been lost on Lee. Without the services of these two men, one killed and the other severely wounded by the fire of their own troops, Lee was not only forced to scramble to find adequate replacements but was also deprived of their wisdom and counsel for the duration of the war.

5 Generals Killed by Friendly Fire

Name	Army	Battle
1. Albert Sidney Johnston	Confederate	Shiloh
2. Thomas J. "Stonewall" Jackson	Confederate	Chancellorsville
3. Micah Jenkins	Confederate	Wilderness
4. Jesse Reno	Union	South Mountain
5. Thomas Williams	Union	Baton Rouge

☆☆☆

Most tactical decisions on the battlefield were not made by generals or colonels. At a time when communications systems were still incredibly primitive, high-ranking officers had to rely upon the judgment of majors, captains, and lieutenants. In the heat of battle, these men not only had to lead, but they also had to transmit accurate information up the chain of command. The 11th Virginia Cavalry was organized in June 1862 and participated in numerous skirmishes and battles until the end of the war. During its time in the field, the 10 companies of this cavalry regiment were officered by a colonel, four majors, 26 captains, and 75 lieutenants. Of these officers, 61 percent were either killed, wounded, or captured. This high casualty figure was typical for frontline officers, especially in Confederate units.

Made up mostly of men from the Shenandoah Valley, the 11th Virginia Cavalry, a member of the Laurel Brigade, was a star-crossed unit. Its shining moment occurred on the fields of Brandy Station, where the 11th Virignia fought gallantly to hold the field and eventually fend off the unusually aggressive Federal horsemen. However, in 1864, with many of their veteran officers gone by the wayside, the 11th Virginia was also a part of Jubal Early's army and his disastrous attempt to hold off Phil Sheridan's advance up the

Union General Jesse Reno, mortally wounded by his own men during the battle of South Mountain. (National Archives)

Shenandoah Valley. Time and again, the Rebel cavalry was routed by their Union counterparts and after a particularly poor performance at Tom's Brook, Early acidly commented: "The laurel is a running vine." Like many veteran units in the Confederate army, the 11th Virginia suffered late in the war from poor leadership, especially the loss of frontline officers. The following is a list of the captains who served in the 11th Virginia Cavalry and their actions during the war:

26 Captains of the 11th Virginia Cavalry

Name	*Actions During War*
1. Mottrom M. Ball	Hospitalized for acute diarrhea and scabies; wounded once.
2. Albert Braxton	Hospitalized for scabies; paroled as captain of Company B.
3. Mordecai B. Cartmell	Killed in action at Sangster's Station, December 1863.
4. Thomas K. Cartmell	Wounded at Linville Creek; captured three times.
5. Thomas Chipley	Resigned June 1862 after being accused of cowardice.

Name	*Actions During War*
6. Foxall A. Daingerfield	Wounded six times and captured once.
7. James H. Daugherty	Wounded twice, left leg amputated.
8. R. G. Findley	Captured and paroled May 1865.
9. James M. Hanger	Promoted to major and joined J.E.B. Stuart's staff.
10. William H. Harness	Cited for gallantry; resigned under charges of neglect of duty.
11. Addison Harper	Resigned in February 1862 at age of 53.
12. James L. Hooff	Served as assistant quartermaster.
13. Dr. Alexander McChesney	Resigned May 1862, returned to medical practice.
14. Edward McDonald	Wounded at Amelia Springs, Virginia, April 1865.
15. Hugh H. McGuire	Died of wounds received at Amelia Springs, April 1865.
16. David Meade	Awarded Cross of Honor, March 1910.
17. George Myers	Resigned under charges of neglect of duty.
18. John R. Pendleton	Wounded three times and captured twice during war.
19. Adolphus M. Pierce	Wounded at Upperville, Virginia, June 1863.
20. Archibald Richards	Lost election in May 1862; transferred.
21. William Taylor	Resigned to join General Lomax's brigade.
22. Willam Tayolor	Wounded at Haw's Shop, Virginia; captured, sent to Point Lookout.
23. John A. Turner	Captured and sent to Fort Delaware.
24. Andrew J. Ware	Suffered from chronic rheumatism and diarrhea.
25. Octavious Weems	Cashiered for getting drunk and using abusive language.
26. Thomas J. Wills	Resigned June 1863 after being accused of cowardice.

43 Foreign-Born Union Generals

1. Jacob Dolson Cox, Canada. Future Secretary of the Interior under President Grant.
2. John Franklin Farnsworth, Canada. General Elon Farnsworth's uncle.
3. John McNeil, Canada. Discharged after battle of Westport because he had one lame arm.
4. Gustave Paul Cluseret, France. Was placed under arrest and resigned from the army in March 1863.
5. Philippe Regis Denis de Keredern de Trobriand, France. Defended the Peach Orchard at Gettysburg.
6. Alfred Napoleon Alexander Duffie, France. Captured by Confederate partisans in 1864.
7. Ludwig Blenker, Germany. Died as the result of injuries suffered in a fall from his horse.
8. Henry Bohlen, Germany. Killed in action at Freeman's Ford on the Rappahannock River.

9. August Valentine Kautz, Germany. Led a division of black troops into Richmond in April 1865.
10. Karl Leopold Matthies, Prussia. Wounded while charging up Missionary Ridge.
11. Peter Joseph Osterhaus, Prussia. Fought with Sherman's army in Georgia.
12. Friedrich Salomon, Prussia. Brother of wartime Governor of Wisconsin.
13. Alexander Schimmelfennig, Prussia. Hid in a pigsty for two days to avoid capture at Gettysburg.
14. Carl Schurz, Prussia. Vigorous abolitionist and noted orator.
15. Franz Sigel, Germany. Helped recruit thousands of Germans.
16. Adolph von Steinwehr, Duchy of Brunswick. Fought well at Chancellorsville and Gettysburg.
17. Max Weber, Achern, Grand Duchy of Baden. Was severely wounded at Antietam.
18. August Willich, Prussia. He was captured at Stones River and wounded at Resaca.
19. Edward Dickinson Baker, Great Britain. Close friend of Lincoln, he was killed at Ball's Bluff.
20. John Wallace Fuller, England. Served as a brigade and division commander.
21. John McArthur, Scotland. Cited for conspicuous gallantry and efficiency at the battle of Nashville.
22. Joshua Thomas Owen, Wales. Charged with disobedience of orders at Cold Harbor.
23. William Henry Powell, South Wales. Cavalry commander, wounded and captured in July 1863.
24. Alexander Sandor Asboth, Hungary. Wounded at Pea Ridge, Arkansas, and Marianna, Florida.
25. Julius (Szamvald) Stahel, Hungary. Awarded the Congressional Medal of Honor for bravery.
26. Richard Busteed, Ireland. Appointed Judge of the U.S. District Court for Alabama in 1863.
27. Patrick Edward Conner, Ireland. Commanded the District of Utah.
28. Michael Corcoran, Ireland. Wounded and captured at First Bull Run.
29. William Gamble, Ireland. Severely wounded at Malvern Hill, served conspicuously at Gettysburg.
30. Richard Henry Jackson, Ireland. He served in the capture of Pensacola, Florida, in 1861.
31. Patrick Henry Jones, Ireland. He was wounded and taken prisoner at Chancellorsville.
32. James Lawlor Kiernan, Ireland. Resigned due to health problems.
33. Michael Kelly Lawler, Ireland. Led a charge at Vicksburg that captured 1,100 Rebel prisoners.
34. Thomas Francis Meagher, Ireland. Organized and led the Irish Brigade.

35. James Shields, Ireland. Defeated Stonewall Jackson at the first battle of Kernstown, Virginia.

36. Thomas Alfred Smyth, Ireland. He was mortally wounded by a sharpshooter in April 1865.

37. Thomas William Sweeny, Ireland. After the war he led the aborted "invasion" of Canada.

38. Wladimir Krzyzanowski, Poland. Was instrumental in recruiting Germans and Poles in 1861.

39. Albin Francisco Schoepf, Poland. Served as commander of the Federal prison at Fort Delaware.

40. John Basil Turchin (Ivan Vasilovitch Turchinoff), Russia. Fought bravely at Chickamauga.

41. Edward Ferrero, Spain. His habit of being drunk during battles was, for some reason, overlooked.

42. Charles John Stolbrand, Sweden. Distinguished officer of artillery.

43. John Eugene Smith, Switzerland. Served bravely at Fort Donelson, Shiloh, and Vicksburg.

14 Union Officers Who Ran for President of the United States

	Name	*Party*	*Years*	*Highest Rank*
1.	George McClellan	Democrat	Lost election of 1864	Major-General
2.	Andrew Johnson	Republican	1865-1869	Brigadier-General
3.	Ulysses S. Grant	Republican	1869-1877	Lieutenant-General
4.	Rutherford B. Hayes	Republican	1877-1881	Major-General
5.	James Garfield	Republican	1881*	Major-General
6.	Winfield S. Hancock	Democrat	Lost election of 1880	Major-General
7.	John W. Phelps	Anti-Masonic	Lost election of 1880	Brigadier-General
8.	James B. Weaver	Greenback	Lost election of 1880	Brigadier-General
9.	Neal Dow	Prohibition	Lost election of 1880	Brigadier-General
10.	Benjamin Butler	Greenback	Lost election of 1884	Major-General
11.	Benjamin Harrison	Republican	1889-1893	Brigadier-General
12.	James B. Weaver	People's Party	Lost election 1892	Brigadier-General
13.	Clinton B. Fiske	Prohibition	Lost election of 1888	Brigadier-General
14.	William McKinley	Republican	1897-1901*	Major

* Assassinated while in office

8 Future Union Generals and Colonels at Fort Sumter in 1861

	Name	*Final Rank*
1.	Major Robert Anderson	Major-General
2.	Captain Abner Doubleday	Major-General
3.	Captain John Foster	Major-General
4.	Captain Truman Seymour	Major-General

Name	Final Rank
5. Lieutenant Jefferson C. Davis	Major-General
6. Lieutenant George W. Snyder	Colonel
7. Lieutenant Norman J. Hall	Colonel
8. Surgeon Samuel Crawford	Major-General

21 Civil War Nicknames

1. Bull Head - Given to Union General Edwin Sumner because a musket ball once bounced off his skull.
2. Cump - Given to Union General William Tecumseh Sherman; shortened version of his middle name.
3. Fighting Joe - Given to Union General Joseph Hooker. Derived from an Associated Press dispatch.
4. Granny Lee - Given to Confederate General Robert E. Lee early in the war for his elderly appearance.
5. Gray Ghost - Given to Confederate raider John Mosby because he was so elusive.
6. Grumble - Given to Confederate General William Jones, for his generally sour disposition.
7. Jeb - Given to Confederate General James Ewell Brown Stuart; taken from his initials.
8. Little Phil - Given to Union General Philip Sheridan in regard to his short stature.
9. Mudwall - Given to Confederate General William L. Jackson, cousin of Stonewall Jackson.
10. Old Fuss and Feathers - Given to Union General Winfield Scott for his approach to subordinates.
11. Old Pete - Given to Confederate General James Longstreet from an old West Point nickname.
12. Old Snapping Turtle - Given to Union General George Meade for his short temper.
13. Polecat - Given to French-born Confederate General Camille Armand Polignac.
14. Prince John - Given to Confederate General John Bankhead Magruder for his lavish way of entertaining.
15. Sam - Union General Ulysses S. Grant; from an old West Point nickname.
16. Shanks - Given to Confederate General Nathan George Evans because of his small legs.
17. Slow Trot - Given to Union General George Thomas for his careful way of organizing for battle.
18. Virginia Creeper - Given to Union General George McClellan in honor of his slow advances.

19. Uncle John - Given to Union General John Sedgwick for his paternalistic behavior towards his troops.
20. Wooden Head - Given to Confederate General John Bell Hood for his tendency to attack at any cost.
21. Young Napoleon - Given to General George McClellan because of his inflated sense of importance.

Ages of 30 Union Leaders in 1861

1.	General Winfield Scott	75
2.	Secretary of State William Seward	60
3.	Admiral David Farragut	60
4.	Secretary of the Navy Gideon Welles	59
5.	President Abraham Lincoln	52
6.	Vice-President Hannibal Hamlin	52
7.	Vice-President Andrew Johnson	53
8.	Secretary of Treasury Salmon Chase	53
9.	Admiral David Dixon Porter	48
10.	Secretary of War Edwin Stanton	47
11.	General Joseph Hooker	47
12.	General Henry Halleck	46
13.	General George Meade	46
14.	General Nathaniel Banks	45
15.	General George Thomas	45
16.	General Benjamin Butler	43
17.	General William Rosecrans	42
18.	General William T. Sherman	41
19.	General Ulysses S. Grant	39
20.	General John Pope	39
21.	General Ambrose Burnside	37
22.	General Winfield Hancock	37
23.	General John A. Logan	35
24.	General George McClellan	35
25.	General James McPherson	33
26.	General Joshua Chamberlain	33
27.	General Philip Sheridan	30
28.	General John Schofield	30
29.	Colonel Robert Gould Shaw	24
30.	General George Armstrong Custer	22

Ages of 30 Confederate Leaders in 1861

1.	General Albert Sidney Johnston	58
2.	Treasury Secretary Christopher Memminger	58

3.	General Joseph E. Johnston	54
4.	General Robert E. Lee	54
5.	President Jefferson Davis	53
6.	General Sterling Price	52
7.	Admiral Raphael Semmes	52
8.	Secretary of State Judah Benjamin	50
9.	Vice-President Alexander Stephens	49
10.	Secretary of the Navy Stephen Mallory	48
11.	General John C. Pemberton	47
12.	Secretary of War James Seddon	46
13.	General Jubal Early	45
14.	General Braxton Bragg	44
15.	General Richard Ewell	44
16.	General Pierre G.T.Beauregard	43
17.	General Josiah Gorgas	43
18.	General Wade Hampton	43
19.	General Earl Van Dorn	41
20.	General James Longstreet	40
21.	General Nathan Bedford Forrest	40
22.	General John C. Breckinridge	40
23.	Colonel Henry Wirz	38
24.	General Stonewall Jackson	37
25.	General Edmund Kirby Smith	37
26.	General Ambrose P. Hill	36
27.	General George Pickett	36
28.	General Richard Taylor	35
29.	General John Bell Hood	30
30.	General J.E.B. Stuart	28

67 Union Generals: What They Did After the War

20 Politicians

1. Ulysses S. Grant: Became 18th President of the United States in 1868.
2. Carl Schurz: U.S. Senator from Missouri, 1869-75.
3. George McClelland: Governor of New Jersey, 1878-81.
4. Adelbert Ames: Governor of Mississippi, 1868-70 and 74-76. Senator from Mississippi, 1870-74.
5. Francis Channing Barlow: New York Attorney General, 1871-73.
6. Francis Blair: U.S. Senator from Missouri, 1871-73.
7. Ambrose Burnside: Governor of Rhode Island, 1866-68, and U.S. Senator, 1875-81.
8. Benjamin Butler: Massachusetts Congressman and Governor of Massachusetts, 1883.

9.   Joshua Chamberlain: Elected Governor of Maine four times.
10. Powell Clayton: Governor of Arkansas, 1868-71, and Senator, 1871-77.
11. Jacob Cox: Ohio Governor, 1866-67, and Congressman, 1876-78.
12. Charles Devens: Massachusetts Supreme Court, 1873-77, 1881-91.
13. John Adams Dix: Governor of New York, 1873-75.
14. Lucius Fairchild: Governor of Wisconsin, 1866-72.
15. James Garfield: Elected 20th President of the United States.
16. Rutherford B. Hays: Elected 19th President of the United States.
17. Joseph Hawley: Connecticut Governor, 1866; Representative, 1872-75 and 1879-81; and Senator, 1881-95.
18. George Washington Morgan: Representative from Ohio.
19. John Palmer: Governor of Illinois, 1869-73, and Senator, 1891-97.
20. James Shields: Senator from Missouri; only person elected Senator from three different states.

11 Educators

1. Jacob Cox: Dean of the Cincinnati Law School, 1881-97.
2. George Washington Cullum: Superintendent of West Point, 1864-66.
3. Joshua Lawrence Chamberlain: Governor of Maine four times, President of Bowdoin College.
4. Samuel P. Carter: Annapolis Commander of Cadets, 1877-80.
5. Oliver O. Howard: Founded Howard University, 1869-74.
6. Richard W. Johnson: Taught military science in Missouri and Minnesota.
7. Eliakim Scammon: Taught college mathematics.
8. John Schofield: Superintendent of West Point 1876-81.
9. Emory Upton: Commanded the Presidio in San Francisco, California.
10. Adolph Steinwehr: Taught military science at Yale.
11. Alexander Webb: President of City College of New York, 1869-1902.

6 Businessmen

1. William Wood Averell: Manufacturer and inventor of industrial products.
2. Erasmus Darwin Keyes: Business interest in banking, mining, and viniculture.
3. Mortimer Legett: Founded Brust Electric Company.
4. Ely Parker: Became New York businessman.
5. Lewis Parsons: Went into banking and railroads.
6. Henry Hastings Sibley: Became a banker and merchant.

7 Lawyers

1. Francis Channing Barlow: Became New York Attorney General, 1871-73.
2. William Birney: Attorney for District of Columbia.
3. James Deering Fessenden: Portland attorney.

4. Manning Ferguson Force: Became a lawyer and a judge.
5. Mortimer Leggett: Became a lawyer in Cleveland.
6. John McClernand: Resumed legal career.
7. Henry Slocum: A Brooklyn attorney.

11 Appointees

1. Henry Baxter: Minister to Hondurus, 1966-69.
2. William Belknap: Secretary of War under Grant, 1869-76.
3. Rufus King: Minister to the Vatican.
4. Peter Osterhaus: Held consular appointments in France and Germany.
5. Halbert Paine: Commissioner of Patents.
6. William Rosecrans: Minister to Mexico, 1868-69.
7. Robert Schenk: Ambassador to England, 1870.
8. Powell Clayton: Ambassador to Mexico, 1879-1905.
9. Charles Devens: U.S. Attorney General, 1877-81.
10. John Adams Dix: Minister to France, 1866-69.
11. Lucius Fairchild: Ambassador to Spain, 1880-82.

12 Writers

1. Newton Martin Curtis: Wrote *From Bull Run to Chancellorsville*.
2. Jacob Cox: Wrote extensively about the war.
3. Henry Beebe Carrington: Wrote *Battle of the American Revolution*.
4. George Armstrong Custer: Wrote *My Life on the Plains*.
5. George Washington Cullum: Wrote *The Biographical Register of West Point Graduates*.
6. Ulysses S. Grant: Wrote his personal memoirs in 1885.
7. David McMurtrie Gregg: Wrote account of 2nd Cavalry Division at Gettysburg.
8. John Logan: Wrote *The Great Conspiracy* and *The Volunteer Soldier of America*.
9. James Steedman: Became a Toledo journalist.
10. Emory Upton: Wrote *Military Policy of the United States*.
11. Lew Wallace: Wrote *Ben Hur*.
12. Joshua Chamberlain: Wrote *The Passing of the Armies*.

67 Confederate Generals: What They Did After the War

7 Educators

1. Robert E. Lee: President of Washington College.
2. Nathan Evans: School principal in Alabama.
3. Daniel Hill: Head of the University of Arkansas.
4. Bushrod Johnson: Chancellor of the University of Nashville.

5. Henry Lane: Taught at Alabama Polytechnic Institute.
6. George Washington Custis Lee: Taught at VMI. Followed father as head of Washington College.
7. Edmund Smith: Became President of the University of Nashville.

12 Politicians

1. Joseph E. Johnston: Served in U.S. Congress.
2. William Bate: Governor of Tennessee, 1882-86.
3. Simon Buckner: Governor of Kentucky, 1887-91.
4. Thomas Churchill: Arkansas State Treasurer, 1874-80, and Governor, 1881-83.
5. Alfred Colquitt: Governor of Georgia, 1876-82, and U.S. Senator, 1882-94.
6. James Connor: South Carolina Attorney General, 1876-77.
7. John Gordon: U.S. Senator from George, 1873-80 and 1891-97, and Governor, 1886-90.
8. Johnson Hagood: South Carolina Governor, 1880-82.
9. Wade Hampton: South Carolina Governor 1876 and 1878, and U.S. Senator.
10. James Kemper: Governor of Virginia, 1874-78.
11. William Mahone: U.S. Senator, 1881-87.
12. John Marmaduke: Governor of Missouri, 1884-87.

5 Foreign Soldiers

1. William Loring: Served with the Egyptian army.
2. John Magruder: Served Emperor Maximilian in Mexico.
3. Alexander Reynolds: Joined the Egyptian army in 1869.
4. Joseph Shelby: Joined Emperor Maximilian's forces in Mexico.
5. Henry Sibley: Became artillery general with Egyptian army, 1865-74.

5 Engineers

1. Braxton Bragg: Civil engineer in Texas and Alabama.
2. Robert Ransom: A civil engineer.
3. Carter Stevenson: A civil and mining engineer.
4. Isaac Trimble: Engineer in Baltimore.
5. Prince Camille Polignac: A French civil engineer.

20 Lawyers

1. Jubal Early: Legal practice in Lynchburg, Virginia.
2. Rufus Barringer: Practiced law in Concord, North Carolina.
3. Richard Lee Beale: Resumed legal practice in Hague, Virginia.

4. John Breckinridge : Resumed legal practice in Lexington, Kentucky.
5. William Lewis Cabell: Admitted to the bar in Fort Smith, Arkansas.
6. Howell Cobb: Practiced law in Georgia.
7. James Connor: Resumed legal practice in South Carolina.
8. John Imboden: Legal practice in Richmond, Virginia.
9. Alexander Lawton: Practice law in Savannah, Georgia.
10. John Singleton Mosby: Resumed practice in Virginia.
11. William Henry Payne: Maintained legal practice in Virginia.
12. Albert Pike: Wrote legal treatises in Washington, D.C.
13. Roger Pryor: Admitted to the bar in New York in 1866.
14. Pierre Soule: Returned to law practice in New Orleans, Louisiana.
15. Robert Toombs: Resumed legal practice in Georgia.
16. Leroy Walker: Resumed law practice in Huntsville, Alabama.
17. William Taliaferro: Operated legal practice in Virginia.
18. William Wickham: Practiced law in Virginia.
19. Henry Wise: Resumed legal practice in Richmond, Virginia.
20. Marcus Wright: Returned to law practice in Memphis, Tennessee.

8 Farmers

1. Alfred Cumming: Farmed in Georgia.
2. Arnold Elzey: Farmed in Maryland.
3. Richard Ewell: Farmed in Nashville.
4. Nathan Forrest: Returned to cotton farming.
5. Alfred Iverson: Became a farmer.
6. William Mackall: Became a Virginia farmer.
7. John McCausland: Became a West Virginia farmer.
8. John Pemberton: Became a Virginia farmer.

10 Businessmen

1. John Bell Hood: A merchant in New Orleans.
2. John Rogers Cooke: A merchant in Richmond.
3. Zacharias Deas: Cotton merchant.
4. George Dibrell: Businessman.
5. Birkett Fry: Cotton Merchant.
6. William Hardee: Alabama planter and businessman.
7. James Hawes: A hardware merchant.
8. John Marmaduke: A St. Louis businessman.
9. Walter Lane: Became a merchant.
10. Roswell Ripley: Became a manufacturer in England.

CHAPTER 11

Death:
The Currency of War

ESPITE STRONG UNIONIST SENTIMENT in many parts of the state, North Carolina contributed more than 125,000 soldiers to the Confederate army. In addition, North Carolinian units were noted for having gained the most ground during Pickett's Charge and for launching the last charge of the Army of Northern Virginia at Appomattox Court-House. However, the Tar Heel state paid a steep price for this distinction, because more than 17 percent of its entire military population (white males between the ages of 18 and 45) were killed in the war. The only state that sacrificed more young men (23 percent) for the Confederacy was South Carolina. As a means of comparison, the top two Union states, in terms of total deaths, were New York and Pennsylvania, and each lost 'about 10 percent of the men it supplied to the Federal army.

Ulysses S. Grant was called a "butcher" and sharply criticized for the high casualty figures the Army of the Potomac suffered during the Overland campaign in the summer of 1864. It is difficult to determine how many men died during the campaign because, according to General Joshua Chamberlain, the officers "were not called upon or permitted to report casualties during that whole campaign…for fear the country could not stand the disclosure." We do know, however, that during the few short minutes that the battle of Cold Harbor lasted, almost 10,000 men were killed or wounded.

The 26th North Carolina lost over 800 men during the three day battle of Gettysburg. (Library of Congress)

☆ **95** ☆

The site of the mortal wounding of Confederate General Jeb Stuart, near
Yellow Tavern, Virginia. (Library of Congress)

Robert E. Lee, on the other hand, is best remembered as a grand tactician who
was able to win numerous battles despite being outnumbered and outgunned. However, in May 1862, when Lee was called upon to drive the General George McClel-
lan-led Army of the Potomac away from Richmond, Virginia, he also resorted to
frontal assaults at Gaines's Mills and Malvern Hill, and his army suffered more than
20,000 casualties in only seven days. For both Grant and Lee, the price they had to
pay for military victories was the lives of many of their men. The following is a list
of the states with the highest total battle deaths during the war:

15 States with Highest Total of Battle Deaths

	State	Number of Dead
1.	*North Carolina	19,673
2.	New York	19,085
3.	Pennsylvania	15,265
4.	*South Carolina	12,922
5.	Ohio	11,588
6.	Illinois	9,884
7.	*Mississippi	8,458
8.	*Virginia	7,847
9.	Indiana	7,243
10.	*Georgia	7,272
11.	Massachusetts	6,115

THE 3 CAUSES OF WOUNDS DURING BATTLE IN THE CIVIL WAR

1.	Muskets and pistols	93%
2.	Artillery	5%
3.	Bayonets and sabers	1%

State	Number of Dead
12. Michigan	4,448
13. Wisconsin	3,802
14. Iowa	3,540
15. *Louisiana	3,486

*Confederate records are incomplete and the actual totals are probably higher.

☆☆☆

Infantry regiments formed the backbone of both the Union and Rebel armies. A newly recruited regiment in the Union army would typically have between 845 and 1,025 men. That number would swiftly decline when the regiment saw action. For example, the 141st Pennsylvania, which began the war with 1,047 men, carried only 417 men into battle at Chancellorsville. A month later, less than 200 men answered the morning roll call prior to the battle of Gettysburg. Any time an infantry regiment came into contact with the enemy, casualties were to be expected. A unit could reasonably expect to lose as many as 10 percent of its men if heavily engaged in a major battle, but there were times when battle losses went much higher.

The Union regiment that suffered the most men killed, wounded, or captured in a single engagement during the war was the 1st Minnesota. Prior to the battle of Gettysburg, the only distinction that the 1st Minnesota held was that it was the only regiment from that state to serve in the East. That changed late in the afternoon of July 2, 1863, when Union General Winfield Hancock discovered a gap in his lines. Hancock ordered the 1st Minnesota, led by Lieutenant-Colonel William Colville, to plug the gap by charging an advancing Confederate brigade. Alone and unsupported, Colville's brave Minnesotans succeeded in checking the Rebel advance long enough for Hancock to stabilize the line, but at a terrible cost.

Union General Winfield Scott Hancock, commanded the Second Corps of the Army of the Potomac. (Library of Congress)

Of the eight companies engaged, 215 of the 262 men who began the charge were either killed or wounded in it, and the casualties were so severe that the highest-ranking unhurt officer after the battle was Captain H. C. Coates. Of the charge, Coates wrote: "The fire we encountered...was

Bones being collected from the Cold Harbor, Virginia, battlefield. (Library of Congress)

terrible, and, although we inflicted severe punishment upon the enemy, and stopped his advance, we…lost in killed and wounded more than two-thirds of our men and officers who were engaged."

Only the 1st Texas Infantry Regiment, of John Bell Hood's proud Texas Brigade, suffered a higher percentage of casualties. As the shock troops of the Army of Northern Virginia, these men were usually called upon when General Lee needed to storm a strongly held Union position. At the battle of Antietam, this regiment, commanded by Lieutenant-Colonel P. A. Work, was ordered to halt a Union charge heading across a cornfield toward their position near a small Dunker Church. Work's men stormed through the Federal line until they were 150 yards ahead of the rest of the brigade. During the charge, eight separate color-bearers were shot down and, facing fire from the front and flank, Work was forced to order a retreat. Twenty minutes after the charge had begun, four of every five men were killed or wounded. After the battle, when General Hood was asked where his men were, he responded: "Dead on the field."

The regiment that lost the most total men killed or mortally wounded in one engagement was the 26th North Carolina at Gettysburg. At the beginning of the day on July 1, 1863, this unit could count more than 800 muskets ready for action. In spearheading the effort to drive the famed Iron Brigade back through the town, the 26th lost 86 men killed, 502 wounded, and 120 missing and presumed wounded or killed. Incredibly, the 26th was also called upon to participate in Pickett's Charge and, on the following day, mustered only 80 men for duty. The following is a list of the regiments with the highest percentage of casualties in one battle:

Rebel soldier killed in the trenches near Petersburg, Virginia. (National Archives)

20 Regiments with the Highest Casualty Percentage

	Regiment	Battle	Engaged	% Casualties
1.	1st Texas (C)	Antietam	225	82%
2.	1st Minnesota	Gettysburg	262	82%
3.	21st Georgia (C)	2d Manassas	242	76%
4.	141st Pennsylvania	Gettysburg	198	76%
5.	101st New York	2d Manassas	168	74%
6.	26th North Carolina (C)	Gettysburg	820	72%
7.	6th Mississippi (C)	Shiloh	425	71%
8.	25th Massachusetts	Cold Harbor	310	70%
9.	36th Wisconsin	Bethesda Church	240	69%
10.	20th Massachusetts	Fredericksburg	238	68%
11.	8th Tennessee (C)	Stones River	444	68%
12.	10th Tennessee (C)	Chickamauga	328	68%
13.	8th Vermont	Cedar Creek	156	68%
14.	Palmetto Sharpshooters(C)	Glendale	375	68%
15.	81st Pennsylvania	Fredericksburg	261	67%
16.	12th Massachusetts	Antietam	334	67%
17.	17th South Carolina	South Carolina	284	67%
18.	1st Maine Heavy Artillery	Petersburg	900	67%
19.	23rd South Carolina	2d Manassas	225	66%
20.	44th Georgia	Mechanicsville	514	65%

(C) = Confederate army

CHAPTER 12

Outlaws and Raiders

WILLIAM CLARK QUANTRILL WAS probably the most notorious of the raiders and bushwhackers to emerge from the internecine warfare that took place along the Kansas-Missouri border during the war. Together with "Bloody Bill" Anderson and George Todd, Quantrill helped engineer a ruthless campaign against the pro-Union men living in the region. The high point of Quantrill's career occurred on August 11, 1862, when he and his men captured Independence, Missouri. Four days later, Quantrill received a commission as captain, and his men were officially mustered in as partisan rangers in the Confederate army.

Eager for additional accolades, Quantrill traveled to Richmond during the winter of 1862-63, but he was frustrated in his attempts to receive any further official recognition of his activities or his unorthodox approach to waging war. After remaining quiet for most of the summer, in August 1863 Quantrill led his men into Lawrence, Kansas, the strongest abolitionist city in the state. In a few hours of bloody

The sacking of Lawrence, Kansas, by Quantrill's men. (Library of Congress)

work, his men killed more than 150 men and boys and burned most of the city. As a result of Quantrill's action, thousands of families living near the Missouri-Kansas border were forced to leave their homes and the territory was turned into a vast wasteland for the duration of the war.

Quantrill conducted numerous other small raids until being killed in Kentucky on May 10, 1864, while traveling to Washington, D.C. with vague plans to assassinate President Lincoln. Although records of Quantrill's service are scarce, 198 men are known to have officially joined his command. Of these, 70 were reported as killed in action, and only 37 are known to have survived the war. Many of the men who rode and fought with Quantrill were unable to adjust to life after the war and continued their extralegal activities in the post-war era.

The most famous survivors of Quantrill's raiders were Frank and Jesse James. The James brothers began their outlaw career on February 13, 1864, by robbing a bank in Liberty, Missouri. They were joined by the Younger brothers to form the most notorious gang of that era. The James gang robbed banks and trains from Iowa to Texas until being nearly destroyed while trying to rob the First National Bank in Northfield, Minnesota, in 1876. Five years later, Jesse was shot in the back for the $10,000 reward money and, shortly thereafter, Frank gave himself up to the authorities. After being found not guilty of murder, armed robbery, and finally, robbery in three separate trials, Frank was released and retired to a life of farming until quietly dying in 1915.

Jim "Crow" Chiles was another of Quantrill's men who survived and he, according to historian David McCulloch, "conducted his own one-man reign of terror" after the war. Chiles is remembered today because he married Sallie Young, the aunt of future President Harry Truman. Chiles had killed nine men and was under indictment for three additional murders when, in 1873, he was killed in a confrontation with a deputy marshal in Kansas City. The following is a list of men who rode with Quantrill and went on to become criminals after the war:

15 Future Outlaws Who Rode With William Clark Quantrill

1.	Richard Burns	Arrested in 1867 for robbing bank in Richmond, Missouri.
2.	Jim Chiles	Wanted for three murders before being killed by a deputy marshal.
3.	Ike Flannery	Arrested in 1867 for robbing bank in Richmond, Missouri.
4.	Frank Gregg	Robbed bank in Liberty, Missouri, in 1866.
5.	Frank James	Member of James-Younger gang.
6.	Jesse James	Member of James-Younger gang.
7.	Payne Jones	Arrested in 1867 for robbing bank in Richmond, Missouri.
8.	Thomas Little	Lynched in 1867 for robbing bank in Richmond, Missouri.
9.	Allen Parmer	Lynched in 1867 for robbing bank in Richmond, Missouri.
10.	Bud Pence	Robbed bank in Liberty, Missouri, in 1866.

Champ Ferguson, Rebel guerrilla fighter charged with 23 murders
during the war. (*Harper's Weekly*)

11. Donnie Pence   Robbed bank in Liberty, Missouri, in 1866.
12. George Shepherd   Jailed for robbing bank in Russellville, Kentucky, in
                       1868.
13. Oliver Shepherd   Robbed bank in Liberty, Missouri, in 1866.
14. Cole Younger   Member of James-Younger gang.
15. James Younger   Member of James-Younger gang.

☆☆☆

It is generally accepted that Captain Henry Wirtz, commandant of Andersonville Prison, was the only man executed by the Federal government after the war for
crimes committed during the war. However, there was another man, now largely
forgotten, who was also executed for war crimes. Champ Ferguson was a Confederate guerrilla commander who operated, for the most part, in his native Kentucky during the war. By the time he was finally captured and brought to the military prison in Nashville, Tennessee, Federal authorities had decided that Ferguson
would not be given a parole, but instead would be arrested and tried for murder.

While Ferguson's activities in Kentucky were grisly—he was suspected of at
least 21 civilian killings during the war—it was his actions at the battle of Saltville,
Virginia, in October 1864 that brought him to the attention of the Federal government. Apparently outraged at having to fight black soldiers, Ferguson and his men
prowled the field after the battle and killed dozens of wounded Federal soldiers.
Ferguson may have gotten away with this act of brutality if he had not, six days
later, entered the Emory and Henry Hospital in Washington County, Virginia, and
killed Lieutenant E. C. Smith of the 13th Kentucky Cavalry, who was lying desperately wounded on his bunk. At the time, the Confederate hospital was filled with

Union soldiers wounded at Saltville, and several witnesses claimed that Ferguson intended to kill all the Union officers in the hospital that had led black troops, but was only prevented by the insistence of the regimental surgeon.

Champ Ferguson was captured at his home near Sparta, Tennessee, shortly after Robert E. Lee's surrender at Appomattox. His trial lasted several months, and the court reached a verdict on September 26, 1865. Found guilty of murder, Ferguson was hung on October 20, 1865, the only man other than Henry Wirtz to be found guilty of war crimes. The following is a list of the charges that were filed against Ferguson:

The hanging of Champ Ferguson.
(*Harper's Weekly*)

23 Murder Charges Against Champ Ferguson

1. Lieutenant E. C. Smith, 13th Kentucky, shot in the head while a prisoner and lying in the hospital at Emory, Virginia.
2. 12 soldiers, whose names are unknown, at Saltville, Virginia.
3. 2 black soldiers, names unknown, while lying wounded at Saltville in October 1864.
4. 19 soldiers of the 5th Tennessee Cavalry, names unknown, on February 22, 1864.
5. Reuben Wood, near Albany, Kentucky, in 1861.
6. William Frogg, while sick in bed, in 1861.
7. Joseph Stover, private 1st Kentucky, in Clinton County, Kentucky, in April 1862.
8. William Johnson, in Clinton County in 1862.
9. Louis Pierce, in Clinton County in 1862.
10. Fount Zachery, a boy, near Spring Creek, Kentucky, 1862.
11. Elijah Kogier, in Clinton County in 1862. His young daughter was clinging to him when he was shot, pleading for his life, but Ferguson fired several more shots, killing him.
12. James Zachery, in Fentress County, Kentucky, in May 1862.
13. Alexander Huff, in Fentress County in 1862.
14. Joseph Beck, near Poplar Mountain, Kentucky, in summer of 1862.
15. William McGlasson, in Cumberland County, Kentucky, November 1862. Ferguson told him to run, then shot him in the back.
16. Elam Huddleston, shot through the head and in the back in January 1863.
17. Peter Zachery, shot while lying sick in bed in Russell County, Kentucky, in January 1863.

18. Allan Zachery, same time and place.
19. John Williams, killed by being tortured with knives and sharp sticks, afterward being cut to pieces.
20. David Delk, killed by being chopped to pieces in Fentress County in 1863.
21. John Crabtree, a prisoner, near the house of Mrs. Piles, in Fentress County in 1863.
22. A black man, name unknown.
23. Mr. Tabor, in Albany, Clinton County, in 1862.

While the war brought out the worst in the men who became outlaws, it also provided an opportunity for brave and courageous men to show their skills and abilities in a variety of spectacular secret missions. The Confederacy attempted more of these types of missions for the simple reason that it had less raw materials to work with to win the war in a conventional manner. Time and again, Confederate agents were sent north for the purpose of disrupting the Union war effort. The two Union efforts included here were limited operations that had specific military objectives. While the Union missions achieved spectacular success, the Rebels enjoyed only mixed results. This probably resulted from the fact that most of the Rebel schemes were undertaken against much greater odds and were designed to bring the war to the North, with little, if any, military objectives involved.

10 Secret Missions

1. Rebel spies in New York during draft riot. In the wake of the mighty battle of Gettysburg, all the Federal troops garrisoning New York City were rushed to reinforce the Army of the Potomac. The troops were sorely missed when, several days later, the first draft in the city erupted in violence and the city's police force was overwhelmed. In three days of intermittent fighting in early July 1864, more than 1,000 people were hurt or killed and millions of dollars of damage was done. There is evidence that Confederate agents were involved in the riots. A man named John Andrews, who had addressed the crowd on the first day of the riot, was also seen on several other occasions urging further acts of violence. He was later arrested and sent to Fort Warren in Boston Harbor, but he disappeared without a trace before he could be brought back to New York for trial. There were probably other Southern agents in the city working the crowds, but their actions and identities have never been revealed.

2. The plot to capture Maine. The success of Rebel commerce raiders spurred perhaps the most daring and little-known plot of the war. During the summer of 1864, several Confederate topographers were sent to the Maine

Rebel agents were suspected of inciting the 1863 Draft Riot in
New York City. (*Harper's Weekly*)

coast to map isolated bays and harbors. Specially trained troops were to
be brought to Maine by blockade runners and joined by additional troops
sent from Canada. In addition, the raider *C.S.S. Tallahassee* was ordered
to steam up the coast and do as much damage as possible. However,
before the elaborate plan could unfold, three agents were caught after robbing a bank in Calais, Maine, and, after their arrest, gave a complete con-
fession. After a secret inquiry, the entire incident was suppressed until
being discovered in a cache of old papers held in the National Archives
in 1953. Although never able to sail into New York Harbor as originally
planned, the *Tallahassee* succeeded in creating quite a stir by attacking
ships near New York City, Boston, and along the coast of Maine.

3. Explosion at City Point. During the siege of Petersburg in 1864-65, the
    small town of City Point, Virginia, located at the confluence of the James
    and Appomattox rivers, became the central supply depot of the Army of
    the Potomac. On July 26, 1864, Captain Maxwell and his guide, R. K.
    Dillard, left Richmond on a secret mission with what was known as a
    horological torpedo. Traveling mostly at night, they reached City Point
    and crawled past the Union picket lines on their hands and knees. Max-
    well continued to the wharf, which was crowded with tons of supplies
    and ammunition. He waited until the captain of one of the boats left his
    vessel, and then placed his torpedo aboard the ship. A little over an hour
    later, on August 11, the bomb exploded. The blast shook the docks and
    did a tremendous amount of damage, including permanently deafening

Maxwell and Dillard. In addition, falling debris reached the headquarters of General Ulysses S. Grant and narrowly missed injuring, or perhaps even killing, the Union commanding general.

4. John Hunt Morgan makes a daring escape from prison. After being captured at the end of his Ohio raid in July 1863, General Morgan and 68 of the officers of his command were sent to the Ohio State Penitentiary in Columbus. On November 4, 1863, a small group of Morgan's men began constructing a tunnel and making plans for a daring escape from confinement. With the only tools available being two kitchen knives, it took 20 days to complete the tunnel. After securing some Federal money and a train schedule, Morgan and six of his officers managed to escape. Heading south, Morgan was in Cincinnati and across the Ohio River before being missed and, with the help of numerous sympathetic citizens, was able to celebrate Christmas at home.

5. The Greenback raid. Colonel John Singleton Mosby's partisan rangers were so successful in 1863 and 1864 that they laid claim to much of eastern Virginia as Mosby's Confederacy. With only several hundred troopers at his disposal at any one time, Mosby was able to tie down thousands of Union soldiers, disrupt communications behind the lines, and secure valuable information for General Robert E. Lee. On October 14, 1864, Mosby went after a different kind of target. He brought his men to the Baltimore and Ohio Railroad west of Harper's Ferry and attacked a train carrying a Union payroll. Before destroying the engine and cars, the train was looted and a heavy tin box was found. When the box was opened, it was found to contain more than $160,000. This money

Colonel John Singleton Mosby, Confederate Partisan Ranger. (National Archives)

was split among the men, as was the custom of partisan rangers, and each trooper received $2,200 in "crisp new greenbacks, in uncut sheets of various denominations." At a time when food, supplies, and fresh horses were becoming exceedingly scarce and expensive, the spoils of the greenback raid were put to good use.

6. Confederates raid Vermont. Twenty-one-year-old Bennett H. Young had been an integral member of General Morgan's cavalry command early in the war and was captured at the end of the ill-fated raid into Ohio. After

escaping from prison, Young headed for Canada and helped mastermind one of the most audacious secret missions of the war. With a small command of about 20 men, Young took control of St. Albans, Vermont, located 15 miles from the Canadian border, in an effort to get a much-needed infusion of cash for his underground activities. Young's men cleaned out the banks of the town and made a getaway, but a posse of local men were able to capture a dozen of the raiders. However, the capture took place on Canadian soil and the raiders were freed after Canadian authorities ruled that the men were soldiers acting under orders.

7.   Destruction of the *C.S.S. Albemarle.* In April 1864, the newest and most powerful Rebel ironclad, the *C.S.S. Albemarle,* was launched in the Roanoke River and led a successful attack on Plymouth, North Carolina. The sandbars that blocked the entrance of Albemarle Sound prevented Union ironclads from ascending up the river, leaving the Rebel warship in full control of the shallow waters of the Sound. This situation lasted until October, when Lieutenant William Cushing proposed piloting a small steamer armed with a torpedo against the powerful Confederate vessel. Under cover of darkness, Cushing closed in on the *Albemarle* only to discover a log boom surrounding the vessel, and he was forced to circle the vessel before launching his attack. The resulting explosion destroyed the *Albemarle* and forced Cushing and his men to abandon ship. Of the crew, only Cushing was able to escape back to the Union lines with the news that the *Albemarle* had been destroyed.

Union Lieutenant-Commander William Barker Cushing, brother of Gettysburg hero Alonzo Cushing. (Library of Congress)

8.   The burning of New York City. In the fall of 1864, Colonel Robert Martin led a group of eight Confederate agents into New York City. Armed with Greek Fire, which was supposed to blaze uncontrollably on contact with air, Martin planned to burn the business district of the city to the ground. On November 25, 1864, the agents split up, took rooms in different hotels near Broadway, and started a series of fires. Unfortunately for the saboteurs, the Greek Fire they were supplied with was unreliable and the damage to the city was negligible. Only the fire at P. T. Barnum's Museum blazed out of control as Martin and his men made their escape across the

border to Canada.

9. Prison break on Lake Erie. On September 19, 1864, Confederate agent John Beall, commanding a small group of agents, seized control of a steamer on Lake Erie. Beall intended to use the vessel to capture the gunboat *U.S.S. Michigan*, the only Federal warship on the Great Lakes, and use it to liberate the 3,000 Confederate prisoners held at the prisoner-of-war camp located on Johnson's Island. In the rough waters of the lake, Beall was unable to ram the gunboat and was forced to abort the operation.

10. Mock gunboat fools the Rebels. In February 1863, the newest Federal ironclad in the Mississippi River Squadron, the *U.S.S. Indianola*, was sunk in shallow water. The armaments of the ship included two enormous 11-inch Dahlgren rifled cannon and a battery of 24-pounders. The ship's position in a stretch of the Mississippi River that was controlled by the Confederates meant that its valuable guns were available for the taking. To give him time to send an expedition to rescue the vessel, Admiral David Porter ordered the construction of a mock ironclad to be built of wood. The 300-foot long ship was completed in 12 hours and included two huge wheelhouses and portholes sporting wooden guns. An American flag was raised over it, and "Deluded Rebels, Cave In!" was painted along its side to complete the picture. The crewless ship was sent down the river with the current, and news of its impending arrival quickly reached the Rebels working to re-float the *Indianola*. Rather than risk facing this mysterious new Federal warship, it was quickly decided to blow up the *Indianola*. The two Dahlgren rifles were overloaded with powder and swung to face each other, and the resulting explosion completely destroyed whatever was left of the ship.

☆☆☆

Throughout the war, cavalry commanders were sent into enemy territory to disrupt lines of communication, provide accurate information of troop locations, and to wreak havoc on the civilian populace behind the lines. For the first two years of the war, the Confederacy enjoyed a huge advantage in the use and efficiency of its cavalry. Most Union army commanders, like George McClellan and George Meade, had little use for cavalry other than to act as couriers and to protect the picket lines. In addition, it took several years for the Union to organize its cavalry into a corps, a unit large enough to act on its own, and to stand up to the Confederate horsemen. By the summer of 1863, the Union cavalry had shown itself strong enough to match up with their Rebel counterparts and, as the war continued and forage and horses became scarce in the South, the vaunted Rebel cavalry found themselves, more and more, acting on the defensive. Barely able to fend off the increasingly strong Union thrusts, the Rebel cavalry was no longer able to mount raids of its own. The following lists contain five of the most spectacular Rebel raids, and five equally notable Union cavalry raids:

5 Spectacular Rebel Cavalry Raids

Confederate General James Ewell Brown (JEB) Stuart, cavalry commander for the Army of Northern Virginia. (National Archives)

1. Stuart's ride around McClellan, June 12-15, 1862. Shortly after being named the commander of the Army of Northern Virginia, General Robert E. Lee formulated a plan to trap and destroy General George McClellan's Army of the Potomac. With the Union army threatening the gates of Richmond, Lee was convinced that the right flank of the Union army was vulnerable. However, to put his plan into action, Lee needed accurate information about Union troops stationed near the right flank. To get that information, Lee turned to General J.E.B. Stuart, his young hot-blooded cavalry commander. Starting from Hanover Court House, Stuart led 1,000 troopers completely around the Union army. In all, he marched more than 150 miles and captured dozens of prisoners, all at the loss of only one man. Stuart returned with the necessary information three days later, prompting Lee to begin plans for a campaign that would force the Union army to return to its lines in Northern Virginia.

2. Forrest's Tennessee raid, July 6-20, 1862. Knowing that General Don Carlos Buell's army was on the march towards Chattanooga, Tennessee, departmental commander General Kirby Smith ordered Nathan Bedford Forrest's cavalry command into Middle Tennessee in an attempt to cut the railroad supplying Buell's army. Leaving Chattanooga with 1,000 men, Forrest surprised and captured an entire Federal brigade at McMinnville and captured more than $1 million worth of supplies. Continuing the raid, Forrest's men destroyed two important railroad bridges and put the Nashville-Stevenson railroad out of commission for an entire week. Before Forrest was done, Buell's offensive was put on hold and his men, already on half rations, were put to work repairing and guarding their suddenly vulnerable railroad supply line.

3. Van Dorn's Holly Springs' raid, December 20-25, 1862. In the winter

of 1862, General Ulysses S. Grant was planning his first campaign to capture Vicksburg, while Confederate General Earl Van Dorn was licking his wounds after absorbing most of the blame for his disastrous defeat at Corinth, Mississippi. After being demoted from command of an army and given a much smaller cavalry force, Van Dorn determined to restore his reputation by launching a strike against Grant's supply base at Holly Springs, Mississippi. Leading a 3,500-man force, Van Dorn's raid was a complete success and forced Grant to give up his attempt to advance against Vicksburg. In addition, General Sherman, unaware of Grant's predicament, proceeded down the Mississippi River to effect a planned junction of the two Union forces. Sherman also went down to defeat at Chickasaw Bluffs, ending the first phase of the Vicksburg campaign.

4. Stuart's Gettysburg raid, June 24-July 2, 1863. After being stung by a surprisingly strong Union cavalry attack at Brandy Station, J.E.B. Stuart was itching to restore his military reputation. At the beginning of General Lee's second invasion of the North, Stuart was given orders to link up with General Ewell's Corps in Pennsylvania. Instead of taking a direct route, Stuart decided to repeat his earlier success of riding around the entire Army of the Potomac. Things started going wrong almost immediately for Stuart, and he found he had to travel much farther to the east than he had originally planned. Slowed down by captured wagons and prisoners, Stuart had to keep moving to stay ahead of the Federal cavalry, and he was unable to inform Lee that the Union army was on the march. By the time Stuart rejoined the army, Lee had already stumbled into the battle of Gettysburg with disastrous results.

5. Morgan's Ohio raid, July 2-26, 1863. John Hunt Morgan earned a reputation early in the war as an extremely daring and resourceful scout and cavalry commander. By the time General Braxton Bragg authorized Morgan's request to launch a raid in Kentucky in an effort to slow the Federal advance towards Chattanooga, Tennessee, Morgan had already led three remarkably successful cavalry raids. However, instead of heeding Bragg's explicit instructions not to extend his raid into Ohio, Morgan ordered his men across the Green River and into the Buckeye state. Traveling an average of 21 hours a day, Morgan's men defeated numerous Federal militia units and even entered the outskirts of Cincinnati before heading for the safety of the Ohio River. However, before he could get across the river, Morgan found himself trapped near New Lisbon, and he and most of his force were eventually captured as the raid ended in a disastrous defeat.

5 Famous Union Cavalry Raids

1. Grierson's raid, April 17-May 2, 1863. While planning his risky crossing of the Mississippi River south of Vicksburg, Ulysses S. Grant sent Colonel

Benjamin Grierson and 1,600 troopers on a raid to divert the attention of General John Pemberton. To further the deception, Grierson repeatedly sent off small detachments of horsemen in different directions to draw off any Rebel pursuit. Grierson hit the Mobile and Ohio Railroad at Newton Station and, after avoiding an ambush near Union Church, drove off three companies of Rebel cavalry at Wall's Bridge. Covering the last 78 miles in 28 hours, Grierson's men were able to reach the Union lines at Baton Rouge just ahead of the Rebel pursuit. At a loss of only three men killed and seven wounded, Grierson captured more than 500 prisoners and destroyed between 50 and 60 miles of railroad in what Grant called "one of the most brilliant exploits of the war."

2. Stoneman's Chancellorsville raid, April 29-May 8, 1863. One of the first things "Fighting" Joe Hooker did after being named to replace Ambrose Burnside as commander of the Army of the Potomac was to combine his cavalry into one large Cavalry Corps under General George Stoneman. Hooker then devised a clever strategy to trap Robert E. Lee's army using the newly formed Cavalry Corps as a key component of his striking force. After being delayed by rain for several crucial days, Stoneman crossed the Rappahannock River with 10,000 men with orders to cut Lee's supply line. Rather than proceeding boldly according to Hooker's plan, Stoneman quickly lost his nerve and his raid; although causing considerable distress in Richmond, he did little to contribute to Hooker's military plans. A few unimportant bridges were burned, but on the whole, the cavalry exerted no influence on the battle, and, by their absence, contributed mightily to Hooker's embarrassing defeat at Chancellorsville.

3. The Dahlgren-Kilpatrick raid, February 28-March 4, 1863. After receiving information that Richmond was lightly guarded, General Judson Kilpatrick was given permission to organize a raid on the Confederate capital. The primary goal of the expedition was to free the thousands of prisoners being held in the city before they could be transferred farther south, but the capture of President Davis and his cabinet was also considered a viable military option. With approximately 3,500 horsemen, Kilpatrick crossed the Rapidan River at Ely's Ford and made good progress towards Richmond. At Spotsylvania, Colonel Ulric Dahlgren and a 500-man force split off with orders to approach Richmond from the south. When Kilpatrick reached the fortifications outside the capital, he quickly determined that they were too strong to assault and headed back for the Union lines. Unaware of Kilpatrick's decision, Dahlgren's small force was trapped and the colonel was killed in an ambush near King and Queen Court House. When Dahlgren's body was examined, inflammatory papers were found including explicit instructions to kill President Davis and his cabinet. In large part, these papers contributed to the increasingly aggressive tactics taken by the Confederate Secret Service, including a plot to burn New

York City and a plan to kidnap President Lincoln.

4. Sheridan's Richmond raid, May 9-24, 1864. Disgusted with playing such a small role in the Army of the Potomac's advance to Spotsylvania, General Phil Sheridan convinced General Grant that, given the chance, he could "whip Stuart." With Grant's permission, Sheridan took 10,000 troopers, in a column 13 miles long, and headed towards Richmond. His nemesis, J. E. B. Stuart, rushed forward to cut off Sheridan's advance and, at Yellow Tavern, the two forces met. After putting up a stout resistance, Stuart's cavalry was routed and forced to retreat. However, the greatest loss of the day was the fatal wounding of Stuart by Private J. A. Huff. Shortly after the battle, Sheridan realized that an advance on Richmond was unwise and he veered off to join General Benjamin Butler's army at Haxall's Landing. During the raid, his first as an independent cavalry commander, Sheridan rode completely around Lee's army, beat the Rebels in four separate engagements, and destroyed thousands of dollars of supplies and equipment.

5. Wilson's Selma raid, March 22-April 20, 1865. With the war coming swiftly to a close, General James H. Wilson led three cavalry divisions to Selma, Alabama, one of the few remaining industrial centers in the South. To oppose Wilson, General Nathan Bedford Forrest had only 2,500 worn-out cavalrymen. Despite putting up a desperate resistance, Forrest was outmarched and outmaneuvered by Wilson's cavalry in one of the most lopsided Union victories of the war.

CHAPTER 13

Winning and Losing on the Battlefield

ISTORICALLY, THE DEATH, CAPTURE, or wounding of the opposing general was the ultimate goal of a battle, and whichever side was able to accomplish this was considered the day's winner. That tradition slowly changed during the 16th century because the gradual shift from handheld weaponry to more technologically advanced implements of war caused commanders to place more emphasis on directing the battle than in participating in it. Slowly but surely, holding undisturbed possession of the contested field came to signify a battlefield victory.

This theory held sway for many Civil War generals and came to be the accepted rule of thumb during the war. As a result, Robert E. Lee's withdrawal from Antietam after the battle gave the victory to George McClellan, even though he was unable to dislodge Lee's forces during the actual fight. Only a very few generals, like Nathan Bedford Forrest, Stonewall Jackson, and Ulysses S. Grant, were able to see beyond holding the actual battlefield to understand that the destruction of the enemy's forces was of much greater value. Time and again, military commanders from both the North and South frittered away opportunities to strike heavy blows against a retreating and wounded foe. President Lincoln became especially upset with General Meade after Gettysburg for

Confederate General Nathan Bedford Forrest, the Wizard of the Saddle.
(*Battles and Leaders*)

what Lincoln believed to be Meade's inordinate satisfaction in forcing the Army of Northern Virginia to retreat, and his failure to follow up the victory by crushing General Lee's wounded army after the battle.

The following is a list, as compiled by William Fox for his influential 1889 study in the *Regimental Losses in the American Civil War 1861-1865*, of the battles in which the Union armies remained in undisturbed possession of the field:

45 Union Battlefield Victories

1. Rich Mountain, West Virginia: July 11, 1861. General William Rosecrans led four regiments around the flank of Colonel John Pegram's position on the Buckhannon-Beverly Road, forcing his surrender.

2. Mill Springs, Kentucky: January 19, 1862. General George Thomas scored the first major Union victory of the war by defeating General Felix Zollicoffer's force protecting southeastern Kentucky.

3. Roanoke Island, North Carolina: February 8, 1862. General Henry Wise's 2,500-man force defending the island was defeated and forced to surrender.

4. Fort Donelson, Tennessee: February 12-16, 1862. A stunning victory for General Grant, who laid siege to the fort and forced the surrender of the 15,000-man garrison. Only General Nathan Bedford Forrest's cavalrymen were able to escape before the surrender.

5. Pea Ridge, Arkansas: March 7-8, 1862. After completing a 55-mile march in the snow, General Van Dorn's attack against General Samuel Curtis' army stalled near Elkhorn Tavern. Curtis launched a counterattack on the second day of the battle and caused a disorganized Confederate retreat to the Arkansas River.

6. New Berne, North Carolina: March 14, 1862. After leaving a garrison on Roanoke Island, General Ambrose Burnside attacked and captured this important coastal town in North Carolina.

7. Kernstown, Virginia: March 23, 1862. A surprise attack by General "Stonewall" Jackson was turned back by Union forces commanded by General James Shields. Jackson's force was routed and forced to retreat up the Shenandoah Valley.

8. Shiloh, Tennessee: April 6-7, 1862. After being surprised and nearly routed early in the first day of the battle, General Grant, with reinforcements from General Don Carlos Buell's army, counterattacked and forced the Confederate army under General P. G. T. Beauregard to retreat toward Corinth, Mississippi.

9. Williamsburg, Virginia: May 4-5, 1862. General James Longstreet was forced to call up reinforcements to delay the Union advance in this rearguard action. After the two-day battle, the Confederates continued their retreat up the York River Peninsula.

10. Baton Rouge, Louisiana: August 5, 1862. General Thomas Williams successfully defended the city against a force commanded by General Breckinridge.

Dead soldiers after the fighting at Antietam, Maryland, the bloodiest day of the war.
(Library of Congress)

Williams was mortally wounded in the battle, probably by the fire of his own troops.

11. South Mountain, Maryland: September 14, 1862. The advance guard of General McClellan's army seized Turner's and Fox's Gaps despite tenacious fighting by the severely outnumbered force of General D. H. Hill.

12. Crampton's Gap, Maryland: September 14, 1862. In an attempt to save Harper's Ferry, General William B. Franklin's troops forced the retreat of the Rebel soldiers guarding the gap.

13. Antietam, Maryland: September 17, 1862. General George McClellan attacked General Robert E. Lee's position near Sharpsburg, forcing Lee to withdraw after the bloodiest day in American history.

14. Iuka, Mississippi: September 19, 1862. A 17,000-man force commanded by General Sterling Price was forced to withdraw from Iuka after capturing the town several days earlier.

15. Corinth, Mississippi: October 3-4, 1862. Two Confederate troops under General Earl Van Dorn and General Sterling Price joined forces but were unsuccessful in dislodging General Rosecrans' army from Corinth. After being soundly defeated, the Confederates hastily retreated to Holly Springs, Mississippi.

16. Perryville, Kentucky: October 8, 1862. In an engagement that began when both armies struggled to secure a water supply, General Bragg's army withdrew and his invasion of Kentucky ended with defeat.

17. Prairie Grove, Arkansas: December 7, 1862. General James Blunt's division of the Army of the Frontier defeated General Thomas Hindman's 11,000-man force in bitter winter fighting. Only the determined resistance of General Jo Shelby's cavalry allowed Hindman's men to escape.

18. Stones River, Tennessee: December 30, 1862; January 2, 1863. After unsuccessfully attacking General Rosecrans' position near Murfreesboro, General Braxton Bragg was forced to retreat from his position protecting Middle Tennessee.

19. Port Gibson, Mississippi: May 1, 1863. Two Confederate brigades unsuccessfully attempted to stall General Grant's advance on the east side of the Mississippi River. General John Pemberton ordered the evacuation of Grand Gulf and pulled his remaining forces into the vicinity of Vicksburg.

20. Marye's Heights, Virginia: May 4, 1863. In conjunction with General Joe Hooker's Chancellorsville attack plan, General John Sedgwick stormed the heights that had proven to be invulnerable to General Burnside in December 1862.

21. Raymond, Mississippi: May 12, 1863. General James McPherson's corps captured the town, allowing General Grant to prevent reinforcements from Jackson, Mississippi, to form and bolster the Vicksburg garrison.

22. Champion's Hill, Mississippi: May 16, 1863. Two corps commanded by General Grant forced General Pemberton to withdraw from his strategic position blocking the roads to Vicksburg from the east.

23. Gettysburg, Pennsylvania: July 1-3, 1863. General George Meade held off three days of furious attacks by the Army of Northern Virginia before General Lee was forced to withdraw back into Virginia.

24. Rappahannock Station, Virginia: November 7, 1863. In a rare night attack, General Sedgwick stormed and captured the Rebel bridgehead on the Rappahannock River.

25. Lookout Mountain, Tennessee: November 24, 1863. In what became known as the "Battle above the Clouds," General Hooker's corps advanced up the seemingly impregnable mountain slope and dislodged the Rebel defenders in a fierce fight near Craven's Farm.

26. Missionary Ridge, Tennessee: November 25, 1863. An impromptu advance by General George Thomas' Army of the Cumberland straight up the ridge caught General Bragg's defenders by surprise, ending the siege of Chattanooga and forcing Bragg to retreat back into Georgia.

27. Cloyd's Mountain, West Virginia: May 9, 1864. While conducting a raid against the Virginia and Tennessee Railroad, General George

Crook defeated a small Confederate force commanded by General Albert Jenkins.

28. Resaca, Georgia: May 13-16, 1864. After two days of heavy fighting, General Joe Johnston discovered that his line of communications were being threatened and he ordered a withdrawal towards Atlanta.

29. Piedmont, Virginia: June 5, 1864. General David Hunter's army defeated a patchwork Rebel force during his devastating march up the Shenandoah Valley.

30. Fort Stevens, District of Columbia: July 11-12, 1864. General Jubal Early's attempt to probe the defenses of the Union capital were turned away, and Early was forced to begin a hasty retreat back to the safety of the Shenandoah Valley.

31. Carter's Farm, Virginia: July 20, 1864. A sudden attack by a Union cavalry division led by General William Averell caused the Rebel forces under General Stephen Dodson Ramseur to break and resulted in the capture of 267 unwounded Confederate soldiers.

32. Atlanta, Georgia: July 22, 1864. General John Bell Hood's second attempt to dislodge General "Cump" Sherman's army outside the city ended in a dismal failure and cost the lives of more than 8,000 Rebel soldiers.

33. Utoy Creek, Georgia: August 5-6, 1864. General Sherman assaulted the left flank of General Hood's army, forcing the Rebel army back from their position along the creek.

34. Jonesboro, Georgia: August 31-September 1, 1864. General Hood's last attempt to force General Sherman to pull back from Atlanta was repulsed. Sherman then launched a counterattack against General Hardee's corps the following day and forced General Hood to order the evacuation of Atlanta.

35. Opequon, Virginia: September 19, 1864. General Phil Sheridan's army attacked and routed the outnumbered army of General Jubal Early, forcing his retreat to Fisher's Hill.

36. Fort Harrison, Virginia: September 28-30, 1864. A surprise attack ordered by General Grant captured several inportant redoubts along the outer defenses of Richmond, Virginia.

37. Cedar Creek, Virginia: October 19, 1864. After initially catching the Union forces by surprise, General Early's Valley Army was soundly defeated when General Sheridan returned to command the army after his famous 14-mile ride from Winchester.

38. Fort McAllister, Georgia: December 13, 1864. In the final action before the conclusion of General Sherman's march to the sea, his forces quickly subdued the small Confederate garrison and captured the fort during an assault that lasted less than 15 minutes.

39.   Nashville, Tennessee: December 15-16, 1864. General Hood's weakened Army of Tennessee, besieging the city, was soundly defeated and nearly destroyed by a Union army commanded by General Thomas.

40.   Fort Fisher, North Carolina: January 6-15, 1865. The 8,000-man expeditionary force commanded by General Alfred Terry stormed the fort and captured the last Atlantic port open to the Confederacy.

41.   Bentonville, North Carolina: March 19, 1865. In the last major action of the war, two Union corps commanded by General Henry Slocum deflected a desperation attack launched by General Joe Johnston in an attempt to prevent General Sherman's army from linking up reinforcements advancing from the east.

42.   Five Forks, Virginia: March 30-April 1, 1865. General George Picket was soundly defeated while he was off attending a shad bake. The victory by General Sheridan caused General Lee to order the evacuation of Richmond, Virginia, and ended the nine-month siege of the Rebel capital.

43.   Fall of Petersburg, Virginia: April 2, 1865. After General Sheridan's victory at Five Forks, General Grant ordered a general assault all along the lines. Despite stubborn resistance, the attack was successful, although Confederate General James Longstreet was able to hold the city until nightfall.

44.   Sailor's Creek, Virginia: April 6, 1865. General Richard Ewell's rear guard was cut off and forced to surrender during General Lee's desperate attempt to escape after the evacuation of Richmond.

45.   Fort Blakely, Alabama: April 9, 1865. In the last infantry battle of the war, General Edward Canby massed his 45,000-man force against the outnumbered garrison and captured the fort in a brief 20-minute battle.

☆☆☆

It should not be surprising that, when you utilize the rule of holding undisputed possession of the battlefield as the definition of military victory, the Confederacy had far fewer victories than did the Union army. The reason for this is simple: Because ultimate victory for the Union meant the conquest of the Confederate states, the Union armies were forced to act offensively for most of the war. Because control over a strategically insignificant village or field meant little, the Confederate armies usually enjoyed the luxury of remaining on the defensive. In fact, the Rebel army could count only 29 such victories during the war. To give a more accurate assessment of their effectiveness during the war, William Fox expanded the definition of a battlefield victory for the Confederacy to include the occasions in which they were able to successfully repulse a Union attack. The following is a list of Confederate battlefield victories using this expanded definition:

40 Confederate Battlefield Victories

1. First Bull Run, Virginia: July 21, 1861. The first major battle of the war ended after General "Stonewall" Jackson blunted the Union attack on Henry House Hill, and Confederate reinforcements successfully counter-attacked the vulnerable right flank of the Union line.

2. Wilson's Creek, Missouri: August 10, 1861. Despite being outnumbered more than two to one, General Nathaniel Lyon launched an unsuccessful attack against an 11,000-man Confederate force commanded by Sterling Price. During Price's successful counterattack, Lyon was killed and the Union commander, Major Sturgis, ordered a Union withdrawal.

3. Ball's Bluff, Virginia: October 21, 1861. A Union reconnaissance-in-force led by Colonel (and ex-Congressman) Edward Baker across the Potomac River was ambushed and nearly annihilated.

The Union debacle at Ball's Bluff, Virginia cost Colonel Edward Baker his life. (Library of Congress)

4. Belmont, Missouri: November 7, 1861. In his first action as an independent commander, General Ulysses S. Grant was forced to make a hasty retreat after General Leonidas Polk unleashed 10,000 Confederate reinforcements into the battle and threatened to cut off the Federal line of retreat.

5. Front Royal, Virginia: May 23, 1862. Utilizing a mountain path across the Massanutten Mountains, General "Stonewall" Jackson surprised and routed a small Union force commanded by Colonel John Kenly. This was the third battle of Jackson's famed Shenandoah Valley campaign.

6. Port Republic, Virginia: June 9, 1862. In the final battle of his illustrious Shenandoah Valley campaign, "Stonewall" Jackson defeated a Union force of approximately 5,000 men. After the battle, all Federal forces in the valley were ordered withdrawn.

7. Secessionville, South Carolina: June 16, 1862. In an attack made against orders, Union General Henry Benham was soundly beaten by the Confederate garrison commanded by General Nathan Evans. As a result, Benham was arrested, relieved of command, and cashiered by President Lincoln.

8. Cedar Mountain, Virginia: August 9, 1862. In a meeting engagement between the forces of Union commander General Nathaniel Banks and Confederate General "Stonewall" Jackson, Banks' men held the advantage

until reinforcements commanded by General A. P. Hill launched a crushing counterattack late in the day.

9. Manassas, Virginia: August 29-30, 1862. Deftly using "Stonewall" Jackson's corps to penetrate deep within the Union lines, General Robert E. Lee utilized General Longstreet's corps to pummel the exposed flank of General John Pope's army, forcing a harried Federal withdrawal to Centreville.

10. Richmond, Kentucky: August 29-30, 1862. A patchwork Union force commanded by General Mahlon Manson was overwhelmed and completely routed during the initial stages of Kirby Smith's invasion of Kentucky.

11. Shepherdstown, Virginia: September 19-20, 1862. Shortly after the battle of Antietam, as General Lee's army was crossing the Potomac River, a Union force advanced and was poised to capture the bulk of Lee's artillery train when reinforcements, summoned by General "Stonewall" Jackson and led by General A. P. Hill, savagely counterattacked and ended any further Union pursuit of the retreating Rebel column.

12. Pocotaligo, South Carolina: October 22-23, 1862. A reconnaissance-in-force ordered by Union General Ormsby Mitchel was turned back with the help of Confederate reinforcements, which arrived by railroad from nearby Savannah, Georgia.

Burnside's Bridge, on the Antietam, Maryland, battlefield. (National Archives)

13. Fredericksburg, Virginia: December 13, 1862. A foolhardy frontal assault ordered by General Ambrose Burnside against General Lee's almost impregnable line was soundly defeated, resulting in more than 12,000 Union casualties.

14. Chickasaw Bluffs, Mississippi: December 29, 1862. General Sherman's attempt to force a passage to Vicksburg from the Yazoo River was sharply rebuffed by a small Confederate force commanded by General M. L. Smith.

15. Chancellorsville, Virginia: May 1-4, 1863. General Lee blunted the advance of the Joe Hooker-led Army of the Potomac and then launched a devastating counterattack against Hooker's unprotected right flank. Only the fatal wounding of "Stonewall" Jackson tarnished this Confederate victory.

16. Vicksburg, Mississippi: May 19, 1863. General Ulysses S. Grant's first assault against the city was repulsed all along the lines after several hours of heavy fighting.

17. Vicksburg, Mississippi: May 22, 1863. Grant's second attempt to breach the Vicksburg defenses by a frontal assault was again repulsed with heavy losses. After the war, Grant regarded this and the Cold Harbor assault as the only attacks he regretted ordering.

18. Ox Ford, Virginia: May 24, 1863. Union brigade commander General James Ledlie ordered a foolhardy assault against a heavily entrenched Confederate position. After suffering heavy casualties, Ledlie withdrew his unsupported unit to safety.

19. Port Hudson, Louisiana: May 27, 1863. The first unsuccessful attempt by General Banks to carry the fortifications protecting the Mississippi River south of Vicksburg.

20. Winchester, Virginia: June 13-15, 1863. In the first battle in the Gettysburg campaign, the lead elements of the Army of Northern Virginia, commanded by General Richard Ewell, captured the Flag and Star forts protecting the city and forced a midnight evacuation by Union commander General Robert Milroy.

21. Port Hudson, Louisiana: June 14, 1863. General Banks' second unsuccessful attempt to carry the town. After the assault, he resorted to conducting a lengthy siege operation.

22. Fort Wagner, South Carolina: July 18, 1863. A Union assault spearheaded by Colonel Robert Shaw's 54th Massachusetts Colored Infantry and immortalized in the movie *Glory* was handily repulsed by the Confederate garrison of the fort situated on Morris Island.

23. Maryland Heights, Maryland: September 15, 1863. In a prelude to the battle of Antietam, General "Stonewall" Jackson captured the heights overlooking Harper's Ferry and forced the surrender of General Dixon Miles' 12,000-man garrison.

24. Chickamauga, Georgia: September 19-20, 1863. Utilizing reinforcements from the Army of Northern Virginia, General Braxton Bragg scored the most decisive Confederate victory of the war in the West. General William Rosecrans' army was compelled to retreat to Chattanooga, and only the determined resistance of General George Thomas on Snodgrass Hill prevented the total destruction of the Union Army of the Tennessee.

25. Olustee, Florida: February 20, 1864. A politically inspired Union advance into north-central Florida, commanded by General Truman Seymour, was mauled and driven back to Jacksonville by a Confederate force commanded by General Joseph Finnegan.

26. Sabine Cross Roads, Louisiana: April 8, 1864. Confederate General Richard Taylor halted the advance of Nathaniel Banks' army during the Red River Campaign. After the battle, Banks was forced to embark upon a tortuous retreat back to the Mississippi River.

27. Wilderness, Virginia: May 5-6, 1864. The opening battle of General Ulysses S. Grant's Overland Campaign. Forced by General Lee to fight in an area of tangled overgrowth, with few roads, both sides suffered heavy casualties in confused fighting. Spurred by the arrival of General James Longstreet's corps, the Rebel army was able to temporarily halt Grant's advance.

28. Spotsylvania, Virginia: May 9-13, 1864. Despite almost having his defensive line swept during a dawn attack by General Hancock's corps, General Lee held off the determined attacks of General Grant's second major offensive of the Overland campaign.

29. New Market, Virginia: May 15, 1864. General Breckinridge attacked and routed a Federal force commanded by General Franz Sigel in a battle that was punctuated by a charge by a battalion of V.M.I. cadets commanded by Lieutenant-Colonel Scott Shipp.

30. Drewry's Bluff, Virginia: May 16, 1864. General P. G. T. Beauregard launched a successful attack against a Union force ineptly led by General Benjamin Butler. Only an uninspired performance by General Chase Whiting allowed Butler's men to successfully retreat back to their original position at Bermuda Hundred.

31. Cold Harbor, Virginia: June 3, 1864. A disastrous and costly assault ordered by General Ulysses Grant was easily and quickly repulsed. The attack, which by some estimates lasted less than 15 minutes, resulted in the loss of 7,000 Federal soldiers.

32. Brice's Cross Roads, Mississippi: June 10, 1864. A Union raiding column commanded by General Samuel Sturgis was soundly defeated and forced into a tortuous retreat by incessant attacks led by Confederate General Nathan Bedford Forrest.

33. Petersburg, Virginia: June 17-18, 1864. After General "Baldy" Smith threw away an opportunity to capture Petersburg when it was virtually undefended several days earlier, the suddenly reinforced General P. G. T. Beauregard successfully defeated a belated Union attack commanded by General Hancock. In the assault, the 1st Maine Heavy Artillery sustained the highest casualties of any Union regiment in the war.

34. Seven Days' Battles, Virginia: June 25-July 1, 1864. General Robert E. Lee's first campaign as commander of the Army of Northern Virginia. Lee engaged General George McClellan's Army of the Potomac every day for seven days until finally forcing the Union army to take refuge under the shelter of Federal gunboats stationed in the James River.

35. Kenesaw Mountain, Georgia: June 27, 1864. Frustrated in his attempts to outflank General Joe Johnston's Army of Tennessee, General "Cump" Sherman resorted to a frontal assault that resulted in a costly repulse. In

the attack, more than 2,000 of Sherman's men were killed and wounded, while Johnston had fewer than 500 casualties.

Fictional portrayal of Union General George McClellan leading his troops into battle. (*Battles and Leaders*)

36. Monocacy, Maryland: July 9, 1864. General Jubal Early's raid on Washington was delayed for 24 crucial hours by the stubborn resistance put up by a small Union force. Commanded by General Lew Wallace, the bluecoats were finally forced to retreat toward Baltimore, Maryland.

37. Petersburg Mine, Virginia: July 30, 1864. After successfully digging a tunnel under the Confederate trenches along Elliot's Salient, the Union attempt to capitalize on the ensuing explosion ended in a bloody disaster. The military careers of three Union generals (Burnside, Ferrero, and Ledlie) ended after this, in the words of General Grant, "stupendous failure."

38. Deep Bottom, Virginia: August 13-20, 1864. Two Union corps commanded by General Winfield Hancock attempted to crack General Lee's defensive lines north of the James River. A Confederate counterattack forced the Federals to take refuge behind Deep Bottom Creek before Hancock was ordered to withdraw.

39. Ream's Station, Virginia: August 25, 1864. Union General Winfield Hancock's attempt to cut the Weldon Railroad was blunted by a Confederate force commanded by A. P. Hill. The ensuing Rebel counterattack routed several regiments in General John Gibbon's division and resulted in the capture of more than 2,000 Union prisoners.

40. Hatcher's Run, Virginia: October 27, 1864. A General Hancock-led Union attack against the Southside Railroad near Petersburg was stymied by an aggressive Confederate defense commanded by General A. P. Hill.

CHAPTER 14

This Month in 1863

WHILE IMPORTANT EVENTS OCCURRED during each year of the war, 1863 was not only the turning point of the war in terms of military events, it was also a watershed year for the United States as a whole. On the first day of the year, President Lincoln signed the Emancipation Proclamation. While it did not free any slaves, it did shift the focus of the war in a dramatic way. In addition, the nation's first Conscription Act was signed and a national banking system was established. Both of these pieces of legislation forever altered the political and economic landscape of the country.

On the military front, the twin defeats at Gettysburg and Vicksburg crippled the Confederacy. In July, General Lee invaded the North for a second time. He attacked General Meade's army for three days, shattered his own troops, and was forced to retreat back to Virginia. He would never again command an army large enough to mount a full-scale invasion of the North. The loss of Vicksburg and General Pemberton's entire army split the Confederacy in two and gave the Union control of the Mississippi River. Late in the year, Braxton Bragg, after receiving reinforcements

Union Admiral David Farragut, given a heroes welcome upon his return to New York City in August 1863. (Library of Congress)

from the Army of Northern Virginia, launched a successful attack at Chickamauga, Georgia. Bragg's victory was short-lived, however, as he failed to capture Chattanooga, and a month later, he saw his own army defeated and forced to retreat. General Ulysses S. Grant's stock continued to grow with each victory, and his promotion to overall command of the Union armies became only a matter of time.

☆ **January:** President Lincoln releases the Emancipation Proclamation.

☆ **February:** Lincoln signs legislation authorizing a national banking and a national currency system.

☆ **March:** The United States Congress passes a conscription act that authorizes a draft of all men between 20 and 45 years of age.

☆ **April:** Admiral Porter's gunboats run past the Vicksburg batteries to join Grant's army for the second phase of the Vicksburg campaign.

☆ **May:** Lee wins another battle at Chancellorsville, Virginia, despite being vastly outnumbered. Grant's army wins five battles in three weeks but is denied at the gates of Vicksburg.

☆ **June:** Union cavalry surprise General Stuart's horsemen at Brandy Station, Virginia, and hold their own for the first time against the grayback cavalry.

☆ **July:** The three-day battle at Gettysburg, Pennsylvania, ends with the defeat of Pickett's charge. Vicksburg surrenders after a lengthy siege, giving the North complete control of the Mississippi River.

☆ **August:** Captain Quantrill's raiders sack and burn Lawrence, Kansas, killing all the men and boys of the town.

☆ **September:** After receiving reinforcements from Virginia, General Bragg's army attacks and routs the Federal army at Chickamauga, Tennessee. The Union army is forced to retreat to Chickamauga and General Rosecrans is replaced by General "Pap" Thomas.

☆ **October:** General Grant is given command of all the Union forces in the West and is ordered to lift the Confederate siege of Chattanooga.

☆ **November:** Ulysses S. Grant's army charges up Missionary Ridge to rout the Rebels outside Chattanooga and drives General Bragg's army back into Georgia.

☆ **December:** General Bragg is relieved and Joe Johnston is given command of the Confederate Army of Tennessee.

CHAPTER 15

This Day in the Civil War: April 10, 1863

B Y APRIL 1863, THE midpoint of the war, the growing strength of the Union army was beginning to manifest itself. Throughout the war, Confederate President Jefferson Davis was committed to a territorial defense. Davis' primary consideration was political because it was necessary to prove that the South was a viable nation. As a result, Rebel troops were scattered in various departments and were almost always doomed to be outnumbered in any major engagement. This strategy placed 68 percent of the Confederate fighting force in three major departments—Northern Virginia, Vicksburg, and Central Mississippi—against 81 percent of the available Federal armies. Thus, while the Confederacy was outnumbered by only about two to one in the number of troops available in the field, it was outnumbered by about two and a half to one along these major fronts.

Because the Union army was committed to engaging in an offensive strategy, the numerical advantages enjoyed were mitigated somewhat by the great number of men required to defend captured territory and provide garrison troops in strategic locations. As a result, the Union had to dedicate about one-third of its force, approxi-

Confederate President Jefferson Davis (National Archives)

mately 176,000 men, to these types of tasks. The Confederacy, on the other hand, had to commit only 43,000 (one-sixth) of its men to such things as protecting ports and coastal railroads. The following is a list of the troop disposition in April 1863, and shows just where Presidents Lincoln and Davis decided to place their armies:

Troop Disposition in April 1863

Confederate Department	Troops	U. S. Department	Troops
1. Northern Virginia	85,000	Virginia/Washington	224,300
2. Vicksburg	33,000	Western Tennessee	91,000
3. Central Tennessee	57,000	Central Tennessee	96,000
4. Deep South	18,100	Deep South	10,800
5. Alabama/Louisiana	23,600	Alabama/Louisiana	31,000
6. North Carolina	27,000	North Carolina	16,240
7. Western Virginia	6,000	Southwest Virginia	7,000
8. Texas	7,000	Texas	0
9. Trans-Mississippi	15,000	Trans-Mississippi	38,000
10. Total	259,000	Total	529,000
11. Real Troops Available	215,000	Real Troops Available	350,000

☆☆☆

During the four years of the war, only about 120 days were dedicated to major battles. However, the other 1,338 days were filled with engagements, skirmishes, scouts, and all other forms of minor actions. On April 10, 1863, the exact midpoint of the war, Union and Confederate soldiers were engaged in 13 fatal encounters. The largest of these occurred at Franklin, Tennessee, where Earl Van Dorn and Nathan Bedford Forrest led two cavalry divisions toward the city to determine if it had been abandoned by the Federals. Van Dorn was led into a trap and his outnumbered men had to fight fiercely to escape their predicament and retreat to Spring Hill.

However, not all those killed on April 10, 1863, died from enemy gunfire. One of the dead, Captain Alphonso Charles Webster, was (probably) the only Union officer to be executed for violating his parole. He had been a member of a Pennsylvania unit early in the war until being court-martialed and forced to resign. He then joined another unit and was captured in a battle near Waterford, Virginia, on August 27, 1862. He was quickly paroled and returned to the North where he joined up yet again, and he was again captured. This time he was sent to Castle Thunder in Richmond, Virginia. After making several unsuccessful escape attempts, Webster was tried for violating his parole, convicted, and sentenced to death by hanging. The following is a list of the fatal encounters on April 10, 1863:

Captain Alphonso Webster, the only Union officer to be executed for violating the conditions of parole during the war. (Library of Congress)

A wooden engraving of a drawing by Thomas Nast, published in *Harper's Weekly* in 1867. (Library of Congress)

13 Fatal Encounters

	Name	Class	Confederate Army	Union Army
1.	Franklin, Tennessee	Engagement	111	63
2.	Antioch Station, Tennessee	Skirmish	2	32
3.	Waverly, Tennessee	Skirmish	21	0
4.	Germantown, Kentucky	Skirmish	9	1
5.	Edisto Island, South Carolina	Action	9	1
6.	Gloucester Point, Virginia	Action	1	5
7.	Sabine Pass, Texas	Action	4	0
8.	Harpeth River, Tennessee	Action	1	2
9.	Deep Creek, Virginia	Action	0	2
10.	Folly Island, South Carolina	Action	0	2
11.	Deer Creek, Mississippi	Accident	0	1
12.	Northern Missouri	Scout	2	0
13.	Executions		1	1
	Total Casualties		161	110

One of the saddest facts of the Civil War is that many more men died of sickness and disease than were felled in battle. Poor sanitary and medical conditions combined to make hospitals much more deadly than any battlefield. In addition, thousands of young men and boys from rural areas were exposed to diseases for

Union soldiers are cared for in a hospital in Washington, D.C. (National Archives)

the first time, leading to virulent epidemics that spread through military camps. As Confederate records are incomplete, the following is a list, organized by disease, of the number of men who died in Northern military hospitals on April 10, 1863:

Soldiers Killed by Disease

	Disease	*Died*
1.	Typhoid	29
2.	Diarrhea	23
3.	Pneumonia	15
4.	Unknown	6
5.	Brain fever	2
6.	Smallpox	2
7.	Remit. fever	2
8.	Delirium tremens	2
9.	Malaria	1
10.	Hepatitis	1
11.	Disability	1
12.	Peritonitis	1
13.	Serufuld	1

	Disease	*Died*
14.	Bowel obstruction	1
15.	Scurvy	1
16.	Lung inflammation	2
17.	Brain inflammation	1
18.	Pythsis	1
19.	Marasmus	1
20.	Ulcers	1
21.	Chorea	1
22.	Measles	1
23.	Rubeola	1
24.	Periconditis	1
25.	Diphtheria	1
26.	Pyemia	1
27.	Erysipelas	1
28.	Diptherea	1
29.	Bronchitis	1
30.	Apoplexy	1

CHAPTER 16

Women and the War

ROM CAMP FOLLOWERS TO tireless hospital workers, women were vital to the war effort and filled numerous roles on both sides during the Civil War. Even before the fighting started, Harriet Beecher Stowe's book, *Uncle Tom's Cabin,* polarized the nation. Drawn largely from her experiences while living in Cincinnati, separated only by the Ohio River from slavery, Stowe's book was translated into more than 20 languages and performed as a musical to audiences throughout the North.

Another woman whose contributions are well remembered is Clara Barton, who became known as the "angel of the battlefield" for her efforts to rehabilitate the overworked hospital system in the North. She also organized an agency that obtained and distributed supplies for wounded soldiers and, in 1865, set up a bureau of records to aid in the search for missing men. Largely through her efforts, many of the Union soldiers who died at Andersonville Prison were identified and commemorated in a national cemetery.

A woman was also able to influence the outcome of the war's first important battle. Through the efforts of Mrs. Rose Greenhow, Generals Beauregard and Johnston were able to prepare for the Union

Harriet Beecher Stowe, celebrated author of *Uncle Tom's Cabin.* (National Archives)

advance to Manassas in 1861, and the Confederacy was able to win the First Battle of Bull Run. Married to a socially prominent doctor, Mrs. Greenhow was both wealthy and socially connected in Washington, D.C. After her husband's death, Greenhow became one of the premier Washington hostesses and, through her intimate relationship with Massachusetts Senator Henry Wilson, was also able to wield considerable political clout.

When the war began, Greenhow decided to help the Confederate cause and quickly became a member of an elaborate Rebel spy network in the city. On July 10, 1861, using an attractive young woman as a courier, Greenhow sent a secret message to Beauregard that Union forces were preparing to advance. Six days later she sent another encoded dispatch revealing that "the enemy—55,000 strong..., would...advance from Arlington Heights and Alexandria on to Manassas." Beauregard used this information to concentrate his army in time to fight and win the first big battle of the war.

Clara Barton, known as the angel of the battlefield. (Library of Congress)

Mrs. Greenhow's activities soon drew the suspicion of Allan Pinkerton, the head of the Union Secret Service, and on August 23, 1861, she was placed under house arrest. During her early confinement Greenhow continued to funnel information to the South, and she even claimed to have gotten her hands on the minutes of one of President Lincoln's Cabinet meetings. When it became clear that Greenhow was still collecting and transmitting information, Pinkerton transferred her to the more secure Old Capitol Prison and her career as a spy came to an end. After being banished to the South, Greenhow continued her efforts to help the Confederacy by traveling to Europe, publishing her memoir, *My Imprisonment, and the First Year of Abolition Rule at Washington,* and working to drum up foreign support for the Confederacy. On her return trip to America, the blockade runner she was traveling on ran aground and she drowned when her lifeboat capsized in heavy seas. The following is a list of some of the most famous female spies to emerge during the war:

5 Famous Female Spies

1. Rose Greenhow, a Washington society leader, informed General Beauregard of Union plans for First Bull Run. She was arrested and sent to the Old Capital Prison with her small daughter and then sent South. After visiting Europe, her ship ran aground off the North Carolina shore and she drowned.

2. Belle Boyd, a 17-year-old girl, took information on Union troop movements to General Stonewall Jackson during the Valley campaign. She was arrested twice, and in 1863 moved to England after being released from the Old Capital Prison.

Confederate spy Rose O'Neil Greenhow and her daughter being held in the Old Capitol Prison. (Library of Congress)

3. Antonia Ford, a beautiful 23-year-old, helped in gathering information that led to the capture of Union Brigadier-General Edwin Stoughton by John Mosby's men. She was arrested and sent to Old Capital Prison and was eventually released in the fall of 1864.

4. Elizabeth Van Lew, from a prominent Richmond family, stayed loyal to the Union and became one of the most dependable spies of the war. She passed military information to Generals Benjamin Butler and Ulysses S. Grant during the Richmond siege in 1864-65.

5. Pauline Cushman, a commissioned spy for the Federal government, was captured with compromising papers in her possession and sentenced to be hanged. Her sentence was never carried out because the Confederate forces holding her near Shelbyville, Tennessee, were forced to evacuate and she was set free.

☆☆☆

Rose Greenhow was not the only woman arrested for spying for the Confederacy in 1861. During the time she was held under house arrest, in the summer and fall of 1861, at least five other women charged with espionage were also confined in her house in what became know as the "Greenhow Prison." Crowds would gather at her house in hopes of catching a glimpse of the famous ladies, and at least one official believed that lots of money could be made by charging the public $10 for each look. The following is a list of the ladies held in confinement at the Greenhow house:

5 Ladies of "Greenhow Prison"

1. Mrs. John Low, arrested in Detroit, claimed to be a subject of Great Britain and a resident of Virginia. The charges against her were that she conveyed contraband correspondence and information to the Confederate states.

2. Mrs. C. V. Bexley, arrested in Baltimore, was charged with being a spy and transporting numerous letters to Jefferson Davis and others in Richmond.

3. Mrs. Augusta H. Morris was charged with giving information to the enemy regarding the position and strength of the Federal troops and fortifications in and about Washington.

4. Miss Stewart, alias Ellie M. Poole, was arrested in Wheeling, (West) Virginia, but escaped and was recaptured in Louisville, Kentucky. There was "abundant" evidence showing that Miss Poole was a shrewd and dangerous spy and had made several trips to Richmond.

5. Mrs. William H. Norris, arrested in Baltimore, was charged with being a spy after her husband, a noted secessionist, fled the city to avoid arrest.

New Orleans native Pauline Cushman, served as a Union spy during the war. (Library of Congress)

☆☆☆

In addition to the women who worked behind the scenes, there were probably between 500 and 1,000 women who enlisted as full-fledged soldiers during the war. These women marched, fought, and endured the hardships of camp life while keeping their identity a secret. Some wanted the bounty money, some wanted to be with their husbands or a brother, and some joined up because they believed in the cause. Unfortunately, because these women had to keep their identities a secret, much of what they did has been lost to history.

One of the main reasons so many women were able to enlist was that the physical exam most had to pass was cursory at best. In many cases, it consisted of the recruit holding out his hands to demonstrate that he had a working trigger finger and opening his mouth to show he had enough teeth to rip open a musket-ball cartridge. In addition, the rigid dress code of the time period, and the readily held belief that women were physically unfit for military service, reinforced the assumption that anyone in the army was a man. Finally, the large number of boys who were accepted into service allowed women to blend in despite their unusually small stature and lack of facial hair.

One woman who changed sexes to become a soldier was Sarah Rosetta Wakeman. She was the eldest of nine children when, in the summer of 1862, she posed as a man to get a job as a boatman on the Chenango Canal. Her driving motive at the time was to provide money for her hard-pressed family. When she learned that she could pocket $152 in bounty money by enlisting in the army, she jumped at the chance. At the time, she was 17-years-old and only about 5' tall. Her regiment, the 153rd New York, served as part of the garrison force in Washington and was even assigned for a time to guard the Old Capital Prison while Belle Boyd was incarcerated there.

Wakeman had given up on seeing any active duty until February 1864, when her regiment shipped out to Louisiana to take part in the Red River campaign. After surviving the disastrous battle of Pleasant Hill, during which she was under fire for several hours, she was one of the many who got sick during the ensuing arduous retreat. Suffering from chronic diarrhea, she was admitted to the regimental hospital and was ultimately sent to the Marine General Hospital in New Orleans. After battling her sickness for almost a month, she died on June 19, 1864, and was buried in a military cemetery. Incredibly, while she was suffering in the hospital and even after she died, Wakeman was never discovered to be a woman. Wakeman was "discovered" when the letters she wrote home during her military service were published in 1994 n the book *An Uncommon Soldier* (edited by Lauren Cook Burgess). The following is a list of eleven female soldiers about whom there is enough documentary evidence to establish their military service.

11 Women Soldiers

1. Sarah Rosetta Wakeman, a native of Afton, New York, joined Company H of the 153rd New York State Volunteers in August 1862. She served with her unit during the Red River campaign before contracting acute diarrhea and dying. Even in death she remained undiscovered; she was buried at Chalmette National Cemetery in New Orleans with the notation that she "served honestly and faithfully with his company in the field."

2. Sarah Emma Edmonds served in the 2nd Michigan at First Bull Run, and she fought with the Army of the Potomac until the end of 1862. She deserted to protect her identity after falling ill while stationed with her regiment in Kentucky.

3. Jennie Hodgers served under the name of Albert Cashier in the 95th Illinois. She participated in the Vicksburg campaign and the battles in Mississippi and Tennessee without being discovered. She continued to pose as a man after the war until a routine physical exam in 1911 revealed her sex.

4. Emma A. B. Kinsey served with the 40th New Jersey Infantry and claimed to have received an honorable discharge from her regimental commander in July 1864, allegedly with the rank of lieutenant-colonel.

5. Sarah Collins enlisted with her brother in Wisconsin, but was dismissed shortly thereafter for her "unmasculine manner of putting on shoes and stockings."

Madam Velasquez, also known as Confederate Lieutenant Harry T. Buford.
(Library of Congress)

6. Lizzie Cook enlisted with her brother in St. Louis and served until she gave herself away by displaying "refined table manners."

7. "Frank" Martin served in the 2nd East Tennessee Cavalry regiment until being wounded in the shoulder during the battle at Stones River. After her discharge, she re-enlisted and served for several months in the 8th Michigan.

8. Amy Clark served with her husband in a cavalry regiment until his death at the battle of Shiloh. She re-enlisted in the 11th Tennessee and served until being captured and returned to Confederate lines after being discovered as a woman.

9. Frances Clayton served with her husband in a Minnesota regiment until he was killed and she was wounded during a bayonet charge at Stones River. She was hospitalized and was immediately discharged after her discovery as a woman.

10. Frances Hook was a member of the 90th Illinois until being taken prisoner at Florence, Alabama, in late 1863. She escaped and was wounded in the left leg. Upon being examined and discovered to be a women by a Confederate doctor, she was sent back to the North.

11. Sarah Melinda Pritchard Blalock joined Company F of the 26th North Carolina to be with her husband. She revealed her sex after her husband was discharged for a disability.

CHAPTER 17

Black Soldiers

UNTIL HE RELEASED THE Emancipation Proclamation on January 1, 1863, President Lincoln had remained resolutely quiet about the subject of allowing blacks to join the war as soldiers. However, in the proclamation, Lincoln stipulated that blacks could be received in the armed services "to garrison forts, positions, stations, and other places." Shortly thereafter, in New Orleans, the 1st Regiment Louisiana National Guards became the first all-black unit to be formally mustered into the United States

Army. Still, the ultimate question about black soldiers remained unanswered: Will they fight? The answer to that question came on May 27, 1863, during the first Federal assault on the fort at Port Hudson, Louisiana. After the battle, according to their fellow white soldiers, the new black recruits "charged and re-charged and didn't know what retreat meant." Two weeks later, black troops who were stationed at Milliken's Bend, Louisiana, successfully drove off a determined Rebel attack. Their bravery was noted by General Ulysses S. Grant who reported that their behav-

Colonel Robert Shaw leads the doomed charge of the 54th Massachusetts. (Library of Congress)

ior under fire was "most gallant." Grant concluded, if properly led, that blacks "will make good troops." Even after proving themselves in battle, black troops were primarily used as garrison troops. Except on rare occasions, blacks were not trusted by most Union commanders to spearhead assaults or to hold important positions.

An unidentified company of black soldiers in the Union Army. (Library of Congress)

However, when given the opportunity, black soldiers proved themselves to be formidable fighters.

The following is a list of battles in which black soldiers played a significant role:

Black Troops in Action

1. Island Mound, Missouri, October 29, 1862
2. Port Hudson, Louisiana, April 27, 1863
3. Milliken's Bend, Louisiana, June 7, 1863
4. Cabin Creek, Indian Territory, July 1-2, 1863
5. Honey Springs, Indian Territory, July 17, 1863
6. Olustee, Florida, February 2, 1864
7. Poison Springs, Arkansas, April 4, 1864
8. Fort Pillow, Tennessee, April 12, 1864
9. Poison Springs, Arkansas, April 18, 1864
10. Jenkins' Ferry, Arkansas, April 30, 1864
11. Brice's Crossroads, Mississippi, June 10, 1864
12. Battery Wagner, South Carolina, July 18, 1864
13. The Crater, Virginia, July 30, 1864
14. New Market Heights, Virginia, September 29, 1864
15. Fort Gilmer, Virginia, September 29, 1864
16. Saltville, Virginia, October 2, 1864

17. Honey Hill, South Carolina, November 30, 1864
18. Overton Hill, Tennessee, December 18, 1864
19. Natural Bridge, Florida, March 8, 1865
20. Fort Blakely, Alabama, April 9, 1865
21. Palmito Ranch, Texas, May 12-13, 1865

On September 29, 1864, for the first time, black troops fighting in Virginia were given the opportunity to lead an assault. The objective for the night was a Confederate fort at New Market Heights, a stronghold along the James River near Richmond, Virginia. At 5:30 a.m., the 4th and 5th United States Colored Troops advanced in double ranks through the slashings and abatis in front of the fort. Withering Confederate fire quickly dulled the advance, but General Birney, who was commanding the assault, ordered the 5th, 36th, and 38th U.S.C.T. to make another charge. After absorbing almost 30 minutes of steady pounding, the black soldiers made a final victorious charge against the Rebel works. At a cost of approximately 900 men, the Rebel line crumbled and the fort fell into Union hands. Sixteen black soldiers were awarded medals of honor for their efforts during the engagement at New Market Heights:

16 Medal of Honor Winners for Action at New Market Heights

1. Sergeant Christian A. Fleetwood, 4th U.S.C.T.
2. Sergeant Alfred B. Hilton, 4th U.S.C.T.
3. Private Charles Veal, 4th U.S.C.T.
4. Lieutenant William Appleton, 4th U.S.C.T.
5. Sergeant Thomas Hawkins, 6th U.S.C.T.
6. Sergeant Alexander Kelly, 6th U.S.C.T.
7. Lieutenant Nathan H. Edgerton, 6th U.S.C.T.
8. Sergeant James H. Bronson, 5th U.S.C.T.
9. Sergeant Milton M. Holland, 5th U.S.C.T.
10. Sergeant Robert Pinn, 5th U.S.C.T.
11. Sergeant Powhatan Beaty, 5th U.S.C.T.
12. Private James Gardiner, 38th U.S.C.T.
13. Corporal Miles James, 38th U.S.C.T.
14. Private William H. Barnes, 38th U.S.C.T.
15. Sergeant James H. Harris, 38th U.S.C.T.
16. Sergeant Edward Ratcliff, 38th U.S.C.T.

The organization of the 54th Massachusetts Infantry (Colored) Regiment was the brainchild of abolitionist Governor John A. Andrew. After receiving permission to organize the unit in January 1863, Andrew sought out the brightest young white men to command it and sent out dozens of recruiters to find enough young black men to fill the ranks. Andrew was convinced that, because the 54th would be the first black regiment to be raised in the North, "its success or failure will go far to elevate or depress the estimation in which the character of the Colored Americans will be held throughout the World." After some convincing, Colonel Robert Gould Shaw accepted command of the regiment, and he took great care in drilling and preparing them for battle.

After being assigned to duty along the South Carolina coast, Shaw quickly realized that there were no plans to use his regiment in a pitched battle. However, when preparations were being made to assault Battery Wagner, located on Morris Island and designed to protect Charleston Harbor, Colonel Shaw volunteered his men to lead the assault. After a fearsome bombardment, Shaw led his men forward. The attack pierced the Rebel defenses, but the Union soldiers could not hold their ground and were forced back. In the battle the 54th lost heavily, and Shaw and most of his officers were killed or captured. However, Shaw's men were not the only ones to charge the Rebel battery; the following is a list of the casualties suffered by all the Union regiments in the assault:

Unit Casualties During Assault on Battery Wagner

	Unit	*Casualties*
1.	54th Massachusetts	272
2.	48th New York	242
3.	7th New Hampshire	216
4.	100th New York	175
5.	62nd Ohio	151
6.	67th Ohio	126
7.	9th Maine	117
8.	6th Connecticut	138
9.	3rd New Hampshire	46
10.	76th Pennsylvania	24
11.	Staff	2
	Total	1,515

☆☆☆

By the time the war ended, 178,975 black soldiers had joined the Union army, and they had participated in 449 separate engagements. While the lure of fighting to end slavery was great, a potential black soldier faced many hardships that his white counterpart did not have to endure. The first, and perhaps greatest, was poor medical attention. It was understood throughout the army that if a black soldier had the misfortune to get sick, he would receive only the most rudimentary care and, during the war, at least 35,130 black soldiers succumbed to sickness and disease.

The Fort Pillow massacre, as depicted in *Harper's Weekly*. (Library of Congress)

In addition, black soldiers who were unfortunate enough to be taken prisoner could expect to either be killed on the spot, returned to slavery, or, at best, face a long imprisonment under extremely harsh conditions. Of the 180 black soldiers taken prisoner from the 29th U.S.C.T. at the battle of the Crater, only seven survived the harsh conditions imposed upon them while being imprisoned in Danville, Virginia.

The final indignity suffered by many black soldiers was poor leadership. In many cases, the only requirement necessary to gain a command of a black unit was the willingness by a white officer to command black troops. In addition, black units were usually stationed in backwater departments, under general officers who were not deemed fit for service in more important sectors. The following is a list of engagements in which black soldiers toiled under poor commanders, with disastrous results:

5 Disastrous Engagements

1. **The Crater: Generals E. Fererro, J. Ledlie, and A. Burnside.** The attack was poorly planned by the notoriously inept Ambrose Burnside, who chose Ferrero's and Ledlie's units to spearhead the assault. Rather than leading their men, Ferrero and Ledlie spent the battle safely in a bombproof sharing a bottle of medicinal rum. The Rebel counterattack, commanded by General William Mahone, was particularly gruesome as no quarter was given to the black soldiers who tried to surrender. Of the 4,500 black soldiers who fought at the Crater, 1,327 were either wounded or killed before Burnside was ordered to call off the attack.

2. **Saltville, Virginia: General Stephen Burbridge.** The attack against the South's primary source of salt miscarried almost from the very start. For his role in the failure, Burbridge, who lost more than 350 men in the ill-advised assault, was relieved of command in December 1864. After the battle, many of the wounded Union soldiers were left behind and between 12 and 155 wounded black soldiers were murdered by revenge-seeking Confederates.

3. **Fort Pillow, Tennessee: Majors Lionel Booth and William Bradford.** Rather than accepting the surrender terms offered to them by General Nathan Bedford Forrest, the Union commanders decided to fight despite the fact that their outnumbered garrison was trapped in a poorly designed fort. In the aftermath of the battle, Forrest's troops killed many of the black soldiers who tried to surrender. In all, 64 percent of the black troops were killed or mortally wounded, while only about 30 percent of the white soldiers suffered a similar fate.

4. **Brice's Cross-Roads, Mississippi: General Stephen Sturgis.** In another unsuccessful Union attempt to defeat Nathan Bedford Forrest, Sturgis led an expedition of 7,800 men into Mississippi. Despite being outnumbered more than two to one, Forrest attacked and sent Sturgis' men straggling back to Memphis. In the aftermath, 1,623 black troopers were reported missing and local civilians, using bloodhounds, helped Forrest to round up the fleeing Union soldiers and to return many to slavery.

5. **Poison Springs, Arkansas: General Frederick Steele.** Finding his command unsupported and without supplies, Steele dispatched a wagon train to Little Rock. En route, the train and the support column of black cavalry troopers were attacked by Confederate cavalry under General Marmaduke. The train was captured and the supporting column quickly routed in an engagement that quickly degenerated into mass killing. Indians, fighting with Marmaduke's force, reportedly had to be restrained from killing and scalping the black prisoners taken in the fight. However, according to Major Ward, 1st Kansas (Colored), "They took no colored prisoners." Colonel Samuel Crawford, 2nd Kansas (Colored), had this to say about Steele's campaign: "All things considered, the expedition was disastrous; not from any fault of the troops, but for want of a competent commander."

CHAPTER 18

This Month in 1864

THE PROMOTION OF ULYSSES S. Grant to commander of all the Union armies marked the beginning of total war against the Confederacy. Grant designed a strategy that utilized all elements of the Federal army at once against the weakening Confederate armies. While Grant made little headway in the East, his chief subordinate, William Tecumseh Sherman, made swift progress toward Atlanta, Georgia, and then cut a swath through the central part of the state on his march to the Atlantic Ocean. Lee attempted to thwart Grant's plan by sending one of his corps, under General Jubal Early, north against Washington, but Early could not break through the city's defenses and was eventually forced back. General Phil Sheridan was then assigned to the Shenandoah Valley and, in a series of hard-fought battles, thoroughly routed Early's force. As a consequence, the tough-minded Grant ordered the Valley burned to prevent any future Confederate use of this strategic area.

The political landscape was dominated by President Lincoln's renomination by the Republican Party and his campaign against Democratic challenger and former

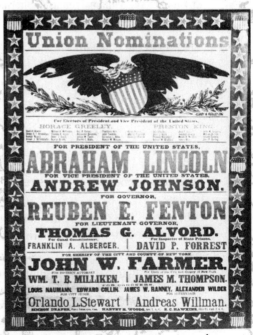

1864 Union Party campaign poster from New York City. (National Archives)

Union General William Tecumseh Sherman, on the outskirts of Atlanta.
(Library of Congress)

Union general George McClellan. Although Lincoln's prospects looked dim for most of the year as the casualty figures under Grant kept climbing, Sherman's capture of Atlanta and Sheridan's subsequent victory at Cedar Creek, Virginia, helped to secure a second term for Lincoln. The Democrats were hampered by McClellan's reluctance to acknowledge the party's peace platform and in November, Lincoln, aided greatly by the votes of the soldiers in the field, won the election by a scant 400,000 votes (he did win the electoral battle in a landslide 212-21).

☆ **January:** General Rosecrans relieves General Schofield as commander of Missouri.

☆ **February:** The Confederate submarine *Hunley* sinks the *U.S.S. Housatonic* in Charleston Harbor, marking the first successful attack of an underwater vessel in wartime.

☆ **March:** General Grant is promoted to lieutenant-general and commander of all the military forces of the Union army. General William "Cump" Sherman is given command of the West.

☆ **April:** Nathan Bedford Forrest's cavalry kills numerous surrendering black soldiers at Fort Pillow. Shortly after the incident, Grant ends all prisoner exchanges with the Confederate government.

General Grant's disastrous assault at Cold Harbor, Virginia. (Library of Congress)

☆ **May:** General Grant begins the Overland campaign in Virginia; Sherman starts his drive on Atlanta.

☆ **June:** After several bloody inconclusive battles, Grant launches an assault at Cold Harbor, Virginia, losing 10,000 men in less than 20 minutes. Sherman is stopped briefly at Kennesaw Mountain, also suffering numerous casualties.

☆ **July:** General Early's raid reaches the outskirts of Washington,D.C., before being turned away. General Hood replaces Joe Johnston as Confederate commander outside Atlanta.

☆ **August:** Fort Morgan, Alabama, falls to Admiral Farragut's gunboats in the battle of Mobile Bay.

☆ **September:** After losing three costly battles, General Hood abandons Atlanta to the Federal forces under Sherman.

☆ **October:** Following the instructions of Grant, General Sheridan implements a scorched earth policy on the fertile farmlands of the Shenandoah Valley.

☆ **November:** Abraham Lincoln wins re-election in an electoral landslide over Democratic candidate George McClellan. Sherman begins his march to the sea.

☆ **December:** General Hood leads a desperate advance into Tennessee that results in the destruction of his army outside Nashville. Sherman ends his march to the sea when he reaches Savannah, Georgia, and re-establishes contact with the rest of the Federal army.

blank

CHAPTER 19

By the Numbers

ONE OF THE MOST overlooked features of the Civil War was the incredible amount of money that was needed to feed, clothe, and equip the armies in the field. For the South, this was a losing proposition almost from the beginning. Because the Confederate government did not possess the means to levy meaningful taxes, they had to rely almost exclusively on manufacturing their own money to pay the bills. With hundreds of millions of dollars of paper money flooding the country, inflation was a constant fact of life for the citizenry. By the end of 1862, the economy of the South had become unmanageable and the rate of inflation was increasing between 10 and 15 percent every month; by the end of the war, the rate of inflation in the Confederate states had increased an astounding 9,000 percent.

The economy of the North was much better suited to the demands of full-scale warfare. Financier Jay Cook made a fortune selling bonds to ordinary people, and his firm brought in more than a billion dollars to the Federal government before the end of the war. In addition, the first Federal income tax was enacted on August 5, 1861, and in February 1862, Congress passed the Legal Tender Act, which authorized the issuance of United States notes. These were soon called greenbacks and were made receivable for all public and private debts. Both of these acts altered the nature of the American economy in a fundamental way, and

Each of these Parrot guns cost the U.S. Government $200. (National Archives)

the prudent fiscal policy prescribed by the Treasury Secretary Salmon Chase limited inflation to a reasonable (for wartime) 80 percent. The following is a list of some of the prices paid for waging the Civil War:

34 Prices During Wartime

- ☆ $0.10: Cost of pamphlet *How to get a discharge* or *How to get a furlough.*
- ☆ $0.40: Price each Union cavalryman was charged each day for the use of his horse.
- ☆ $1.00: Mustering-out pay received by members of General Beauregard's staff.
- ☆ $4.00: Amount Julia Ward Howe was paid for the rights to *The Battle Hymn of the Republic.*
- ☆ $5.00: Price of bulletproof vest, tested at 40 rods.
- ☆ $8.63: Cost to build dummy gunboat sent down the Mississippi River.
- ☆ $10.00: Price of Milligan's patent mess kettle, complete with 18 cooking utensils.
- ☆ $20.00: Cost of a portable army stove.
- ☆ $135.00: Amount in greenbacks that could buy $100 in gold in 1863.
- ☆ $150.00: Amount paid by Grover Cleveland to secure a substitute.
- ☆ $200.00: Price the Federal government paid for each Parrot Rifle.
- ☆ $300.00: Amount paid to avoid service in the Union army.
- ☆ $500.00: Amount paid by President Lincoln to hire a substitute.
- ☆ $678.00: Amount received by a first-time recruit in New York City in 1864.
- ☆ $1,000.00: Amount paid for the use of a buggy to view battle of First Manassas.
- ☆ $1,500.00: Price offered to British soldiers in Canada to desert and join the Union army.
- ☆ $3,265.00: Amount of government vouchers Colonel Frederick D'Utassy was convicted of forging.
- ☆ $10,000.00: Amount in administrative costs needed to form the new state of West Virginia.
- ☆ $28,000.00: Amount paid to purchase enough Enfield rifles for one regiment in the Union army.
- ☆ $60,000.00: Amount stolen by Rebel surgeon R. R. Goode from Farmer's Bank of Kentucky in 1864.
- ☆ $100,000.00: Bond posted to free Jefferson Davis from prison after the war.
- ☆ $125,185.00: Value of supplies captured by Stonewall Jackson in the Shenandoah Valley in 1862.
- ☆ $173,000.00: Amount appropriated by John S. Mosby during the Greenbacks raid.

Union prisoners playing baseball in the prison camp at Salisbury, North Carolina. (National Archives)

- ☆ $300,000.00: Value of coins and bullion evacuated from Richmond just prior to its fall in 1865.
- ☆ $347,374.80: Amount paid to the Phoenix Iron Company for producing 3" rifles.
- ☆ $510,000.00: Largest prize ever split by a Union naval crew during the war.
- ☆ $600,000.00: Amount appropriated by Congress for overseas colonization of former slaves.
- ☆ $2 million: Damage done during General Hunter's raid into Rockbridge County, Virginia.
- ☆ $2.8 million: Amount spent to publish the *Official Records of the War of the Rebellion*.
- ☆ $10 million: Amount in U.S. bonds that Jay Kent Cook sold on an average day.
- ☆ $15.5 million: Amount paid by England after the war to settle damages done by the *C.S.S. Alabama*.
- ☆ $250 million: Amount of Confederate currency in circulation at the end of 1862.
- ☆ $750 million: Total amount paid by the North for bounties.
- ☆ $2 billion: Amount of the national debt at the end of the war.

An unavoidable by-product of combat is prisoners of war. At the beginning of the war, both sides relied upon an informal parole system, in which the captured men promised not to take up arms again until the negotiation of a formal exchange cartel. The agreement, which specified a man-for-man, rank-for-rank exchange for all prisoners, worked well for about 10 months, until Jefferson Davis announced that black soldiers would be re-enslaved rather than exchanged. Although informal exchanges continued, the unwillingness of the Confederate government to bend on this issue doomed any further attempts to negotiate an agreement, and the population of prisoner of war camps soon exploded.

In Andersonville, Georgia, a camp designed for 10,000 prisoners soon became packed with more than 30,000 men. When some of the sick prisoners were exchanged, and the condition of the camp became known, the North exploded with rage. Many demanded retaliation against Rebel prisoners held in Northern prisoner of war camps, and prisoner rations were cut as a result. By the end of the war, however, conditions in the overcrowded Northern camps rivaled the poor conditions found in many of the Southern ones. In January 1865, the Rebels finally gave in and offered to exchange all prisoners and the cartel functioned again until the war ended. The following is a list of the ranks of prisoners captured by Union armies:

Rebels Captured During the War

- ☆ 121,056 Privates
- ☆ 63,563 Non-commissioned officers
- ☆ 5,811 Lieutenants
- ☆ 5,800 Civilians
- ☆ 2,496 Captains
- ☆ 244 Majors
- ☆ 168 Colonels
- ☆ 146 Lieutenant-colonels
- ☆ 25 Brigadier-generals
- ☆ 5 Major-generals
- ☆ 1 Lieutenant-general

Just who fired the first shot of the war and when it occurred has always been a subject for debate. The first shots fired in anger were directed against the ship *Star of the West* in January 1861. The unarmed steamer was bringing supplies and reinforcements to the Federal garrison at Fort Sumter and, unfortunately for its crew, just about everyone in Charleston knew of the ship's impending arrival. As the ship entered the harbor and began to approach Sumter, shots were fired from a masked battery on Morris Island manned by cadets from the Citadel. The ship was forced to return to the North. The Citadel still commemorates the occasion by awarding a small piece of wood from the *Star of the West* to the cadet who graduates at the top of his class each year. The *Star of the of West* was also the first Union vessel to be captured by a Rebel force in Texas three months later, and the ship enjoyed a curtain call later in the war when General William Wing Loring deliberately sank her in the Talahatchie River to block the only channel leading to Fort Pemberton.

There were many men who claimed to have fired the first shot at Fort Sumter early in the morning of April 12, 1861, but only one man was offered the honor and turned it down. That man was Roger Atkinson Pryor, a Virginia native and former Congressman, who resigned his seat in order to travel to Charleston to urge the bombardment of Sumter. When given the opportunity to strike the first blow he had so ardently urged, Pryor declined because his native state had yet to join the Confederacy. Fellow Virginian and noted secessionist Edmund Ruffin also traveled to Charleston and is credited by many with pulling the lanyard that sent the first shell towards Fort Sumter. Although Ruffin had no qualms about being remembered as the man who started the war, that honor probably goes to Captain George James, who fired the initial signal shot of the bombardment at 4:30 a.m. Abner Doubleday, the famed "inventor" of baseball,

Edmund Ruffin, cited by many as the man who fired the first shot at Fort Sumter. (National Archives)

touched off the first answering round at 7:30 a.m., marking this as the first engagement in which both sides took part in the shooting. The bombardment of Fort Sumter ended after 34 hours and is described by many as a bloodless affair. That was small consolation for Daniel Hough, a private from the fort's garrison, who was killed after the surrender by an accidental explosion during the Rebel celebration.

Professor Thaddeus S. C. Lowe achieved notoriety by pioneering the use of balloons as observation platforms for the Union army early in the war. He was also, by his own acclaim, the first prisoner of the Civil War. Before his military service, and only eight days after the fall of Sumter, Lowe took flight in one of his gas-filled balloons from Cincinnati, Ohio. After traveling 900 miles, Lowe landed, much to his surprise, in South Carolina and was arrested as a spy. Luckily for Lowe, he carried proof of his identity as a scientist and was quickly released.

The story of William Harney, the first Union general to be captured in the war, also has a happy ending. A Tennessee native, Harney was stationed

Professor Thaddeus Lowe pioneered the military use of balloons in the Union Army. (Library of Congress)

in St. Louis as the commander of the Department of the West before the war. Doubts about Harney's loyalty caused President Lincoln to relieve him of duty in May 1861, and while en route to Washington, Harney's train was stopped by a Virginia militia unit near Harper's Ferry. At the time of his capture, the 61-year-old Harney was one of only four general officers-of-the-line in the Union Army. Treated more like a guest than a prisoner by his sympathetic captors, Harney was held for only one night before being given his parole and allowed to continue his journey.

14 Famous and Not-So-Famous Firsts

1. January 8, 1861: First shots of the war fired at the *Star of the West* in Charleston Harbor.
2. April 12, 1861: First shot fired at Fort Sumter by Captain George S. James.
3. April 14, 1861: First Union soldier killed was Private Daniel Hough, 27th Pennsylvania.
4. April 17, 1861: First Union vessel captured was the *Star of the West* near Indianola, Texas.
5. April 19, 1861: First Union soldier killed by a bullet was Lieutenant Albert B. Rowland.
6. April 20, 1861: First "spy" captured was Professor Thaddeus S.C. Lowe in South Carolina.
7. April 23, 1861: First Union prisoners of war captured near San Antonio, Texas.
8. June 1, 1861: First Rebel officer killed was Lieutenant John Q. Marr at Fairfax Court House.
9. June 10, 1861: First Rebel private killed in battle was Henry L. Wyatt at Big Bethel, Virginia.
10. June 27, 1861: First Union naval officer killed was Commander James H. Ward.

14 MOST FREQUENTLY USED TERMS IN THE OFFICIAL RECORDS

1. Skirmish
2. Scout
3. Reconnaissance
4. Expedition
5. Affair
6. Raid
7. Action
8. Occupation
9. Engagement
10. Attack
11. Battle
12. Siege
13. Campaign
14. Operations

11. July 13, 1861: First Rebel general killed was Robert S. Garnett near Corrick's Ford, Virginia.
12. July 21, 1861: First woman killed was Judith C. Henry during battle of Bull Run.

13. July 21, 1861: First shots fired at Bull Run were by Captain J. Howard, 2nd Union Artillery.

14. Nov. 14, 1861: First cavalry raid of the war was led into Kentucky by Nathan Bedford Forrest.

CHAPTER 20

Notable and Quotable

ONE OF THE MOST FASCINATING figures to emerge from the Civil War era, and one of the very few good fiction writers who actually saw combat, was Ambrose Bierce. In the spring of 1861, Bierce was the second man in Elkhart County, Indiana, to enlist when he joined the 9th Illinois Volunteers. He quickly proved himself to be a competent and courageous soldier and, after the battle of Shiloh, was promoted to lieutenant. Bierce's military career came to an end in the summer of 1864 when he was shot in the head while leading a skirmish line near Kennesaw Mountain, Georgia. Against all odds, Bierce survived, but his outlook on life was forever changed. He spent the rest of his life writing misanthropic short stories and newspaper columns laden with a biting and sardonic wit for the *San Francisco Argonaut* (1879-1880), the *San Francisco Wasp* (1881-1886), and the *San Francisco Examiner* (1887-1896.) After moving to Washington D.C, Bierce grew tired of life in America and made plans for a trip to Mexico. Bierce then mysteriously disappeared, and some theorize that he was killed in 1913 while taking part in Pancho Villa's revolution in Mexico during the siege of Ojinaga.

Ambrose Bierce, earned the nickname 'Bitter Bierce' for his writing style and temperament. (National Archives)

Along with his chilling ghost stories, Bierce is best remembered today for his autobiographical depictions of what he saw during the war and his caustic lexicon entitled *The Devil's Dictionary*. The following is a list of some of the military-oriented definitions found in that work.

19 Entries from *The Devil's Dictionary*

1. Abatis: Rubbish in front of a fort, to prevent the rubbish outside from molesting the rubbish inside.
2. Admiral: That part of a warship that does the talking while the figurehead does the thinking.
3. Barrack: A house in which soldiers enjoy a portion of that which it is their business to deprive others.
4. Battle: A method of untying with the teeth a political knot that would not yield to the tongue.
5. Capital: The seat of misgovernment.
6. Corporal: A man who occupies the lowest rung on the military ladder.
7. Diplomacy: The patriotic art of lying for one's country.
8. Dragoon: A soldier who combines dash and steadiness in so equal measure that he makes his advances on foot and his retreats on horseback.
9. Epaulet: An ornamental badge, serving to distinguish a military officer from the enemy—that is to say, from the officer of lower rank to whom his death would give promotion.
10. Flag: A colored rag borne above troops. It appears to serve the same purpose as certain signs that one sees on vacant lots in London— "Rubbish may be shot here."
11. Gunpowder: An agency employed by civilized nations for the settlement of disputes that might become troublesome if left unadjusted.
12. Hash: There is no definition for this word—nobody knows what hash is.
13. History: An account mostly false, of events mostly unimportant, which are brought about by rulers mostly knaves, and soldiers mostly fools.
14. Hostility: A peculiarly sharp and specially applied sense of the earth's overpopulation.
15. Insurrection: An unsuccessful revolution.
16. Peace: A period of cheating between two periods of fighting.
17. Projectile: The final arbiter in international disputes.
18. War: A byproduct of the arts of peace.
19. Yankee: In Europe, an American. In the Northern States of our Union, a New Englander. In the Southern States, the word is unknown.

All of the men who rose to greatness during the Civil War are long dead. Although many left voluminous tomes describing their actions during the war, most are remembered for their deeds and for a few select quotes that have stood the test of time. The man best remembered for his quips and quotes is Abraham Lincoln. His sense of humor and gift with the English language has been well preserved. Many of the humorous anecdotes about Lincoln, like his well-reported comment about General Grant's drinking, "Tell me what brand of whiskey he drinks, and I'll send a barrel of it to all my other generals," are apocryphal, but the majority are true, and give us an inkling of what type of man he was.

The following is a list of quotes from some of the major figures from north and south of the Mason-Dixon Line:

20 Yankee Quotes

1. "The dogmas of the past are inadequate to the stormy present. The occasion is piled high with difficulty, and we must rise to the occasion."
   —President Abraham Lincoln, Message to Congress

2. "Then hen is the wisest of all the animal creatures because she never cackles until after the egg is laid."
   —Lincoln, describing the boastful General Joe Hooker

3. "Our Army held the war in the hollow of their hand and they would not close it."
   —Lincoln, after Gettysburg

4. "If General McClellan does not want to use the army, I would like to borrow it, provided I could see how it could be made to do something."
   —Lincoln, expressing his impatience with his top general

5. "Wherever the enemy goes let our troops go also."
   —General Ulysses S. Grant, in a dispatch from the front in 1864

6. "No terms except unconditional and immediate surrender can be accepted. I propose to move immediately on your works."
   —Grant, while negotiating for the surrender of Fort Donelson

Union General Joshua Chamberlain, hero of the Gettysburg battle. (National Archives)

7. "War is cruelty. You cannot refine it."
   —General William Tecumseh Sherman, in a letter

8. "There is many a boy here today who looks on war as all glory, but, boys, it is all hell."

—Sherman, in a speech after the war

9. "A crow could not fly over it without carrying his rations with him."

—General Philip Sheridan, after his men burned most of the Shenandoah Valley

10. "The only good Indians I saw were dead."

—Sheridan, after the war

11. "Bayonet!"

—General Joshua Chamberlain, before his charge from Little Round Top

12. "Damn the torpedoes! Captain Drayton, go ahead! Jouett, full speed!"

—Admiral David Farragut, during attack on Mobile Bay

13. "They couldn't hit an elephant at this distance."

—General John Sedgwick, just before being killed by a sharpshooter at Spotsylvania Court House

Admiral Farragut, commanded the Union forces to victory at Mobile Bay, Alabama; Battles and Leaders)

14. "Alas, my poor country! I know in my innermost heart she never had a truer servant."

—General George McClellan, after being relieved of command

15. "All right men, we can die but once. This is the time and place. Let us charge."

—General William Lytle, shortly before his death at Chickamauga

16. "Our country, right or wrong."

—General Carl Schurz, in a speech to German-Americans

17. "I urge you to fly to arms, and smite with death the power that would bury the government and your liberty in the same hopeless grave."

—Frederick Douglass, in a recruiting speech

18. "My business is stunting blood and feeding fainting men; my post the open field between the bullet and the hospital."

—Clara Barton, in a letter

19. "The real war will never get in the books."

—Walt Whitman, from a poem

20. This is a beautiful country."

—John Brown, on his way to be executed

20 Rebel Quotes

1. "We are fighting for existence, and by fighting alone can independence be gained."

—President Jefferson Davis, in a speech in Mississippi

2. "He has lost his left arm, but I have lost my right arm."

—General Robert E. Lee, after Stonewall Jackson's wounding

3. "It is well that war is so terrible—we should grow too fond of it."

—Lee, after battle of Fredericksburg

4. "Ah here is Longstreet; here is my old warhorse! Let us hear what he has to say." —Lee, after battle of Antietam

5. "I would fight them if they were a million. Gentleman we shall attack at daylight tomorrow."

—General Albert Sidney Johnston, staff meeting before battle of Shiloh

6. "Arms is a profession that, if its principles are adhered to for success, requires an officer do what he fears may be wrong, and yet, according to military experience, must be done, if success is to be attained."

—General Stonewall Jackson, in a letter to his wife

7. "It is the Lord's day, my wish is fulfilled. I have always desired to die on Sunday. Let us cross over the river and rest under the shade of the trees."

—Jackson, on his deathbed

8. "My duty is to obey orders."

—Jackson, favorite saying

9. "I would not give the life of a single soldier of mine for a barren victory."

—General James Longstreet, to General Lee

10. "If General Lee doesn't know when to surrender until I tell him, we will never surrender."

—General James Longstreet, at Appomattox

11. "It was thought to be a great thing to charge a battery of artillery or an earthwork lined with infantry. We were very lavish with blood in those days."

—General Daniel Harvey Hill, reflecting on the battle of Gaines's Mill, Virginia

12. "Give them the cold steel."

—General Lewis Armistead, during Pickett's Charge

13. "Each State has the right of revolution. The secession of a State is an act of revolution."
—General Alfred Iverson, before the war

14. "We gained nothing but glory and lost our bravest men."
—Unknown soldier, after battle of Gettysburg

15. "When a fellow's time comes, down he goes. Every bullet has its billet."
—Private E.E. Patterson, diary entry

16. "If you can't feed us, you had better surrender, horrible as the idea is."
—Letter to General Pemberton during the siege of Vicksburg, signed by "Many Soldiers"

17. "Sic semper Tyrannis! The South is avenged."
—John Wilkes Booth, after assassinating President Lincoln

18. "We are poor men and are willing to defend our country but our families [come] first."
—Mississippi private, after deserting his unit

19. "Yesterday we rode on the pinnacle of success—today absolute ruin seems to be our portion. The Confederacy totters to its destruction
—General Josiah Gorgas, diary entry after the defeats at Gettysburg and Vicksburg

20. "The shedding of blood will serve to change many votes in the hesitating states. If you want us to join you, strike a blow."
—Edmund Ruffin, just prior to the attack on Fort Sumter

Ages of 34 Notables in 1861

1.	Roger Taney, Supreme Court Justice	84
2.	Viscount Palmerston, British Prime Minister	77
3.	Edmund Ruffin, Secessionist	67
4.	Dred Scott, Slave	66
5.	Sojourner Truth, Ex-slave, abolitionist	64
6.	Robert Barnwell Rhett, "Father of Secession"	61
7.	Gail Borden, Invented condensed milk	60
8.	Dorothea Dix, Superintendent of Female Nurses	59
9.	Former President Franklin Pierce	57
10.	William Lloyd Garrison, Abolitionist	56
11.	Charles Francis Adams, Ambassador to Great Britain	54
12.	Napoleon III, Emperor of France	53
13.	Justin Smith Morrill, Vermont Congressman	51
14.	Harriet Beecher Stowe, Writer	50
15.	Horace Greeley, Abolitionist editor	50
16.	Charles Sumner, Massachusetts Senator	50
17.	Lyman Trumbull, Illinois Senator	48
18.	William Yancy, Southern diplomat	47

19.	Elizabeth Cady Stanton, Women's rights advocate	46
20.	Mary Bickerdyke, Nursing pioneer	44
21.	Frederick Douglas, Abolitionist	44
22.	Mary Todd Lincoln, Lincoln's wife	43
23.	Herman Melville, Writer	42
24.	Walt Whitman, Poet	42
25.	Susan B. Anthony, Women's rights movement	41
26.	Clement Vallandigham, Prominent Copperhead	41
27.	Clara Barton, Founder of the American Red Cross	40
28.	Jay Cooke, Financier	40
29.	Harriet Tubman, ex-slave, abolitionist	40
30.	Mathew Brady, photographer	38
31.	Mary Chesnut, Plantation wife, diarist	38
32.	Varina Howell Davis, wife of Confederate president	35
33.	Winslow Homer, painter	25
34.	John Wilkes Booth, actor/assassin	23

CHAPTER 21

Stories from the Telegraph Office

DAVID HOMER BATES WAS only 17 years old when he began working for the United States Military Telegraph Corps. Because the telegraph office was located only a short distance from the White House, President Lincoln became a familiar figure to Bates. The President made it a habit to walk over to the telegraph office, sometimes several times in a single day, to read the latest telegrams from the front. During the fall of 1862, while Lincoln was laboriously writing the Emancipation Proclamation, he would often go to the cipher room to free himself from his official duties to work on the historic document in peace. Bates was able to observe the commander-in-chief during times of crisis and also in a more relaxed setting while waiting for fresh news from the front. During these quiet times, Bates was privy to many of the stories that Lincoln became famous for. Bates described his perception of Lincoln during these times: "To those of us who watched him day after day, it was clear that the telling of stories...gave him needed relaxation from the severe strain and heavy burden resting upon him." The following is a list of some of the stories President Lincoln told while visiting the telegraph office:

President Abraham Lincoln, frequent visitor to the Military Telegraph Office. (National Archives)

5 Stories from the Telegraph Office

1. This story was Lincoln's attempt to explain why he could not break himself from telling stories. Lincoln explained that the habit was formed in his younger days, and he could not resist the temptation of telling a story to prove a point or win an argument.

   This was like the story of the old black man on the plantation, who neglected his work in order to preach to the other slaves, who often idled their time away listening to the old man's discourses. His master admonished him, but all to no purpose, for the good old man had the spirit of the gospel in him and kept on preaching, even when he knew the lash awaited him; but finally he was ordered to report at the big house, and was berated soundly by his master and told that he would be punished severely the very next time he was caught in the act of preaching. The old man, with tears in his eyes, spoke up and said, "But marsa, I jest cain't help it; I allus has to draw infrunces from de Bible textes when dey comes into my haid. Doesn't you, marsa?" This reply interested the master, who was a religious man, and who said, "Well, uncle, I suspect I do something of that kind myself at times, but there is one text I never could understand, and if you can draw the right inference from it, I will cancel my order and let you preach to your heart's content." "What is de tex,

President Lincoln with his son Tad.
(National Archives)

   marsa?" said the old man. The master replied, "The ass snuffeth up the east wind." He continued, "Now uncle, what inference do you draw from such a text?" After thinking a while, the old man spoke, "Well marsa, i's neber heerd dat tex befo, but I 'spect de infrunce is she gotter snuff a long time befo she git fat."

2. This was perhaps the last story told by Lincoln before his assassination. The story was told after he had read a military dispatch that conveyed information on two subjects in very curt terms.

That reminds me of the old story of the Scotch country girl on her way to market with a basket of eggs for sale. She was ford-ing a small stream in scant costume, when a wagoner approached from the opposite bank and called: "Good morning, my lassie; how deep's the brook, and what's the price of eggs?" "Knee deep and a sixpence," answered the little maid, who gave no further attention to her questioner.

3. This story described Lincoln's unhappiness with General Schenck, who was in command of the Union forces in West Virginia early in the war. Schenck had a habit of reporting numerous small skirmishes, with no defi-nite results.

Union General Robert Schenck, skew-ered in a story told by Lincoln.
(Battles and Leaders)

That reminds me of two snappy dogs, separated by a rail fence and barking at each other like fury, until, as they ran along the fence, they came to an open gate, whereupon they suddenly stopped barking, and after look-ing at each other for a moment, turned tail, and trotted off in opposite directions.

4. Many of the stories told by Lin-coln were in response to a story that had been told to him. When he heard the story of Tom Hood's spoiled child, squashed flat by an oversize aunt, Lincoln was quick with a story of his own.

A man enters a theater with a high silk hat in his hand. He becomes so interested in the movements on the stage that involun-tarily he places his hat, open side up, on the adjoining seat without seeing the approach of a fat dowager who, nearsighted, like a fat aunt of the spoiled child, does not observe the open door of the hat. She sits down, and there is a crunching noise, and the owner of the spoiled hat reaches out to rescue his property as the fat women rises, and holding the hat in front of him says: "Madam, I could have told you that my hat would not fit before you tried it on."

5. After reading a storybook to his son Tad, Lincoln told this story to the cipher operator. At the time there were numerous rumors and allegations of fraud in the Paymaster's Department.

A mother hen tried to raise a brood of chicks, but was much disturbed over the conduct of a sly old fox who ate several of the youngsters while still professing to be an honest fox. So the anxious mother had a serious talk with the old reynard about his wickedness. The fox reformed, and became a highly respected paymaster in the army, and I am now wondering which one he is.

CHAPTER 22

On and
Under the Water

HEN STEPHEN MALLORY WAS appointed as the Confederate Secretary of the Navy on February 21, 1861, he faced a daunting task. While the Confederacy did possess a modern naval shipyard in Norfolk, Virginia, the South had no machine shops capable of building an engine powerful enough for a warship, and it lacked the necessary resources to build enough vessels to ever hope to challenge the Union Navy. Mallory quickly decided to focus on a few specialized weapons that he hoped would maximize the South's limited resources. These included the development of torpedoes and half-submerged torpedo boats, the use of commerce raiders to disrupt Union shipping, and the construction of large ironclad warships.

In June 1861, Mallory authorized the rebuilding of the captured remains of the *U.S.S. Merrimack* into the first Confederate ironclad, the *C.S.S. Virginia*. After only 101 working days, the *Virginia* was commissioned into the Confederate navy on January 30, 1862. Under the command of Captain Franklin Buchanan, the *Virginia* sailed into Hampton Roads on March 8, 1862, to engage the wooden ships of the Union blockading fleet. In less than three hours, the Virginia sank the 30-gun *U.S.S. Cumberland*, forced the surrender of the 50-gun *U.S.S. Congress*, and had chased the rest of the Union fleet to the safety of the open sea.

However, Buchanan's victory was short-lived, as the Union navy had also been working on a "secret weapon." The brainchild of Swedish-born inventor John Ericsson, the *U.S.S. Monitor*, a shallow draft ironclad featuring a circular turret mounted on a raft-like deck, was waiting when the *Virginia* returned to Hampton Roads early the next morning. In an engagement that lasted two hours, the *Monitor* and the *Virginia* exchanged dozens of shots at almost point-blank range to little effect before the *Virginia* pulled out of range. The timely arrival of the *Monitor* returned the balance of power in the Virginia coastal waterways to the Union navy, an advantage they would not relinquish for the duration of the war.

First battle involving iron-clad warships, the *U.S.S. Monitor* and *C.S.S. Virginia.* (National Archives)

The *Monitor* and *Virginia* shared one final trait: They both suffered ignoble ends. When the Confederacy was forced to abandon the Norfolk naval yards to the advancing Union army, the *Virginia* no longer had access to a deep water port. It was destroyed on May 9, 1862, because it could not sail up the James River and was not considered seaworthy enough to sail to another Confederate-held port. The *Monitor* participated in several more engagements before she foundered and was lost at sea in a gale off Cape Hatteras on December 31, 1862. However, Ericsson's design was conducive to mass production, and the Union navy soon featured an array of similar-style ironclads. Before the conclusion of the war, 48 Monitor-class ironclads were in service in the Union navy and an additional seven large seagoing monitors were in various stages of construction. Ericsson's design proved to be so formidable that none of the Monitor-class ships were ever sunk in an engagement with Confederate warships or coastal guns. The monitors were very small targets for Rebel gunners due to the revolutionary design of the ship, in which only the 9'-high turret and the 4'- high pilothouse were above the waterline. However, the monitors remained very unpopular with Union naval captains because they were difficult to maneuver in shallow water, vulnerable to capsizing in heavy seas, and sank very quickly when they did take on water.

4 Monitors That Sank

1. *U.S.S. Monitor* (commissioned 2/25/62): Participated in actions on the James River; sank off Cape Hatteras during a gale, December 31, 1862.
2. *U.S.S. Weehawken* (commissioned 1/18/63): Saw extensive service

around Charleston, South Carolina, and captured the *C.S.S. Atlanta* on June 17, 1863; sank in a gale off Morris Island, Charleston, December 6, 1863, while at anchor.

3. *U.S.S. Tecumseh* (commissioned 4/19/64): Operated in the James River, then in the Gulf of Mexico. She struck a mine in Mobile Bay on August 5, 1864 and sank in 25-30 seconds.

4. *U.S.S. Patapsco* (commissioned 1/2/63): Saw extensive service around Charleston, South Carolina. Mined in the Charleston River on January 16, 1865, and sank in 15 seconds.

☆☆☆

Secretary of the Navy Mallory's efforts with underwater torpedoes was more effective than his efforts to build large ironclads. Stationary marine torpedoes were placed in all the major harbors of the Confederacy, and they proved to be as much of a deterrent to Union naval activities as they were dangerous to Federal warships. Mallory also authorized the development and implementation of specially designed half-submerged David-class vessels that were equipped with spar torpedoes. However, the most revolutionary concept of Mallory's tenure was the design of a fully submergible torpedo boat.

The first submarine ever built and used in wartime was the *Turtle*. Invented by David Bushnell in 1776, the *Turtle* attacked and was nearly successful in sinking a British man-of-war anchored in New York Harbor during the Revolutionary War. Further undersea efforts languished until 1861, when James R. McClintock and Baxter Watson attempted to build a submarine in New Orleans. When New Orleans fell to the Union, they shifted their base to Mobile, Alabama, where their efforts were greatly aided by financier Horace L. Hunley. When it became apparent that their experimental vessel, dubbed the *Hunley*, could not withstand the choppy waters of Mobile Bay, she was offered to General Beauregard in Charleston, South Carolina. Because Beauregard had already had some success with cigar-shaped torpedo boats, he readily accepted and the *Hunley* was transported east during the summer of 1863.

Confederate submarine *H.L. Hunley*, completed first successful underwater attack in military history.
(Naval Official Records)

Lieutenant John Payne was given command of the ship, and he immediately recruited a crew of volunteers and began trials in Charleston Harbor. Twice the *Hunley* swamped and sunk, and Payne and 14 crew members were killed. A disappointed Beauregard was about to abandon the project when Horace Hunley arrived in Charleston. With the belief that navy crews did not understand how to operate the vessel, Hunley convinced Beauregard to give the submarine another try. However, when the submarine dove under the water on October 15, 1863, and never came back to the surface, Hunley and another crew were lost, bringing the death total up to 21. Lieutenant George Dixon, who had helped build the boat, then took over the project with yet another new crew of volunteers for the submarine, now nicknamed the "peripatetic coffin." The following list includes the specifications for the submarine *Hunley:*

5 Specifications for the *H. L. Hunley*

1. Acquisition: Built in Mobile, Alabama, at 1863, in the shops of Park & Lyons.
2. Description: Submarine torpedo boat.
3. Dimensions: Internal, height 5'; breadth 4'.
4. Speed: In smooth water and light current, 4 miles an hour.
5. Remarks: Motive power, a hand propeller, worked by eight men.

Before General Beauregard allowed Dixon to resume testing with the *Hunley*, he insisted that the submarine should stay on or just beneath the surface, and he ordered a switch to a spar torpedo like the one used by the *David*. For weeks he trained his crew and tested the vessel while waiting for the right conditions to attack an enemy warship. Rather than attack a Federal ironclad, now fitted with special netting to prevent a torpedo attack, Dixon decided to focus on one of the more vulnerable wooden blockading vessels. Finally, on February 17, 1864, the conditions were right for the attempt. Using the ebb tide to draw his vessel out to sea, Dixon quietly approached the *U.S.S. Housatonic* before the unsuspecting crew had time to respond. After the torpedo detonated, the Federal ship quickly sank, leaving behind only an immense cloud of black smoke. However, the *Housatonic* was anchored in such shallow water that all but five of her crew members were able to survive the attack. The *Hunley* was not so fortunate. Dixon was able to get his vessel turned around and headed back to port, but the submarine was swamped on the return voyage and all hands were lost. The following list includes the last crew of the *Hunley:*

7 Members of the *Hunley's* Last Crew

1. Lieutenant Dixon
2. Seaman Arnold Becker
3. Seaman James A. Wicks
4. Seaman C. Simkins
5. Seaman F. Collins
6. Seaman Ridgeway
7. Corporal C. F. Carlsen

☆☆☆

The *C.S.S. Alabama* destroyed 69 Union vessels before being sunk off the coast of France.
(National Archives)

Secretary Mallory's most successful endeavor of the war was his effort to secure large warships from British shipyards for conversion into Confederate commerce raiders. The success of these Rebel cruisers was so great that, after the war, the United States government filed a formal grievance against England for repayment of $19,021,000 for the damage done by the 11 Confederate vessels originally constructed in England. It wasn't until 1872 that an international board ruled that England had failed in her responsibilities as a neutral and awarded the United States $15,500,000 in gold.

On June 4, 1861, Captain James Bulloch arrived in Liverpool, England, with instructions from Secretary Mallory to buy, or have constructed, six "steam propeller" ships suitable for use as commerce raiders. The first of these vessels, the *C.S.S. Florida,* was delivered before the end of the year, and Bulloch was soon at work securing enough capital to begin construction of a bigger and faster ship for the Confederate navy. Finally, on May 15, 1862, the *C.S.S. Alabama* was launched. After being fitted with guns, ammunition, and coal, Captain Raphael Semmes took command of the ship and began a remarkable streak of successes against American shipping in the Atlantic Ocean.

Raphael Semmes entered active duty in the United States Navy in 1832. He fought in the Mexican War and resigned his commission when the war began. His first ship in the Confederate navy, the *C.S.S. Sumter,* scored 18 prizes during six months at sea before he was forced to abandon it in Gibraltar. As skipper of the *C.S.S. Alabama*, Semmes captured or destroyed 69 ships before being sunk by the *U.S.S. Kearsage* in the waters off Cherbourg, France. The following list details the cost of building the *Alabama:*

Cost of the *C.S.S. Alabama*

1. Hull, spars, sails, boats, anchors, cables, and all equipment   £ 47,500
2. Battery   £ 2,500
3. Magazine tanks   £ 616
4. Ordnance stores   £ 500
5. Small arms   £ 600
6. Total   £ 51,716
7. Cost in dollars (£51,716 at $4.84) $ 250.305.44

The last vessel purchased by the Confederacy and successfully converted into a commerce raider early in 1865 was the *Sea King*. After being fitted with weapons and a crew, the newly renamed *C.S.S. Shenandoah* set sail for the Pacific Ocean. Under the command of Lieutenant J. I. Waddell, the raider headed for a whaling fleet in the Bering Sea in February 1865. Unaware that General Lee's army had surrendered, Waddell proceeded to decimate the unprotected fleet until learning, in August 1865, of the collapse of the Confederacy. Rather than surrendering his vessel to the hated Union navy, Waddell sailed for Liverpool, England, by way of the Cape of Good Hope. After a voyage of three months, Waddell turned the *Shenandoah* over to British authorities. With Waddell's action, the last vestiges of the Confederacy finally submitted.

29 Whaling Ships Destroyed by the *C.S.S. Shenandoah*

	Date	Name of vessel	Disposition	Total value
1.	April 1	*Edward Cary*	Burned	$15,000
2.	April 1	*Hector*	Burned	$58,000
3.	April 1	*Pearl*	Burned	$10,000
4.	April 1	*Harvest*	Burned	$34,759
5.	May 27	*Abigail*	Burned	$16,705
6.	June 22	*William Thompson*	Burned	$40,925
7.	June 22	*Euphrates*	Burned	$42,320
8.	June 22	*Milo*	Bonded	$20,000
9.	June 22	*Sophia Thornton*	Burned	$70,000
10.	June 22	*Jirch Swift*	Burned	$61,960
11.	June 23	Susan Abigail	Burned	$6,500
12.	June 25	*General Williams*	Burned	$44,740
13.	June 26	*Nimrod*	Burned	$29,260
14.	June26	*William C. Nye*	Burned	$31,512
15.	June 26	*Catharine*	Burned	$26,174
16.	June 26	*General Pike*	Bonded	$20,000

	Date	Name of vessel	Disposition	Total value
17.	June 26	*Gipsey*	Burned	$34,369
18.	June 26	*Isabella*	Burned	$38,000
19.	June 28	*Waverly*	Burned	$62,376
20.	June 28	*Hillman*	Burned	$33,000
21.	June 28	*James Maury*	Bonded	$37,000
22.	June 28	*Nassau*	Burned	$40,000
23.	June28	*Brunswick*	Burned	$16,272
24.	June 28	*Isaac Howland*	Burned	$75,112
25.	June 28	*Martha*	Burned	$30,607
26.	June 28	*Congress*	Burned	$55,300
27.	June 28	*Nile*	Bonded	$41,600
28.	June 28	*Favorite*	Burned	$57,896
29.	June 28	*Covington*	Burned	$30,000
		Total cost of vessels battled		$1,172,223

Due to the relative weakness of the Confederate Navy, there were relatively few pitched naval battles in the Civil War. While the Confederacy was able to build or obtain more than one hundred and thirty vessels during the war, these vessels were more that outmatched by the six hundred ships operated by the Union Navy. The Confederacy diverted a great deal of money and scarce resources into the construction of twenty-six ironclads. Of these, however, only about half actually saw action, and they combined to sink only three Union vessels. This poor performance was mainly due to the fact that most of the Confederate ironclads were severely underpowered as well as mechanically unreliable. Rather than face almost certain destruction by seeking to engage the blockading Federal warships, most Rebel captains kept their ships in the relative safety of Confederate held ports and harbors. Although the Union Navy enjoyed great success during the war in a variety of roles, its most noteworthy accomplishment was the implementation of a blockade over 3,000 miles of Southern coastline. While the blockade provided few spectacular naval victories, it did contribute significantly to the overall Union triumph. The following is a list of seventy-one important naval events during the war.

70 Important Naval Events of the War

(Engagements involving both Union and Confederate warships are in boldface.)

1861

1. April 17: The *U.S.S. Star of the West* was seized by Texas troops commanded by Colonel Earl Van Dorn.
2. April 19: President Lincoln issued proclamation declaring blockade of Southern ports.

3.   April 21 : The Gosport Navy-Yard was abandoned by Union officers and seized by Virginia state troops.

4.   June 27: An engagement occurred between Union gunboats and Confederate batteries at Mathias Point, Virginia.

5.   **July 7**: The *U.S.S. South Carolina* captured or destroyed 10 Confederate vessels off Galveston, Texas.

6.   Aug. 3: John LaMountain made first ascent in a balloon from the Union ship *Fanny* at Hampton Roads, Virginia.

7.   **Oct. 12**: Five Confederate gunboats and the ram *Manassas* seriously damaged the Union fleet at the passes of the Mississippi River.

8.   Nov. 7: Seventy-seven Union vessels under Flag Officer DuPont helped capture Forts Walker and Beauregard in South Carolina.

9.   Nov. 9: *U.S.S. San Jacinto*, commanded by Captain C. Wilkes, stopped the British steamer *Trent* and captured Confederate Commissioners James Mason and John Slidell.

10.   Nov. 11: The *Fingal,* purchased in England, entered Savannah harbor with military supplies; it was the first blockade runner commissioned by the Confederate government.

11.   Dec. 20: The first Union "stone fleet" was sunk in an effort to obstruct Charleston Harbor.

1862

12.   Jan. 16: Seven armored gunboats were commissioned by the Union navy for service on the Mississippi River.

13.   Jan. 30: The newly constructed *U.S.S. Monitor* was launched at Greenpoint, New York.

14.   Feb. 6: Flag Officer Andrew Foote captured Fort Henry on the Tennessee River.

15.   Feb. 8: A Union flotilla under Flag Officer Goldsborough helped capture Roanoke Island, North Carolina.

16.   **Feb. 10**: Gunboats from Foote's flotilla captured the *C.S.S. Eastport* and destroyed all other Confederate craft on the Tennessee River between Fort Henry and Florence, South Carolina.

17.   Feb. 14: Foote's gunboats unsuccessfully attacked Fort Donelson on the Cumberland River.

18.   **March 8**: The ram *C.S.S. Virginia*, the first Confederate ironclad, defeated and sunk two Union vessels in Hampton Roads.

19.   **March 9**: The *U.S.S. Monitor* engaged the *C.S.S. Virginia* in the first battle of ironclads; the battle ended in a draw.

20.   March 14: A joint Union amphibious assault captured New Bern, North Carolina.

21. April 4: The ironclad *U.S.S. Carondelet* dashed past Rebel batteries on Island No. 10 in the Mississippi River.

22. April 7: Aided by the *U.S.S. Carondelet*, the naval force under Flag Officer Foot captured Island No. 10.

23. **April 24**: Flag Officer David Farragut's fleet ran past the forts protecting New Orleans and destroyed the Confederate flotilla protecting the city, including the ram *C.S.S. Manassas*.

24. April 25: New Orleans, the largest city in the Confederacy, surrendered to Farragut.

25. **May 10**: Flag Officer Davis' gunboats were attacked by the Confederate River Defense Squadron near Fort Pillow on the Mississippi River; the *U.S.S. Cincinnati* and *Mound City* were damaged.

26. May 11: The *C.S.S. Virginia* was destroyed to prevent her capture by advancing Union forces.

27. May 13: Robert Smalls, an escaped slave, commandeered the steamer *Planter* and ran it out of Charleston Harbor to the safety of the Union blockading fleet.

28. May 15: The Union James River Flotilla unsuccessfully attacked Confederate batteries protecting Richmond at Drewry's Bluff.

29. **June 6**: Rams commanded by Colonel Ellet destroyed the Confederate River Defense Fleet protecting Memphis, helping to force the surrender of the city.

30. June 28: Flag Officer Farragut's fleet passed the Vicksburg batteries joining the freshwater fleet of Flag Officer Davis.

31. **July 15**: The ironclad ram *C.S.S. Arkansas* ran through the Union fleet on the Yazoo River above Vicksburg and disabled the *U.S.S. Carondelet* and *Tyler*.

32. July 16: David Farragut was promoted to Rear Admiral, the first officer to hold that rank in the U.S. Navy.

33. **July 22**: The Union ram *U.S.S. Queen of the West* and ironclad *U.S.S. Essex* unsuccessfully attacked the *C.S.S. Arkansas* at Vicksburg, Mississippi.

34. Aug. 6: Due to mechanical failures, the disabled *C.S.S. Arkansas* was destroyed by her commander near Baton Rouge, Lousiana, to avoid capture.

35. Aug. 24: Commander Raphael Semmes assumed command of the cruiser *C.S.S. Alabama*.

36. Oct. 31: The Confederate Torpedo Bureau was established under Lieutenant Davidson.

37. Dec. 12: The gunboat *U.S.S. Cairo* was the first vessel to be sunk by a Confederate torpedo in the Yazoo River.

38. Dec. 31: The *U.S.S. Monitor* foundered in a storm and was lost at sea off Cape Hatteras, North Carolina.

1863

39.   **Jan. 1**: The *C.S.S. Bayou* and *Neptune* engaged the Union fleet off Galveston, Texas, forcing the Union withdrawal from that city; the *U.S.S. Harriet Lane* was captured and the *U.S.S. Westfield* was destroyed.

40.   **Jan. 11**: The *C.S.S. Alabama* engaged and sank the *U.S.S. Hatteras* off Galveston.

41.   **Jan. 14**: Four Union gunboats engaged and destroyed the Confederate ironclad gunboat *C.S.S. J.A. Cotton* on the Bayou Teche, Louisiana.

42.   **Jan. 17**: The *C.S.S. Josiah Bell* and *Uncle Ben* captured the *U.S.S. Morning Light* and *Velocity*, temporarily lifting the blockade off Sabine Pass, Texas.

43.   **Jan. 31**: The armed ironclad rams *C.S.S. Palmetto State* and *Chicora* attacked the blockading fleet off Charleston Harbor; the *U.S.S. Mercedita* and *Keystone State* were heavily damaged.

44.   **Feb. 24**: The *C.S.S. William H. Webb* and *Queen of the West* sank the ram *U.S.S. Indianola* near Warrenton, Mississippi.

45.   April 7: The Union gunboat fleet commanded by Rear Admiral DuPont unsuccessfully attacked the Rebel forts in Charleston Harbor; the *U.S.S. Keokuk* sank from damages incurred in the attack.

46.   **April 14**: The Confederate ram *Queen of the West* was destroyed by the gunboat *U.S.S. Estrella* in Berwick Bay, Louisiana.

47.   April 16: Rear Admiral Porter's fleet of eight gunboats ran past the Vicksburg batteries.

48.   May 3: Rear Admiral Porter's fleet helped General Grant force the evacuation of Grand Gulf, Mississippi, opening the road to Vicksburg for Grant's forces.

49.   **June 17**: The *C.S.S. Atlanta* engaged the *U.S.S. Weehawken* and *Nahant* in Wassaw Sound, Georgia; the *Atlanta* grounded and was forced to surrender.

50.   Aug. 23: The Union gunboats *U.S.S. Satellite* and *Reliance* were captured by Confederate raiders in the Rappahannock River, Virginia.

51.   **Sept. 8**: The *C.S.S. Uncle Ben* helped turn back a Union expedition to take Sabine Pass, Texas; the *U.S.S. Clifton* and *Sachem* were disabled and surrendered.

52.   Sept. 9: A 20-vessel fleet under Commander Stephens unsuccessfully assaulted Fort Sumter.

53.   Nov. 2: A second Union naval attempt to capture Fort Sumter was unsuccessful.

54.   **Oct. 8**: The torpedo boat *C.S.S. David* exploded a spar torpedo against the *U.S.S. Ironsides*, damaging, but not destroying, the Union vessel.

The torpedo-boat *C.S.S. Davis* was unsuccessful in attack against the powerful *U.S.S. Ironsides.* (National Archives)

1864

55. Feb. 2: Confederate raiders captured and destroyed the *U.S.S. Underwriter* in the Neuse River, North Carolina.

56. **Feb. 17**: The submarine *H.L. Hunley* sunk the Union blockader *U.S.S. Housatonic* off Charleston Harbor.

57. **April 19**: The ram *C.S.S. Albemarle* engaged and sank the *U.S.S. Southfield* and helped land forces capture Plymouth, North Carolina.

58. **May 5**: The *U.S.S. Sassacus, Wyalushing,* and *Mattabesett* unsuccessfully engaged the *C.S.S. Albemarle* near Plymouth, North Carolina.

59. May 13: Rear Admiral Porter's Mississippi River Squadron escaped the low waters of Alexandria Falls on the Red River .

60. June 19: The sloop of war *U.S.S. Kearsage* engaged and sank the cruiser *C.S.S. Alabama* off the coast of Cherburg, France.

61. Aug. 5: Rear Admiral Farragut's fleet steamed through a torpedo field and into Mobile Bay; the ram *C.S.S. Tennessee* was captured and the monitor *U.S.S. Tecumseh* was blown up by a Confederate torpedo.

62. Aug. 8 : Fort Gaines, Alabama, protecting Mobile Bay, surrendered to Rear Admiral Farragut.

63. Oct. 7: The *U.S.S. Wachusett* captured the cruiser *C.S.S. Florida* at Bahia, Brazil.

64. Oct. 27: A torpedo launch commanded by Lieutenant Cushing destroyed the *C.S.S. Albemarle* in the Roanoke River.

65. Dec. 25: Rear Admiral Porter's fleet aided General Butler's unsuccessful attempt to take Fort Fisher, North Carolina.

1865

66. Jan. 15: Porter's fleet engaged Fort Fisher for a second time in the successful Union assault of Fort Fisher.

67. Jan. 24: A small Confederate fleet attempted to steam down the James River to attack City Point, Virginia; the attack failed when the gunboats were unable to run past obstructions in the river.

68. April 4: The James River Squadron was destroyed as per the orders of Secretary of the Navy Mallory.

69. June 28: The cruiser *C.S.S. Shenandoah* captured 11 American whalers in the Bering Strait.

70. Nov. 6: The commander of the *C.S.S. Shenandoah*, Lieutenant Waddell, surrendered her to British authorities in Liverpool, England.

Chapter 23

Accidental Deaths

A T 2:04 A.M., ON April 26, 1865, the steamship *Sultana*, carrying hundreds of paroled survivors from Rebel prisoner of war camps in Andersonville, Georgia, and Cahaba, Alabama, exploded in flames. The *Sultana* had left New Orleans five days earlier with stops scheduled in Vicksburg, Memphis, Cairo, Evansville, Louisville, and finally Cincinnati. In Vicksburg, the *Sultana* was boarded by soldiers heading home from the war. Although it was only licensed to carry 376 passengers, the *Sultana* accepted as many as 2,300 returning soldiers, 80 crewmen, and 70 paying passengers on its fateful voyage. In addition, a leaky boiler was discovered and repaired during the ship's layover, although the local boilermaker warned the

ship's captain that the repair was only temporary and that "two sheets adjoining the leak should have been taken out."

While the *Sultana* was docked, two additional packet boats arrived in Vicksburg, but Captain George Williams, the Assistant Adjutant General of the Department of the Mississippi, continued to load passengers aboard the *Sultana* until the hurricane deck began to sag and deckhands had to bolster it with

The sinking of the *Sultana* was the worst maritime disaster in United States history. (Library of Congress)

stanchions. Despite its heavy load and a strong rain-fed current, the *Sultana* steamed to Memphis at its normal pace of nine to 10 knots. After a six-hour layover, the *Sultana* continued its journey, with the next stop scheduled for Cairo, Illinois. An hour into the journey, an explosion in the *Sultana's* boilers rocked the night and hundreds of passengers were killed almost instantly. Those who survived the explosion threw themselves overboard and scrambled for any debris that would float. In all, only about 800 of the unfortunate passengers survived.

The official death count for the *Sultana* disaster was 1,238, but other estimates range between 1,500 and 1,700, making it the worst maritime disaster in United States history. An official investigation after the accident, conducted by Judge-Advocate General Joseph Holt, exonerated everyone connected with the fateful voyage, but both senior Union officers, Colonel R.B. Hatch, the Chief Quartermaster of the department, and Major-General Napoleon Dana, the officer in charge of prisoner exchange at Vicksburg, resigned from the service shortly after the investigation ended. In the hue and cry over the assassination of President Lincoln, the *Sultana* disaster received precious little media attention, and the entire sordid affair quickly disappeared from view.

Although the most spectacular and deadly, the *Sultana* disaster was only one of many incidents in which soldiers lost their lives through accident rather than on the battlefield. On a much smaller scale, another deadly accident occurred on April 15, 1861. While attempting to cross the Shenandoah River at Berry's Ferry, 61 men from the 75th Pennsylvania drowned when their boat capsized. A disgusted Colonel Bohlen described the incident in his official report: "There was no danger whatever of the boat sinking, but a panic struck the men and they rushed to the starboard side, causing it to keel over, precipitating its entire contents into the river. Only two small skiffs were at hand to save the drowning men, who were rapidly carried down the stream."

Most accidental deaths during the war were caused by the careless use of firearms, ammunition explosions, or railway accidents. On other occasions the deadly accident was the result of young men acting like boys, and often the untimely death was ignored and all but forgotten. On June 28, 1863, Private Harrison Jones of the 3rd Vermont was excused from the march toward Gettysburg because of his recent illness. However, Private Jones, after resting for a while, continued along on the road heading north. Seven days later, his body was found along the road and, upon examination of the body, a wound was found on the head. It was determined by Colonel Samuel Buck that Jones had been murdered, probably by a local civilian, while traveling alone along the road, and he was buried in an unmarked grave nearby. The following is a list the official causes of deaths in the Union army that were unrelated to the war:

Union Deaths Unrelated to the War

	Cause	Total killed
1.	Drowning	4,944
2.	Accident	4,114
3.	Murder	520
4.	Suicide	391
5.	Sunstroke	313
6.	Military execution	267
7.	Killed after capture	104
8.	Executed by the enemy	64
9.	Unclassified causes	2,034
10.	Cause not stated	12,631
	Total	25,382

29 Union Generals Who Died of "Other" Causes During the War

1.	John Garland	Natural causes
2.	George Gibson	Natural causes
3.	Frederick Lander	Pneumonia
4.	Charles F. Smith	Leg infection
5.	William Keim	Fever
6.	Joseph Plummer	Exposure
7.	William "Bull" Nelson	Murdered by Union General Jefferson C. Davis
8.	Ormsby Mitchel	Yellow fever
9.	Charles Jameson	Fever
10.	Francis Patterson	Accidental self-inflicted gunshot
11.	Slyvester Churchill	Natural causes
12.	Edwin Sumner	Natural causes
13.	James Cooper	Fever
14.	Andrew Foote	Bright's disease
15.	Henry Morris	Poor health
16.	Thomas Welsh	Malaria
17.	John Buford	Exposure
18.	Michael Corcoran	Horse fell on him
19.	Joseph Totten	Natural causes
20.	William Porter	Poor health
21.	Friend Rutherford	Exposure
22.	Joseph Taylor	Natural causes
23.	Daniel Woodbury	Yellow fever

24.	Joshua Howell	Fall from horse
25.	Thomas J.C. Amory	Yellow fever
26.	David Birney	Malaria
27.	Thomas Ransom	Typhoid
28.	Charles Wheelcock	Disease
29.	David Shunk	Disease

19 Confederate Generals Who Died of "Other" Causes During the War

1.	John Grayson	Lung disease
2.	Philip S. Cocke	Suicide
3.	Joseph Hogg	Dysentery
4.	Davis Twiggs	Lung infection
5.	William D. Smith	Yellow fever
6.	Allison Nelson	Fever
7.	John Villepigue	Fever
8.	Johnson K. Duncan	Typhoid
9.	David R. Jones	Heart attack
10.	Daniel Donelson	Natural causes
11.	Earl Van Dorn	Murdered by a jealous husband
12.	John Bowen	Dysentery
13.	John B. Floyd	Poor health
14.	Lucius Walker	Killed in a duel
15.	Claudius Wilson	Camp fever
16.	William Baldwin	Fall from horse
17.	James J. Archer	Effects of being held in prisoner of war camp
18.	John Winder	Exhaustion
19.	John Wharton	Murdered in a private feud

CHAPTER 24

The Legend of Stonewall

WHEN THOMAS J. JACKSON arrived at West Point in 1842 as a tall, raw-boned, relatively uneducated young man, he was quickly dubbed "the General" by his new classmates. This early nickname was a play off his ungainly appearance and the fact that he shared his last name with the great Andrew Jackson. Through hard work and single-minded study, Jackson was able to pull himself up in the class rankings in each of his four years at the Point until he graduated at number 17 in a class of 59 members.

After leaving the army to become a professor at the Virginia Military Institute, Major Jackson proved himself to be a poor instructor, and his extreme nervousness opened him to many humorous nicknames. The cadets greatly enjoyed drawing caricatures of him during class, usually focusing on his exceptionally large feet, which earned him the nickname "Square Box."

General Stonewall Jackson, from Tom Fool to the Old Testament Warrior. (*Battles and Leaders*)

After his tragic death at Chancellorsville, Jackson's life and military career took on an almost saintly character, and he was remembered as the "Old Testament Warrior." The following is a list of some of the great Stonewall Jackson's nicknames:

The 84th Pennsylvania advances against Jackson's position at Kernstown, Virginia.
(Library of Congress)

9 Nicknames of Thomas Jonathan Jackson

	Nicknames	Time Period
1.	The General	Cadet at West Point
2.	Tom Fool	Teacher at VMI
3.	Square Box	Teacher at VMI
4.	Old Hickory	Teacher at VMI
5.	Stonewall	During the war
6.	Old Jack	During the war
7.	Old Blue Light	During the war
8.	The Gallant Jackson	After his death
9.	Old Testament Warrior	After his death

☆☆☆

Stonewall Jackson's most notorious characteristic, before he became a famous Civil War general, was that he was a chronic hypochondriac. During the war, he would ride his horse while keeping one of his arms in the air in a position supposedly designed to provide better blood circulation. However, his primary medical complaints were weak and painful eyes, a recurrent infection of his throat and right ear, and chronic dyspepsia.

The medical community could do little for his eyes, and Jackson resorted to bathing them in cold water to little effect. For his throat, he used a vial of chloroform liniment externally and a preparation of ammonia internally. He even had one of his tonsils removed in 1858, again, with little effect. His greatest complaint, dyspepsia, is no longer considered a medical condition, but is seen by modern doctors as a symptom of stomach gastritis, peptic ulcers, a hiatus hernia, or even cancer of the stomach.

Like many people of the time, Jackson was a firm believer in hydropathy, and he followed a strict regimen of cold-water baths and large amounts of water drinking. He also visited numerous mineral springs in such places as Saratoga Springs, New York; Brattleboro, Vermont; and Northampton, Massachusetts, before the war. There is little evidence that Jackson derived any long-lasting benefits from his efforts. The following list details some of Jackson medical complaints:

11 Medical Complaints of Stonewall Jackson

1. Rheumatism
2. Dyspepsia
3. Chilblains
4. Poor eyesight
5. Cold feet
6. Nervousness
7. Neuralgia
8. Impaired hearing
9. Tonsillitis
10. Biliousness
11. Distortion of the spine

Thomas J. Jackson earned the sobriquet "Stonewall" during the first battle of Bull Run in 1861. At a critical point in the contest, General Barnard Bee, after his own brigade had been routed, shouted to his men: "Yonder stands Jackson like a stone wall!" Because Bee was killed shortly thereafter, it has never been determined if Bee's comment was meant as a compliment or a disparagement, but the name stuck.

After earning his spurs at Bull Run, Jackson was sent to the Shenandoah Valley with a small force, and it was here that Stonewall Jackson earned his place in American history. At the start of the campaign, Jackson's main goal was to hold as many of Union General Nathaniel Banks' soldiers in the Shenandoah Valley as possible. When he learned that some of Banks' men were leaving Winchester, Jackson ordered a forced march and attacked the Union force at nearby Kernstown. Jackson's attack was a failure, but the Federal high command, assuming that Jackson would not have attacked unless he had been reinforced, rushed additional troops to the Valley. For the next two months, Jackson succeeded in outmarching and outgeneraling the Union commanders sent to track him down until he found himself trapped between two larger armies at Port Republic. Rather than retreating to the safety of the Blue Ridge Mountains, Jackson held off General Fremont's force at Cross Keys with a portion of his army, and then crossed the river at Port Republic to defeat the advance guard of General Shields' division.

Jackson's exploits drew a force of 50,000 Union troops into the Shenandoah Valley and immobilized Irvin McDowell's 40,000-man corps at a time when General McClellan was desperately calling for reinforcements. In addition, President Lincoln and Secretary of War Edwin Stanton were so concerned about Jackson's whereabouts that they insisted that strong forces be kept near Washington, D.C., at all times to protect the capital city.

Jackson added to his fame later in 1862 when he captured Harper's Ferry during the Maryland campaign. It would not be until May 1942, when Corregidor Island fell to the Japanese, that Jackson's record of capturing 12,000 United States soldiers at one time would be eclipsed.

There were other factors that enhanced Jackson's enduring fame besides his military record. During his years in Lexington, Virginia, teaching at V.M.I., Jackson became a zealous and ardent Presbyterian. Even during the war, Sundays were sacrosanct, except when a battle was in the offing. When he was informed on his deathbed that he would soon die, Jackson responded: "It is the Lord's Day; my wish is fulfilled. I have always desired to die on Sunday."

In addition, Jackson had an odd array of personal quirks that only became more exaggerated as his fame grew. Colonel A. J. L. Freemantle, an observer from the British army, had this to say about Jackson in 1863: "I heard many anecdotes of the late 'Stonewall Jackson.' When he left the U.S. service, he was under the impression that one of his legs was shorter than the other, and afterward his idea was that he only perspired on one side, and that it was necessary to keep the arm and leg on the other side in constant motion in order to preserve circulation." Other stories about Jackson are purely myth, such as the persistent story of Jackson sucking on lemons while on the battlefield. While Jackson did eat lemons on occasion when they were captured from a Union camp, there is no evidence that he had any particular penchant for them. His other eccentric habits, like refusing to let his back touch the spine of a chair, which marked Jackson as a sort of clown in his early years, have only served to nourish his fame after his death.

9 Battles That Made "Stonewall" Jackson Famous

1. First Bull Run, Virginia (July 21, 1861)

After the initial Confederate position had been pushed back, "Stonewall" Jackson's brigade formed the nucleus of a new line on Henry House Hill. This line held long enough for reinforcements to arrive from the Shenandoah Valley and organize a counterattack that forced Union General Irvin McDowell to order a retreat that quickly turned into a disastrous rout.

2. Front Royal, Virginia (May 23, 1862)

Operating behind an effective screen provided by General Turner Ashby's cavalry, Jackson fooled Union commander General Nathaniel Banks into thinking he was heading up the North Fork of the Shenandoah River. Instead, Jackson crossed the Massanutten Mountains, joined forces with General Ewell's command, and fell up the unsuspecting Union garrison at Front Royal.

3. Winchester, Virginia (May 25, 1862)

Seizing the advantage he had gained by capturing Front Royal, Jackson doggedly pushed his "foot cavalry" toward Winchester. Jackson's swift advance prevented General Banks from organizing an effective defense. The battle ended with Banks' men fleeing from the Shenandoah Valley, and only a breakdown in the Confederate pursuit allowed their escape to Harper's Ferry.

4. Cross Keys, Virginia (June 8, 1862)

Despite having enjoyed a series of victories in the Shenandoah Valley, Jackson found himself trapped between two larger Federal forces. Instead of ordering a retreat, Jackson turned and faced the larger force commanded by General Fremont. Jackson calmly allowed General Ewell to direct the battle, in which the cautious Fremont did little more than probe the Rebel lines before being checked by General Trimble's brigade.

5. Port Republic, Virginia (June 9, 1862)

With General Fremont's force held in check, Jackson turned his attention to the Union forces advancing down the South Fork of the Shenandoah River. The battle was hotly contested until the strong Union battery positioned in the Lewiston coaling on the left of the line was overrun in a desperation attack by General Richard Taylor's brigade. After the defeat, all Union forces were withdrawn from the Shenandoah Valley, and Jackson's army was transferred to General Robert E. Lee's Army of Northern Virginia.

6. Second Bull Run, Virginia (August 29-30, 1982)

After destroying the Federal supply dump at Manassas, Jackson faced the entire brunt of General Pope's Federal army while General Longstreet's corps marched to join his position. Despite almost running out of ammunition and suffering fearful casualties, Jackson's line held until a fearsome counterattack could be launched by Longstreet. The Union army was forced to make a humiliating retreat, and Pope was soon replaced by General George McClellan.

7. Harper's Ferry, West Virginia (September 15, 1862)

Once again using the talents of his "foot cavalry," Jackson swiftly marched from Frederick, Maryland, to Harper's Ferry and trapped the Union garrison commanded by General Miles. Converging on the Union position from three sides, Jackson forced Miles to surrender.

8. Antietam, Virginia (September 17, 1862)

In perhaps his finest hour as a defensive commander, Jackson directed the left of General Lee's line and held off a series of furious Union assaults before General McClellan turned his attention to the center and then to the right of Lee's defensive line.

9. Chancellorsville, Virginia (May 2, 1863)

Faced by almost overwhelming odds, General Lee directed Jackson to make a flank march and strike the vulnerable right flank of General McClellan's Army of the Potomac. Jackson's attack was a smashing success as the Union line was driven back in great confusion. Just as Jackson was attempting to reorganize his men for a final attempt to cut off the Federal retreat route, he was accidentally shot while reconnoitering between the lines. Although his wounds were not considered mortal, Jackson's left arm was amputated on the battlefield and he was transported to nearby Guiney's Station to recuperate. Even as he seemed to be recovering quickly from his wounds, Jackson contracted a severe case of pneumonia and, eight days after being wounded, he died.

CHAPTER 25

The Cult of Robert E. Lee

ROBERT E. LEE SPENT most of his life attempting to live up to the legend of his father, while at the same time being acutely aware of the checkered legacy "Lighthorse" Harry Lee left behind. Without question the elder Lee was one of the best cavalry commanders of the Revolutionary War and a favorite of General George Washington. However, Harry Lee also had extreme financial difficulties after the war and was in debtor's prison when young Robert was born. Harry left the family under mysterious circumstances when Robert was 6 years old, and he died on his return trip to America five years later before being able to reunite with his family. Harry Lee's quixotic adventures had a deep impact on his son and probably were the basis for Robert's decision to accept a career in the peacetime army when many of his fellow officers, like William Sherman and Thomas J. Jackson, left the military to pursue more lucrative career options.

Robert E. Lee's only real combat experience in his 18-year career prior to the start of the Civil War came in the Mexican War in 1846. Serving as an engineer on the staff of General Winfield Scott, Lee earned his first accolades by finding a path through the seemingly impassable Pedregal, a barren wasteland of congealed

General Robert E. Lee conducting his first offensive as the commander of the Army of Northern Virginia. (Library of Congress)

lava. Scott described this as a great "feat of physical and moral courage." Fifteen years later, in April 1861, Winfield Scott, now the general-in-chief of the U.S. Army, remembered his young engineer officer. After describing him as "the very best soldier that I ever saw in the field," Scott suggested that now-Colonel Robert E. Lee be put in command of the Federal force being assembled to put down the rebellion.

Robert E. Lee did not accept Scott's offer and instead resigned his commission and volunteered his services for the fledgling Confederacy. Instead of being given a command assignment, Lee served as a military advisor for President Davis. When General Joe Johnston was hit in the shoulder by a shell fragment during the battle of Seven Pines, Davis quickly tapped Lee as the next commander of the Army of Northern Virginia. Prior to June 1, 1862, General Robert E. Lee had only commanded troops in battle on one occasion in his entire career. Several years earlier, Lee was placed in command of the U.S. Marines and militia troops that were assembled at Harper's Ferry to put down John Brown's raid.

Robert E. Lee's Command Experience Prior to the Start of the Civil War

Date	Troops	Location
1. October 1859	2,000 troops	Harper's Ferry, W. Va.

☆☆☆

General Lee's greatest victories came when he emulated his old commander Winfield Scott's tactics at the battle of Cerro Gordo, Mexico. Although a flank attack was a staple of Napoleonic tactics, the victory at Cerro Cordo clearly showed the devastating impact that such an attack can have when it was not expected. At Second Manassas and Chancellorsville, Lee used this tactic and succeeded in achieving his greatest battlefield victories. On several occasions, Lee eschewed the "Cerro Gordo" style and resorted to full-fledged frontal assaults. At these times, like during Pickett's Charge at Gettysburg, or at Malvern Hill during the Peninsular campaign, Lee suffered harsh defeats. However, Lee's greatest strength as a military commander was during defensive battles. Throughout his tenure as commander of the Army of Northern Virginia, Lee exceled at making his opponents pay dearly in blood for any ground they were able to capture. The following is a list of Lee's defensive victories:

Lee's 7 Defensive Gems

	Battle	Union troops	Lee's troops
1.	Antietam, Md.	75,316	40,000
2.	Fredericksburg, Va.	106,007	72,497

	Battle	Union troops	Lee's troops
3.	Mine Run, Va.	69,643	44,426
4.	North Anna, Va.	80,000	45,500
5.	Wilderness, Va.	101,895	61,025
6.	Spotsylvania, Va.	83,000	50,000
7.	Cold Harbor, Va.	108,000	59,000

☆☆☆

In October 1870, weakened by years of hard service in the field and by a diseased heart, Robert E. Lee quietly passed away. While his war record insured his long-lasting fame as a military general, Robert E. Lee was destined to become much more. In the next 20 years, Lee would go from being the South's wartime hero to a cultural icon for the fabled "Lost Cause of the Confederacy." In the process, Lee's humanity would be stripped away and he would become, in the words of historian Thomas L. Connelly, a "marble man."

Robert E. Lee in later life as president of Washington College in Lexington, Virginia. (National Archives)

After his death, a small group of Virginians with wartime links to Lee wrote hundreds of articles, published dozens of books, and gave uncountable speeches and talks, all lauding Lee's achievements and personality. In their version of the history of the war, Lee was never defeated in battle, only overwhelmed by numbers or let down by incompetent subordinates. The primary architect of this group was former Confederate General Jubal Early.

When the war ended, Early's reputation was in tatters. Not only had he presided over an army that was defeated time and again in battle, Early, perhaps the original unreconstructed Rebel, fled the country and when he finally returned to Virginia in 1869, he was remembered primarily for deserting the South after Appomattox. Although he had opposed secession before the war, Early turned himself into one of its more ardent defenders during the Reconstruction Era. In 1875, he became the permanent president of the

Southern Historical Society, and he did not hesitate to use his position to further the reputation of Lee and the myth of the Lost Cause. He remained at his post until his death in 1894, and, in the process, became one of the most feared men in the South.

One of the key components of Early's strategy to free Lee from any and all human flaws was to find a way to shift the blame for his defeat at Gettysburg. In this Early had a dual purpose, for his own conduct during the battle had been seriously criticized by fellow General J. E. B. Stuart. It was Stuart's belief that Early failed, despite having instructions from Lee, to watch for Stuart's cavalry in the crucial days prior to the Gettysburg battle. In the end, the supporters of Stuart and Early made a deal in which each agreed not to criticize the other, and in turn place the blame for the defeat on General James Longstreet. To achieve this, Stuart's original battle report was released with the paragraph describing Early's failure omitted. General James Longstreet became the ideal choice to take the blame for the defeat because he had dared to criticize Lee's generalship during the battle and, perhaps more importantly, had joined the hated Republican Party after the war. In so doing Longstreet became, in the eyes of Early and company, a traitor to the South. The following is a list of the men who created and maintained the image of Robert E. Lee in the post-war years and created the cult of Lee:

10 Creators of the "Lee Cult"

Name	Occupation
1. Jubal Early	Confederate general
2. William H. Pendleton	Confederate general
3. Fitzhugh Lee	Confederate general
4. Henry Heth	Confederate general
5. Eppa Hunton	Confederate general
6. Walter Taylor	Lee's chief-of-staff
7. Charles Marshall	Member of Lee's wartime headquarters staff
8. Charles Venable	Member of Lee's wartime headquarters staff
9. A. L. Long	Lee's military secretary
10. J. William Jones	Baptist minister and family confidant

☆☆☆

The next major figure to take a turn at molding the reputation of Robert E. Lee was historian Douglas Southall Freeman. In 1935, Freeman released a four-volume biography of Lee that became the backbone of all subsequent studies of Lee and the war. According to Freeman, "it took five generations of clean living and wise mating to produce such a man." In the eyes of Freeman, Lee was a military com-mander without equal this side of George Washington, and an uncomplicated man who personified self-control, self-denial, and self-discipline. Like Early and his cohorts, Freeman blamed all of Lee's military failures on his subordinates. In addi-tion, according to Freeman's analysis, Lee was doomed by his own human kindness to refrain from taking action against them. In the years since the publication of Freeman's work, there has been some critical re-evaluation of Lee's generalship, but his status as an icon for the South and as a hero for the country has remained intact. The following is a list of the personal qualities of Robert E. Lee as found in the index of Freeman's biography:

136 Personal Qualities of Robert E. Lee

1. Ability to preserve morale	36. Dislike of strong drink
2. Abstemiousness	37. Dislike of unconfirmed rumors
3. Accessibility	38. Dislike of writing
4. Accurate reasoning	39. Distrust of politicians
5. Accuracy	40. Energy
6. Admiration for his men	41. Engineering skill
7. Affection	42. Enthusiasm
8. Affection for his army	43. Equanimity
9. Alertness	44. Excitement
10. Amiability	45. Fairness
11. Aptitude for collecting data	46. Faith in God
12. Aptitude for reconnaissance	47. Frankness
13. Audacity	48. Friendliness
14. Boldness	49. Frugality
15. Calmness	50. Generosity
16. Caution	51. Gentlemanliness
17. Charm of manner	52. Gentleness
18. Cheerfulness	53. Good judgment
19. Composure	54. Good looks
20. Confidence	55. Goodness
21. Consideration	56. Grace
22. Courage	57. Gratitude
23. Courtesy	58. Gravity
24. Courtliness	59. Grief
25. Critical analysis	60. Hatred of waste
26. Daring	61. Heroic character
27. Desperation	62. High spirits
28. Determination	63. Humility
29. Devotion to duty	64. Humor
30. Dignity	65. Ingenuousness
31. Diligence	66. Integrity
32. Diplomacy	67. Intelligence
33. Disappointment	68. Interest in women
34. Dislike of debt	69. Intuition
35. Dislike of greediness	70. Joking

71. Justice
72. Kindness
73. Logic
74. Love of animals
75. Love of children
76. Love of civil life
77. Love of family
78. Love of horses
79. Love of nature
80. Love of perfection
81. Love of reading
82. Love of social life
83. Love of teasing
84. Loyalty
85. Magnanimity
86. Mercy
87. Military ability
88. Military judgment
89. Modesty
90. Neatness
91. Nervous stamina
92. Observation
93. Optimism
94. Patience
95. Poise
96. Politeness
97. Practicality
98. Precipitancy
99. Precision
100. Pride
101. Promptness
102. Pugnacity
103. Punctiliousness
104. Quickness
105. Reasonableness
106. Reasoning power
107. Recklessness
108. Resentment at sufferings of non-combatants
109. Reserve
110. Resignation
111. Resourcefulness
112. Respect of constituted authority
113. Restlessness
114. Restraint
115. Self-abnegation
116. Self-confidence
117. Sense of duty
118. Serenity
119. Silence
120. Simplicity
121. Sincerity
122. Spirituality
123. Stoicism
124. Stubbornness
125. Submission of spirit
126. Swiftness
127. Sympathy
128. Taciturnity on public questions
129. Tact
130. Temper
131. Tenderness
132. Thoughtfulness
133. Thrift
134. Understanding
135. Urge to excel
136. Wisdom

CHAPTER 26

The Strange
Journey of Sam Grant

ESSE ROOT AND HANNAH Simpson Grant gave birth to a baby boy and christened him Hiram Ulysses in Point Pleasant, Ohio, on April 27, 1822. Seventeen years later, at the urging of his father, young Ulysses was appointed to a spot in the United States Military Academy. However, Congressman Thomas Hamer, who sponsored Grant's appointment, carelessly wrote the name Ulysses S. Grant when he forwarded his name to West Point. When young Grant arrived at the Point in May 1839, he was informed that if he was to accept his appointment, it would have to be under the name it was given.

Despite bringing this inadvertent name change to the attention of the army on three separate occasions, he officially remained Ulysses S. Grant. It was not long, however, that he found his name was changed yet again. This time by the upperclassmen of West Point. According to William Tecumseh Sherman, who was three years ahead of Grant, he and several other upperclassmen saw the name U.S. Grant on the bulletin board and immediately began searching for a proper nickname: "One said, 'United States Grant.' Another 'Uncle Sam' Grant. A third said 'Sam' Grant. That name stuck."

It wasn't until after his first major campaign as a general in the Civil War that Grant was given a more impressive appellation. After his army had successfully captured Fort Henry

Union General Ulysses "Sam" Grant, supreme commander of the Union Army.

☆ **199** ☆

General Grant's headquarters in City Point, Virginia. (National Archives)

and trapped the Confederate army in nearby Fort Donelson, Grant entered surrender negotiations with General Simon Bolivar Buckner. Because they had been old friends and he had loaned money to Grant in 1854, Buckner had hoped for generous terms. He was stunned when he read the terms Grant proposed: "No terms except unconditional and immediate surrender can be accepted. I propose to move immediately upon your works." Lacking an alternative, Buckner accepted these terms and became the first Confederate commander to surrender an entire army to the Federals. Overjoyed by the news of this unexpected victory by an unknown general, the new hero of the war was dubbed "Unconditional Surrender" Grant. It wouldn't be until he defeated Democrat Horatio Seymour in the presidential election of 1868 that Grant would earn an even more impressive name—President Ulysses S. Grant.

5 Names for a Future President

Name	Years
1. Hiram Ulysses Grant	1822-1836
2. Ulysses S. Grant	1837
3. "Sam" Grant	1838-1861
4. "Unconditional Surrender" Grant	1862-1867
5. President Ulysses S. Grant	1868-1885

☆☆☆

Of all the men who rose to greatness in the Civil War, none was more obscure than Sam Grant. After leaving the army in 1854, Grant tried and failed at being a farmer, a real estate salesman, a rent collector, and a businessman. In 1861, Grant was working as a lowly clerk in a leather goods store run by his two brothers.

The one attribute that the freshly minted General Grant showed early in the war, and that was sorely lacking among many of his fellow officers, was a willingness to fight. In November 1861, Grant changed what was supposed to be merely a diversionary maneuver into a full-fledged battle at Belmont, Missouri. He achieved some success and even drove the Rebels from their camps before being forced to quickly withdraw when enemy reinforcements arrived. The aggressive attitude that Grant showed at Belmont would be repeated with greater degrees of success throughout the war.

The 9 Battles and Campaigns of Grant

1. Belmont, Missouri (November 7, 1861)

After initial success, Grant was forced to withdraw before superior Confederate forces.

2. Fort Henry, Tennessee (February 6, 1862)

Operating with the naval forces of Flag Officer Foote, the partially flooded Confederate fort surrendered before Grant was able to mount an assault.

3. Fort Donelson, Tennessee (February 12-16, 1862)

After stubborn resistance, the 12,000-man Confederate army surrendered en mass to Grant's army.

4. Shiloh, Tennessee (April 6-7, 1862)

After being surprised and nearly driven into the Tennessee River, Grant, with reinforcements from General Buell's army, counterattacked and drove the Confederate army back.

5. Iuka, Mississippi (September 19, 1862)

Grant directed this battle as the Department Commander.

6. Vicksburg Campaign (October 1862-July 1863)

After numerous failures, Grant succeeded in getting his army below Vicksburg and, after winning five battles in two weeks (Port Gibson, Raymond, Jackson, Champion's Hill, and Big Black River Bridge), he placed the Confederate fortress under siege. Six weeks later, General Pemberton surrendered and the last Rebel bastion on the Mississippi River was in Union hands.

7. Chattanooga, Tennessee (November 23-25, 1863)

Summoned to the rescue of General Rosecrans' army after the disaster at Chickamauga, Grant opened the "cracker line" to get food and supplies into the city. He then launched a three-pronged attack that sent General Bragg's Confederate army stumbling back into Georgia.

8. Overland Campaign (May-June 1864)

Matched against General Lee for the first time, Grant resorted to a series of costly frontal assaults until pinning the Confederate army in the trenches surrounding Richmond and Petersburg.

9. Appomattox Court House (April 2-9, 1865)

After forcing General Lee to evacuate Richmond, Grant staged a dogged pursuit until trapping Lee's army and forcing the surrender of the Army of Northern Virginia.

☆☆☆

The one major flaw that followed Grant throughout his military career was his alleged penchant for alcohol. The first known reference to his drinking was his decision in 1848 to join the Sons of Temperance and to take a pledge to cease drinking. However, it was his resignation from the army in 1854, at the behest of his commander Captain Robert Buchanan, who charged that Grant had been under the influence while on duty, that forged Grant's reputation as a drunkard. Thereafter, whenever a fellow officer sought to sully Grant's military achievements, or a newspaperman wanted a quick and controversial story, tales of Grant's drinking episodes, true and untrue, were trotted out. The following is a list of the most popular and widespread drinking stories about Grant:

9 Drinking Stories

1. Cairo story (January 1862)

A steamboat captain named William J. Kountz, upset that Grant had ordered him out of his office, spread rumors that Grant was a drunk. These stories eventually were reported to Washington and were soundly refuted by Grant's Chief-of-Staff, John Rawlins, who promised to resign should Grant ever become "an intemperate man or a habitual drunkard."

A very sober General Grant at Cold Harbor, Virginia. (National Archives)

2. Halleck story (March 1862)

In the aftermath of Grant's victories at Forts Henry and Donelson, Halleck demoted Grant from command of the army and alleged that "General Grant has resumed his former bad habits." When pressed by President Lincoln for proof, Halleck restored Grant's command.

3. Shiloh stories (April 1862)

After the bloody battle, Whitelaw Reid, a correspondent for the *Cincinnati Gazette*, and Joseph Medill, from the *Chicago Tribune*, published stories that Grant had been drunk during the battle. Staff officers testified to Grant's sobriety before, during, and after the battle.

4. Iuka rumors (September 1862)

Newspaper correspondent William Bickham of the *Cincinnati Commercial*, a longtime Grant antagonist, published several columns implying that Grant was drunk during the campaign.

5. Kountz's story (March 1863)

Kountz again reported to Washington that Grant had been gloriously drunk and promised to have proof to back up his claim. Murat Halstead picked up the story and penned this in his column for the *Cincinnati Commercial*: "Our noble army of the Mississippi is being wasted by the foolish, drunken, stupid Grant."

6. Steamer story (May 1863)

Recounted years after the war by newspaperman Sylvanus Cadwallander. Grant, on a trip up the Yazoo River, got "as stupidly drunk as the immortal nature of man would allow." This story was refuted by Charles Dana, a representative of Secretary of War Edwin Stanton, who swore that Cadwallander was not even aboard the steamer during the trip.

7. General Banks' story (September 1863)

While Grant was in New Orleans inspecting the troops commanded by General Banks, he was thrown by his horse and seriously injured. Banks confided in a letter to his wife: "I am frightened when I think he is a drunkard." However, other witnesses swore that Grant was not intoxicated when the accident occurred.

8. "Baldy" Smith's story (June 1864)

According to General Smith, Grant arrived at his headquarters and asked for several drinks before vomiting over his mount. At the time, Smith was seeking a leave of absence, which was immediately granted.

9. William Franklin's story (July 1864)

While visiting Grant's headquarters in search of a new command, General Franklin reported that Grant had been drinking with General Rufas Ingalls, an old West Point classmate. Two days later Franklin was captured by the Confederate raiding column commanded by General Jubal Early.

CHAPTER 27

Court-Martials

HEN THE CIVIL WAR broke out, the Union army grew quickly until, at its peak, it included nearly two million men. The army was eventually organized into 2,500 regiments, each in need of a colonel. Because the vast majority of the officers from the old army were quickly promoted to command of brigades or divisions, the bulk of these new regimental commanders had to come from the civilian ranks. This led to an almost inevitable conflict between the professionally trained general officers and the new amateur colonels, and it resulted in more than 140 court-martials in the first 18 months of the war. The burden placed on these new colonels was very heavy. Not only were they placed in charge of 800 new recruits, they also had tremendous responsibilities placed on them during combat. The following is a list of the five principle types of court-martials:

4 Most Frequent Court-Martial Offenses

1. Insubordination.
2. Conduct unbecoming an officer.
3. Failure of leadership.
4. Cowardice in battle.

During the war, there were more than 100,000 general court-martials in the Union army. All the records that remain are handwritten, and the only name index that still exists, prepared in the 1880s, is located on six rolls of crumbling microfilm. In 1994, an organization called The Index Project, Inc., organized by author

Munson's Hill, Virginia, the site of cowardice under fire by Union Colonel James
Kerrigan (*Battles and Leaders*)

Beverly Lowery, began transcribing this information and entering it into a com-
puter database. By March 1997, more than 24,000 court-martials had been sum-
marized and entered into their database. The following is a list of several of the
court-martials uncovered by The Index Project:

6 Union Court-Martials

1. Colonel Francis Quinn.

Charges: Shamefully deserting his command on the battlefield of Shiloh.

At the heart of the charges against Quinn was a long-running feud between
him and Lieutenant-Colonel William Graves. Prior to and during the battle,
Quinn and Graves refused to cooperate and effectively split the 12th Michigan Infantry Regiment into two separate units. In the battle, both segments
were forced to retreat, although most of the men escaped capture and the unit
did see action on the second day of the battle. Austin Blair, the governor of
Michigan, called Quinn the "worst colonel I ever saw," and the officers of the
12th Michigan filed charges against Quinn after the battle. To avoid a court-
martial, Quinn resigned from the army. He attempted to withdraw his resignation shortly thereafter, but Secretary of War Stanton refused his request and
Quinn had to return to Michigan as a civilian. For his part in the affair, Graves
was promoted to colonel and he led the regiment capably until it was mustered out of the army. Quinn attended the first post-war reunion of the 12th
Michigan, but was branded a liar in a formal resolution and wisely chose not
attend any future reunions.

2. Colonel Michael K. Lawler.

Charges: 1. Sending a bottle of whiskey laced with ipecac (a strong emetic) to several soldiers serving time in the guardhouse for drunken rowdiness. 2. Striking and beating with his fist Private Allen Brock of the 18th Illinois.

These were just several of the many charges lodged against Lawler in a five-month period in 1861. He was eventually found guilty, but the charges were disapproved by General Henry Halleck and Lawler was restored to duty. After returning to command, he led his unit admirably at Fort Donelson, Champion Hill, and during the siege of Vicksburg, and suffered several wounds in combat. He was eventually promoted to brigadier-general before being declared medically unfit for duty as a result of his wounds and sent home in January 1864.

3. Colonel James Kerrigan.

Charges: Shamefully abandoning his post and habitual neglect of duty.

These were just two of the 42 charges lodged against Kerrigan early in 1861. Kerrigan's downfall began during a skirmish in August 1861 near Munson's Hill, Virginia, when he withdrew his pickets while a Confederate force was advancing despite having orders to hold the position. He was also accused of leaving camp to visit and communicate with the nearby Rebels. During the trial, General Martindale testified that, during an inspection of Kerrigan's camp, he found many of the men to be running around with their pants unbuttoned and dirty, without shirts, and with very foul weapons. The court-martial board recommended that Kerrigan resign his commission, which he did. He went on to serve in Congress and as an active member of the Fenian Brotherhood. As part of this Irish organization, Kerrigan participated in several abortive attempts to invade Canada, and he even secured a battlefield victory north of the border at the battle of Limestone Ridge in 1866. Despite these activities, he escaped arrest and returned to live in the United States until the ripe old age of 86.

4. Colonel Dixon S. Miles.

Charges: Drunkenness during the battle of First Bull Run.

The charge against Miles was lodged by Colonel Israel Richardson, who commanded a brigade during the battle. According to Richardson, Miles' speech during the battle was "guttural and his language incoherent." Several other witnesses took the stand, but their opinion of Miles' state of intoxication was mixed. In their final determination, the court-martial board determined that Miles was drunk during the battle, but that his condition was the result of medicinal brandy the colonel had consumed earlier in the day. Miles was returned to duty and given the command of the garrison at Harper's Ferry. Unfortunately for Miles, he soon found himself besieged by a Confederate force led by Stonewall Jackson, and, after a short artillery barrage, he surrendered the 11,500-man garrison to Jackson. In an investigation of the Union disaster, Miles' incapacity was described as bordering on "imbecility." Miles escaped censure for his action at Harper's Ferry only because he had been killed by one of the very last shells directed at the town before the surrender.

5. Colonel David Williams.

Charges: 1. Becoming frightened and confused under fire. 2. Cowardice under fire to the extent of hiding behind a tree stump during a skirmish.

In his first engagement at Fair Oaks Station, Virginia, Williams was found behind a stump while under fire, despite being given orders to take the usual position of a regimental commander. Williams' cowardice emerged again a week later when he was discovered hiding behind a tree during a skirmish. Finally, on July 1, 1862, Williams was unable to exercise command because he was lying paralyzed behind another tree stump. Despite overwhelming evidence, the court-martial board found him not guilty and restored him to duty. He continued to command the 82nd Pennsylvania Infantry until his colonel's commission expired on March 4, 1863, and he was discharged from the army.

6. Colonel Newton B. Lord.

Charges: Drunkenness on duty, cowardice under fire, and disobedience of orders.

Lord was actually court-martialed on two separate occasions. The first time, for disobeying the orders of General Wadsworth, he escaped with only an official admonition. The next time, he was arrested for cowardice during the battle of South Mountain. Before the court-martial could begin, additional charges were added for his behavior at Alexandria, Virginia. While on duty, he was so drunk he fell off his horse and "he made an indecent exposure of his person in the presence of a lady." Lord then outdid himself by riding his horse into a bar and procuring a drink of brandy for himself and his horse. When the charges were finally heard in February 1863, they were dropped in lieu of his resignation from the army. However, Lord did not exit the war quietly. He returned to his home in Jefferson County, New York, recruited enough men to form the 20th New York Cavalry, and served until the end of the war.

CHAPTER 28

This Month in 1865

The battle of Petersburg ended when Union forces under the command of Phil Sheridan severely defeated a much smaller force commanded by General Pickett. Pickett was caught by surprise while attending a shad bake when the battle began. General Lee quickly ordered the evacuation of Richmond and began an arduous retreat in a desperate attempt to link up with Joe Johnston's army in North Carolina. After a week of hard marching, Grant trapped the remnants of Lee's army at Appomattox Court House and, after a brief exchange of notes, accepted the formal surrender of the Army of Northern Virginia. Unfortunately, the victory celebration was cut short by the assassination of President Lincoln by an actor named John Wilkes Booth. Lincoln's Vice President, Andrew Johnson, a former Southern Democrat, was inaugurated as the 17th President of the United States.

At Appomattox, Gettysburg hero General Joshua Chamberlin was tapped to accept the official surrender of Lee's army. After the surrender, the victorious Army of the Potomac and General Sherman's western armies marched to Washington, DC, to participate in a spectacular Grand Review. After his capture in Irwinville, Georgia, while trying to escape to Mexico, Jefferson Davis was brought as a prisoner to For-

Andrew Johnson, the seventeenth President of the United States. (National Archives)

tress Monroe, Virginia. Davis would not be released from custody until 1867, when the United States government finally decided that he could not be convicted of treason or in complicity with the assassination of President Lincoln.

General Custer leads the charge that broke the Rebel lines at the battle of
Five Forks in April 1865. (Library of Congress)

☆   **January:**   The 13th Amendment to the Constitution abolishing slavery is passed and sent to the states for ratification. Fort Fisher, North Carolina, the last major Rebel port, falls to Union forces.

☆   **February:**   General Sherman's forces capture Columbia, South Carolina; Charleston is abandoned, and the American flag is raised over Fort Sumter.

☆   **March:**   The remnants of the vaunted Valley Army is destroyed in a battle near Waynesboro, Virginia.

☆   **April:**   Richmond and Petersburg fall to the Union army, and General Lee's army is forced to surrender at Appomattox; Joe Johnston also surrenders the last major Confederate army in the field in North Carolina. President Lincoln is assassinated and Andrew Johnson takes over as the 17th president of the United States.

☆   **May:**   Confederate President Jefferson Davis is captured and imprisoned. A final Grand Review is held in Washington, D.C., as the armies of the East and the West parade through the city before being mustered out of service.

☆   **June:**   Nine people are implicated in the plot to assassinate President Lincoln; they are found guilty and sentenced to death by hanging. Cherokee Stand Watie is the last Confederate general to surrender.

☆   **July:**   President Johnson proclaims amnesty for all but the most high-ranking Confederates who consent to sign an oath of loyalty.

☆ **August:** Henry Wirtz, commandant of the prisoner-of-war camp at Andersonville, is found guilty by a military commission and sentenced to death by hanging.

☆ **October:** After being found guilty of murder, Confederate guerilla Champ Ferguson is sentenced to death by hanging in Tennessee.

☆ **December:** The 13th Amendment, after being ratified by 27 states, is formally proclaimed to be in effect. President Johnson declares that the Union is restored.

CHAPTER 29

The Death of Abraham Lincoln

BRAHAM LINCOLN'S FATALISTIC ATTITUDE toward his presidency began very early in his term. Threats to his life before his inauguration in 1860 convinced Lincoln, en route to Washington, D.C., to accept the advice of his security chief Allen Pinkerton and sneak through Baltimore, Maryland, ahead of his announced schedule. Lincoln hated this concession to fear, and, in a culture that prized manliness above all other male qualities, he was mocked unmercifully in the press. In many ways, Lincoln spent the rest of his presidency refuting the image of his skulking through the streets of Baltimore. For most of the first four years of his Presidency, there were no guards at the Executive Mansion. When two guards were finally assigned to duty there in August 1864, it was done without consulting Lincoln. Shortly afterward, when General Benjamin Butler warned Lincoln about the possible dangers he faced, the Chief Executive laughed if off by replying: "Oh, assassination is not an American crime."

President Lincoln's seemingly cavalier attitude toward his own mortality may also have been related to his own premonitions. He always believed that if "the Richmond people... wanted to get at me, no vigilance could keep them out." In addition, Lincoln had a dream in early April 1865 that he

President Lincoln did not allow guards in the Executive Mansion until August 1864. (National Archives)

described to Ward H. Lamon, one of the men assigned to him as a bodyguard. In the dream, Lincoln entered the East Room and discovered a "throng of people...gazing mournfully upon [a] corpse." When the president demanded who had died, one of the soldiers responded: "The president. He was killed by an assassin." Lamon worried extensively about a possible assassination attempt and even occasionally slept in the hall outside Lincoln's bedroom. Unfortunately, Lamon was in Richmond, Virginia, attending the state convention during the second week of April 1865.

John Wilkes Booth, world famous actor and presidential assassin. (National Archives)

The historical events that put John Wilkes Booth and President Abraham Lincoln on a collision course began as early as July 26, 1864. On that date Booth was recruited by Confederate Secret Service agents in Boston, Massachusetts. By September 1864, Booth was putting his own team together to help him capture the President. A month later, Booth was in southern Maryland organizing an escape route, and by January, he had associates procuring boats to get the President across the Potomac River. During this time, Booth contributed almost $4,000 of his own money to forward his clandestine endeavor. When it became clear that the Confederacy was collapsing, Booth called all his conspirators together on March 17, 1865. A plan to capture Lincoln the following Monday, while he was on the road to the Soldier's Home outside Washington, D.C., was agreed upon, but was foiled when the President failed to make the trip. The conspiracy would have died that day had not Booth learned, early on April 14, that the President would be taking in a play that evening at Ford's Theater.

The Timeline: April 14, 1865

	Lincoln	*Booth*
7 a.m.	Gets up; works in office.	Gets up; leaves National Hotel.
8 a.m.	Breakfasts w/Mrs. Lincoln, Robert, and Tad.	Goes to nearby barbershop.
9 a.m.	In office, takes visitors.	Returns to the National Hotel.
10 a.m.	In office, more visitors.	Leaves hotel; posts letter. Goes to Ford's Theater and learns of Lincoln's plans to attend that evening.
11 a.m.	Convenes cabinet meeting on Reconstruction. General Grant is invited to attend.	
Noon	Cabinet meeting continues.	Hires a horse at Pumphrey's Stable to be saddled at 4 p.m.

The Presidential Box at Ford's Theater in Washington, D.C. (National Archives)

1 p.m.	Cabinet meeting continues.	Walks to the Herndon House to see Lewis Paine.
2 p.m.	Lunches with Mrs. Lincoln.	
3 p.m.	In office, takes visitors.	Walks to the Kirkwood House to see George Atzerodt.
4 p.m.	Goes to War Department to see Secretary of War Stanton.	Gets horse; rides to Deery's Tavern for a drink.
5 p.m.	Takes carriage ride with Mrs. Lincoln.	
6 p.m.	Returns from carriage ride, has dinner with Mrs. Lincoln, Robert, and Tad.	Has a drink at Taltaud's bar, goes to Ford's Theater; examines Presidential box and makes preparations for the attack.
7 p.m.	John Parker takes over as Presidential bodyguard.	Eats dinner at National Hotel.
8 p.m.	Leaves for the theater. Picks up guests Major Rathbone and Miss Harris.	Arrives at 8:25 p.m. Meets fellow conspirators at the Herndon House. Finalizes the plans for the evening.
9 p.m.	Watches *My American Cousin*.	Returns to Ford's Theater.

10:17 p.m.   **ASSASSINATION**

First doctors on the scene examine Lincoln's wound:
Dr. Charles Lamb,
Dr. Charles Taft, Dr. Albert King.
Lincoln is brought to William Peterson's house on 435 10th Street, across from the theater

Despite being injured during the attack, heads for escape route; 9th Street, to Pennsylvania Ave. to New Jersey Ave.
Crosses the Navy Yard Bridge into Maryland.

| 11 p.m. | Surgeon-General Barnes takes charge of Lincoln's case. Stanton orders arrest of all Ford's Theater employees. | Rides up Good Hope Hill, is overtaken by David Herold. They head for Surrattsville. |
| 12 am | Arrangements are made for Gen. Grant's return. VP Andrew Johnson is notified that Lincoln's wound is mortal. | After reaching Surrattsville (11 mi. west of Ford's.) Booth and Herold are directed to Dr. Mudd's residence to treat Booth's broken leg. |

☆☆☆

Throughout his life, Abraham Lincoln was an avid reader. Stories abound of Lincoln's quest for interesting reading material as a young boy living on the prairie where books were a scarce commodity. According to David Homer Bates, a telegraph officer during the war, one of Lincoln's favorite authors was William Shakespeare. Bates described a scene from the winter of 1865: "He carried in his pocket a well-worn copy in small compass of *Macbeth,* and one of *The Merry Wives of Windsor,* selections from both of which he read aloud to us in the telegraph office." In addition, Lincoln was drawn to the writings of the great humorists of the day, including Petroleum V. Nasby and Artemus Ward. During a cabinet meeting on the day he presented the Emancipation Proclamation, Lincoln occupied himself by reading Ward's *High Handed Outrage in Utica.*

Although he was an avid reader, Lincoln himself never owned many books and, after his election in 1860, he left most behind in Springfield, Illinois. Unfortunately, Lincoln was never able to return to collect his books, and the following is a list of the ones he left on his desk at his old law office:

9 Books Lincoln Left Behind

1. *Religious Truth: Illustrated from Science*
2. *Gibbon's History of the Decline and Fall of the Roman Empire, Volume 1*
3. *Gibbon's History of the Decline and Fall of the Roman Empire, Volume 2*
4. *Gibbon's History of the Decline and Fall of the Roman Empire, Volume 3*
5. *Gibbon's History of the Decline and Fall of the Roman Empire, Volume 4*
6. *Dictionary of Congress*
7. *The Works of William Paley*
8. *Limitations by James Burrill Angell*
9. *The Republican Party, Summer 1860*

☆☆☆

The joyful celebration of the surrender of Richmond and the army of Robert E. Lee came to an abrupt end when news of Abraham Lincoln's assassination began to spread. The streets of Washington, D.C., were suddenly crowded with people, and it seemed as if everyone was in tears. After his death, Lincoln's body was carried to the White House by a company of soldiers, and his corpse was laid in a room on the north side of the second story. Six physicians attended the post-mortem, and Dr. Woodward and assistant surgeon Edward Curtis cut open Lincoln's skull in order to remove the brain. As Curtis was lifting the brain from the skull, the bullet dropped out. Curtis described the moment: "There it lay upon the white china, a little black mass no bigger that the end of my finger—dull, motionless and harmless, yet the cause of such mighty changes in the world's history as we may perhaps never realize."

Senators William Stewart of Nevada and Solomon Foot of Vermont found Chief Justice Salmon Chase and hurried to the Kirkwood House to bring news of the tragedy to Vice President Andrew Johnson. The Vice President was in his bare feet and only partially dressed when he came to the door, but upon hearing the news, he quickly prepared to take the oath of office. After Chase delivered the oath, the still stunned Johnson went back to his bedroom and retired. The following is a list of items that President Lincoln was carrying in his pocket at the time of his death.

President Lincoln's rocker from Ford's Theater. (National Archives)

9 Items in Lincoln's Pocket When He Died

1. A pocketknife.
2. A linen handkerchief.
3. A sleeve button.
4. A fancy watch fob.
5. Two pairs of spectacles.
6. A tiny pencil.
7. A leather wallet.
8. A Confederate five-dollar bill.
9. Nine old newspaper clippings.

In an effort to properly commemorate the passing of Abraham Lincoln, Benjamin B. French, the Commissioner of Public Works, designed an 11'-high "Temple of Death" in the East Room. When Lincoln's body was brought down for public viewing, a series of levels were constructed so that all who attended could get a view of their fallen President. While only 600 people could attend this ceremony, around the nation 25 million others held services for the President in thousands of local churches.

An enormous procession followed Lincoln's body to the Capitol. All through the gray and rainy day, thousands of people slowly filed past Lincoln's open casket to say goodbye. Newspaperman Noah Brooks described the scene: "Directly beneath me lay the casket in which the dead President lay at full length, far, far below; and like atoms moving over a sheet of gray paper, the slow-moving mourners...crept silently in two dark lines across the pavement of the rotunda, forming an ellipse around the coffin and joining as they advanced toward the eastern portal and disappeared."

A nine-car funeral train carrying Lincoln's body home left Washington, DC, at dawn of April 21, 1865. The first stop on the 1,700-mile trip to Springfield, Illinois, was Baltimore, a city Lincoln had avoided on his journey to Washington four years earlier because of death threats. In hard rain and thunderstorms, services were held at almost every stop along the way. In Philadelphia there were riots as the line of mourners stretched across three miles. Only the citizens of Trenton, New Jersey, were disappointed, because theirs was the only state capital on the journey where a funeral procession and public viewing were not scheduled. The following is a list of the cities that held official funerals for President Abraham Lincoln:

11 Funerals for a Fallen President

1. Washington, D.C.
2. Baltimore, Maryland
3. Harrisburg, Pennsylvania
4. New York, New York
5. Albany, New York
6. Buffalo, New York
7. Cleveland, Ohio
8. Columbus, Ohio
9. Indianapolis, Indiana
10. Chicago, Illinois
11. Springfield, Illinois

The death of John Wilkes Booth in a tobacco barn in Caroline County, Virginia, did little to appease the anger caused by the death of Lincoln. Secretary of War Edwin Stanton, exercising his usual zeal, spearheaded a massive investigation, with his main goal to prove that the Confederate government was responsible for the assassination plot. Despite his best efforts, Stanton was never able to prove that Jefferson Davis' government had any ties to the plot, but he did capture seven men and one woman who aided Booth in one way or another. They were fitted with arm and leg manacles, placed in tiny cells, and forced to wear padded canvas head bags. They were given a military trial, and all were found guilty. Four of them, Mary Surrat, David Herold, Lewis Paine, and George Atzerodt were sentenced to death, while the others, also found guilty, were given lengthy prison sentences. Even Edmond Spangler, who was only guilty of holding Booth's horse on the fateful night, was given a prison term for his innocent action.

The 8 Conspirators

1. Mary Surratt (Managed a boarding house, sentenced to death by hanging)
Was convicted of conspiracy for providing food and lodgings for Booth and his companions.

2. Lewis Paine (Unemployed, sentenced to death by hanging)
Attacked and severely injured Secretary Steward. Was convicted of this and of conspiracy for his role in the assassination plot.

3. David E. Herold (Unemployed, sentenced to death by hanging)
Served as a guide for Paine, escaped Washington, D.C., and was captured with Booth. Convicted of conspiracy for his role in the assassination plot.

4. George Atzerodt (Carriage maker, sentenced to death by hanging)
Failed to carry out his assignment of assassinating Vice President Johnson. Was convicted of conspiracy for being a major figure in Booth's plan.

Lewis Paine, sentenced to death by hanging for his role in Lincoln's assassination. (Library of Congress)

5. Dr. Samuel Mudd (Country doctor, sentenced to life in prison)
Convicted of conspiracy for helping set Booth's leg. He was sentenced to Albany Penitentiary, but was transferred at Secretary Stanton's insistence to Fort Jefferson, Dry Tortugas Prison off Key West Florida. In August 1867, after the prison doctor died during a Yellow Fever epidemic, Dr. Mudd volunteered his services. For this he was granted a pardon in February 1869.

6. Michael O'Laughlin (Ex-Confederate soldier, sentenced to life in prison)
Convicted of conspiracy for aiding Booth's first plot to capture Lincoln. Sent to Albany Penitentiary and then Fort Jefferson. Died during Yellow Fever epidemic in 1869.

7. Sam Arnold (Store clerk, sentenced to life in prison)
Convicted of conspiracy for aiding Booth's first plot to capture Lincoln. Sent to Albany Penitentiary and then Fort Jefferson. Pardoned in 1869.

The hanging of Mary Surrat, Lewis Paine, David Herold, and George Atzerodt.
(Library of Congress)

8. Edmond Spangler (Stage hand, sentenced to six years in prison)

Convicted of conspiracy for holding Booth's horse during the assassination. Was sent to Albany Penitentiary and then Fort Jefferson. Was pardoned in 1869 when he was diagnosed with tuberculosis.

CHAPTER 30

The Top 50 Influential Figures of the War

I

N 1998, ROBERT WOOSTER, a professor of history at Texas A&M University—Corpus Christi, published a book titled *The Civil War 100: A Ranking of the Most Influential People in the War Between the States*. Instead of restricting his list to people who were prominent during the war years, Wooster included those who influenced "events that led to and resulted from the conflict." As a result, a man like John Brown (#14), who was hung for leading the Harper's Ferry raid before the war began, was included. According to Wooster, Brown's influence on events in Kansas in the 1850s, his role as one of the country's most radical and activist abolitionists, and his influence on the coming of the conflict warranted his inclusion.

Wooster's list also embraced some of the war's major villains, as well as some of the most influential social reformers of the era. However, his main focus was on the military aspects of the war, and a good portion of the list encompasses figures who "either saw active military duty or were engaged in organizing or supplying the Union and Confederate armies and navies."

The following lists include 50 of the figures cited by Wooster. However, they have been split into three separate and distinct categories: political leaders, military commanders, and civilians. This was done to address the difficulty in comparing people from such a broad spectrum of backgrounds. Although the rankings have been somewhat modified, most of the figures cited by Wooster as the most influential in the war are included.

All wars are fought for political ends and the Civil War was no exception. The two men who had the most direct influence on the war were also the two men with the most political power during the war: Presidents Lincoln and Davis. The only non-American on the list, Viscount Palmerston, favored British recognition of the fledgling Confederacy until General Lee's defeat at Antietam. After that, Palmerston was instrumental in forging a more neutral position for England.

A Dozen Political Leaders

Name	Side	Ranking
1. *James Buchanan, President	USA	26
2. Salmon Chase, Secretary of the Treasury	Union	21
3. Jefferson Davis, President	Confederate	5
4. *Stephen Douglas, Politician	USA	10
5. Andrew Johnson, Vice President	Union	6
6. Abraham Lincoln, President	Union	1
7. Stephen Mallory, Secretary of the Navy	Confederate	64
8. Viscount Palmerston, British Prime Minister	England	39
9. William Seward, Secretary of State	Union	8
10. Edwin Stanton, Secretary of War	Union	9
11. *Roger B. Taney, Chief Justice Supreme Court	USA	32
12. Gideon Welles, Secretary of the Navy	Union	23

* Major pre-war figure

☆☆☆

Without question, Ulysses S. Grant and Robert E. Lee were the two strongest and most influential military commanders during the war. However, while Grant had an effective coterie of subordinate commanders, many of Lee's most valuable lieutenants, including James Longstreet and "Stonewall" Jackson, were disabled or killed relatively early in the war. In addition, the Confederacy was saddled with poor commanders, including Joe Johnston, Braxton Bragg, and John Bell Hood, whose military legacy did more to hurt the Confederacy than to help it. In fact, it is hard to overstate Bragg's negative impact on the Rebel war effort. Not only did he lose important battles in Tennessee and Kentucky, Bragg was also instrumental in handing over the command of the Army of Tennessee to John Bell Hood prior to his disastrous attacks against General Sherman's army outside of Atlanta, and he reappeared in time to preside over the military defeats in Savannah, Georgia, and at Fort Fisher, North Carolina, later in the war.

Confederate General Pierre Gustave Toutant Beauregard, selected as the 35th most influential figure of the war. (*Battles and Leaders*)

23 Influential Military Generals

	Name	Side	Ranking
1.	Pierre G. T. Beauregard	Confederate	35
2.	Braxton Bragg	Confederate	30
3.	David Farragut (Admiral)	Union	13
4.	Nathan Bedford Forrest	Confederate	44
5.	Josiah Gorgas	Confederate	28
6.	Ulysses S. Grant	Union	2
7.	Henry Halleck	Union	27
8.	Herman Haupt	Union	66
9.	John Bell Hood	Confederate	38
10.	Joseph Hooker	Union	36
11.	Thomas J. Jackson	Confederate	20
12.	Joseph E. Johnston	Confederate	11
13.	Robert E. Lee	Confederate	4
14.	James Longstreet	Confederate	19
15.	George McClellan	Union	7
16.	George Meade	Union	22
17.	Montgomery Meigs	Union	45
18.	David Dixon Porter (Admiral)	Union	42
19.	Winfield Scott	Union	37
20.	Philip Sheridan	Union	18
21.	William T. Sherman	Union	3
22.	James Ewell Brown Stuart	Confederate	33
23.	George Thomas	Union	29

☆☆☆

Shortly after the surrender of General Lee's army at Appomattox Court House, the celebratory mood of the North was shattered by the news that President Lincoln had been assassinated. Thus, in a single blow John Wilkes Booth did as much, if not more, to influence the outcome of the war than many of the great political or military leaders. While it is difficult to gage what path Lincoln may have chosen during Reconstruction, his death left Andrew Johnson, a Southern Democrat and an almost immediate lame-duck president, in command during one of the most tumultuous times in American history. In examining the causes of the war, John Brown and Edmund Ruffin are almost exact mirror images. While Brown sacrificed his life for the cause of abolition, the ardent secessionist Ruffin committed suicide in June 1865 rather than submit to the Northern victory. They both represent the forces that drove the South and the North into the bloody Civil War.

15 Important Civilians

Name	Side	Ranking
1. Susan B. Anthony, Suffragette	Union	41
2. Mary Bickerdyke, Head of Sanitary Commission	Union	90
3. John Wilkes Booth, Actor/Assassin	Confederate	26
4. Mathew Brady, Photographer	Union	34
5. *John Brown, Abolitionist	USA	14
6. Jay Cooke, Financier	Union	48
7. Frederick Douglas, Journalist and Author	Union	10
8. William Lloyd Garrison, Newspaper Owner	Union	24
9. Horace Greeley, Newspaper Editor	Union	31
10. Robert Barnwell Rhett, Secessionist	Confederate	16
11. Edmund Ruffin, Secessionist	Confederate	72
12. Elizabeth Cady Stanton, Suffragette	Union	40
13. Harriet Beecher Stowe, Author	Union	15
14. Charles Sumner, Senator	USA	43
15. William Yancey, Diplomat	Confederate	17

* Major pre-war figure

CHAPTER 31

Reenacting: The Spice of Life

CIVIL WAR REENACTING BEGAN almost as soon as the shooting stopped because many veterans were anxious to demonstrate to their family and friends their activities during the war. The largest reenactments ever held took place during the Civil War Centennial celebration from 1961. Although the authenticity of the equipment and uniforms used at the time was not a highly prized commodity, the reenactment of First Bull Run in 1961, in front of an audience of 50,000 people, was, militarily speaking, probably the most authentic that has ever been staged. Reenacting as a hobby began to grow during the 1960s, even drawing the interest of President John F. Kennedy. The President was invited to attend the reenactment of the Gettysburg Address in November 1963, but chose to travel to Dallas instead, with tragic results.

The quest for authenticity grew during the 1970s until many reproduction items became so realistic that they needed identifying marks to prevent

The reenactor's role model, Private Ira Fish, 150th New York. (Library of Congress)

them from being resold as originals. Although the hard-core reenactor still refuses to use any modern materials, the general rule of thumb is that, if they are to be used, modern items should be kept hidden or covered by period items. According to R. Lee Hadden, author of *Reliving the Civil War*, "Authenticity liberates you to do anything and be anyone in a simpler world that existed 130 years ago." The following is a list of equipment that is considered essential for a modern-day Civil War reenactor:

15 Pieces of Essential Equipment for a Reenactor

	Description	*Cost*
1.	Three-banded musket	$350-525
2.	Bayonet	$28-35
3.	Bayonet scabbard	$20-25
4.	Uniform coat	$70-120
5.	Uniform pants	$60-95
6.	Shirt	$30-45
7.	Belt with buckle	$25-35
8.	Brogans or bootees	$80-120
9.	Canteen	$30-65
10.	Rice bag or haversack	$20-35
11.	Cap box	$20-30
12.	Cartridge box	$50-65
13.	Sling	$15-25
14.	Slouch hat or kepi	$30-60
15.	Brass insignia	$15-25
	Totals	$843-1,305

☆☆☆

Like their counterparts more than a century ago, modern-day reenactors use *Hardee's Rifle and Infantry Tactics* for drill instruction. This book was originally written in the 1850s by Colonel William Hardee when he was an instructor at West Point. Hardee went on to become a general in the Confederate army and was dubbed "Old Reliable" for his strict reliance on the necessity of steady drilling. In 1863, Congress appropriated $350,000 to purchase copies of the manual for the plethora of new and untrained officers. Today, almost any time a reenactment is held, firing demonstrations are arranged for the spectators, and the commands and instructions that are used are usually drawn straight from Hardee's manual. The following is a list of the commands usually used to load and fire Civil War-era muskets:

12 Loading and Firing Commands

1. Load
2. Handle cartridge
3. Tear cartridge

4. Charge cartridge
5. Draw rammer
6. Ram cartridge
7. Return rammer
8. Prime
9. Ready
10. Aim
11. Fire
12. Recover arms

When large numbers of well-armed men (and women) gather together to reenact a battle, safety is always a key concern. All hand-to-hand combat must be carefully scripted to avoid injury, and care must be taken even when firing a weapon that is loaded with only a powder charge. However, occasionally things do get out of control. When this happens, the unit commander will order his company to stand still at right shoulder shift. To the offending reenactors, this is seen as a stinging rebuke and usually puts an end to the offending action. The following is a list of rules for reenactors as found in *Reliving the Civil War*.

17 Rules for the Reenactor

1. There should be no hand-to-hand fighting unless prearranged and scripted.
2. Stay with your regiment.
3. Stay in your rank.
4. Never try to touch the enemy flag.
5. Don't charge artillery head-on.
6. Don't touch a horse without the permission of the rider.
7. When loading a rifle, never insert the paper wad unless on specific orders.
8. While on the field, never use the ramrod to ram cartridges home.
9. Bayonets should be drawn or fixed only for parade.
10. Do not take antiques on the field.
11. Don't insult the enemy.
12. Take hits.
13. If you plan to simulate wounds, let your unit know beforehand.
14. When taking a hit, fall forward on your face.
15. When down, lie still.
16. If you face a choice of dying or being taken prisoner, become a prisoner.
17. If you take prisoners, don't harass them.

☆☆☆

The popularity of reenacting peaked in 1986-1990 during the 125th anniversary of the Civil War. This popularity was reflected by the use of footage taken from these reenactments for movies and Civil War documentaries. Reenactors then began to be invited to participate in major motion pictures, including *Gettysburg* and *Glory*. This created a split in the reenactment and living-history community, because many reenactors are willing to work for free for the opportunity to appear in a movie. However, some regiments refuse to participate without receiving a fair wage and assurance that the project will be historically accurate. Still, reenacting remains a fun and fulfilling hobby for many thousands of Civil War enthusiasts. The following is a list of nine periodicals available for the Civil War reenactor:

9 Periodicals for Reenactors

1. *Camp Chase Gazette*, Box 707 240, Marietta, OH 45750, (614) 373-1865
2. *The Civil War Lady: Women in Reenacting*, 622 3rd Avenue, S.W., Pipestone, MN 56164, (507) 825-3182
3. *The Civil War News Route 1*, Box 36, Tunbridge, VT 05077, (800) 222-1861
4. *The Courier* 2503 Delaware Avenue, Buffalo, NY 14216, (716) 873-2594
5. *The Lady Reenactor* Patrick Publishing, P.O. Box 1864, Varna, IL 61375, (309) 463-2123
6. *Living History; The Journal of Historical Reenactment and Interaction* P.O. Box 77, Fairfax, VA 22030, (800) 294-5559
7. *Reenactor's Journal* P.O. Box 283, Mount Prospect, IL 60056
8. *Smoke and Fire News* P.O. Box 166, Grand Rapids, OH 43522, (419) 832-0303
9. *The Watchdog* P.O. Box 4582, Frankfort, KY 40604

☆☆☆

Civil War reenactments and living history demonstrations have become so popular that events are now scheduled on a regular basis in every state except Hawaii. Every year Gettysburg, Pennsylvania, and Leesburg, Virginia, approximately 30 miles from the Manassas battlefield, host large events with thousands of reenactors in historically accurate representations of the battles. In addition, the annual reenactment of the battle of Cedar Creek in Middletown, Virginia, offers the unique opportunity for the Confederate reenactors to enjoy victory during Saturday's event, while the Union reenactors get to enjoy their revenge on Sunday. The following are events that are scheduled every year. Please note that the dates will change for these events, as most will be scheduled on the weekend nearest the anniversary of the respective battle.

35 Annual Reenactments

1. February 16-18: Battle of Olustee, Florida.

Proceeds benefit the Olustee Battlefield Citizens Support Organization and the Olustee Battlefield Historic Site, P.O. Drawer G, White Springs, FL 32096

2. March 9-11: Anniversary of the Battle of Fork Jackson, Louisiana.

Sponsored by the Plaquemines Parish Economic Development and Tourism Department and hosted by the Washington Artillery of New Orleans.

3. March 9-11: Annual Battle of Averasboro at Herndon Farm, North Carolina.

All proceeds from event will benefit historical preservation. Hosted by the Robeson Rifle Guards, in association with the Southeastern Historical Preservation Society and Drowning Creek Living History Society.

4. March 10-11: Picacho Pass, Picacho, Arizona (westernmost battle of the Civil War).

Sponsored by the Arizona Division of Sons of Confederate Veterans and the Arizona Civil War Council. Picacho Peak State Park, Picacho, AZ 85241.

5. March 16-18: Anniversary of the Battle of Ft. DeRussy.

On part of the original battlegrounds of the Red River Campaign in Marksville, Louisiana. Hosted by the Cenla Historical Reenactment Group.

6. March 17-18: Battle at Narcoosee Mill, East Lake Tohopekaliga near St. Cloud, Florida.

Sponsored by the Jacob Summerlin Camp #1516, Sons of Confederate Veterans.

7. March 17-18: Annual Battle of Kelly's Ford Reenactment, Culpeper County, Virginia. On original site.

Proceeds to be donated Station Battlefield. Contact: Inn at Kelly's Ford, 16589 Edwards Shop Rd., Remington, VA 22734.

8. March 23-25: Siege at Bridgeport, Alabama. On an original site in Jackson County.

All profits to benefit the preservation of local history. Contact: Siege at Bridgeport, P.O. Box 280, Bridgeport, AL 35740.

9. March 24-25: Anniversary of The Battle of Williamsburg at Endview, Newport News, Virginia.

Proceeds to support preservation efforts of Newport News Civil War sites. Sponsored by 32nd Virginia Volunteer Infantry and the Civil War at Endview.

10. April 6-8: The Battle for Pleasant Hill, Louisiana.

For more information, contact: Battle of Pleasant Hill Reenactment Committee, P.O. Box 384, Pleasant Hill, LA 71065.

11. April 7-8: First Battle of Richmond near historic Mt. Zion Church in central Madison County, Kentucky.

On part of original August 1862 battlefield where 4000 Federals were captured.

12. April 21-22: Annual Civil War on the Border, Mahaffie Stagecoach Stop, Olathe, Kansas.

Historic site on border of Territorial Kansas. William Quantrill raided the farmstead and sacked Olathe.

13. April 27-29: Battle of Selma, Alabama.

Artillery night-firing along Alabama River, tactical fighting in woods, assaults against Mahan-correct earthwork fortifications. Part of proceeds go to conservation of Alabama's Confederate flag collection and preservation of Sturdivant Hall.

14. April 28-29: Battle for The Charleston/Savannah Railroad, South Carolina.

Sponsored by The South Carolina Foothills Heritage Committee.

15. May 3-6: Vicksburg Campaign II in Raymond, Mississippi

All proceeds to defray cost of Raymond Battlefield land acquisition and park development. Sponsored by 2001 Raymond Reenactment Committee of the Friends of Raymond Inc. Hosted by Stanford's Mississippi Battery, Inc.

16. May 4-6: Battle of McDowell Living History and Reenactment in McDowell, Virginia.

All proceeds benefit the Highland Historical Society. Sponsored by Highland Historical Society, Highland County Chamber of Commerce, and 5th Battalion. Contact: McDowell Reenactment, 424 South Loudoun St., Winchester, VA 22601.

17. May 11-13: Annual Thunder of the Bay, Fort Gaines, Alabama.

For more information, contact: Fort Gaines Historic Site, 51 Bienville Blvd., Dauphin Island, AL 36528.

18. May 18-20: Battle of Sacramento, Kentucky.

The anniversary of "Forrest's First" action of Dec. 28, 1861, in and near Sacramento. For more information, contact: *battleofsac@mcleanliving.com*; *www.battleofsac.com*.

19. May 19-20: Annual Battle of Resaca, Georgia.

First major battle of Atlanta campaign, on 600 acres of original battlefield. A donation will be made to The Friends of Resaca for battlefield preservation.

Hosted by the Georgia Division Reenactors' Association. Sponsored by the City of Resaca, Gordon County C.O.C. and Historical Society P.O. Box 919, Resaca, GA 30735-0919.

20. May 19-20: Annual Confederate Attack on Fort Pocahontas at Wilson's Wharf on James River at Sherwood Forest Plantation Charles City, Virginia.

Hosted by plantation owner Harrison Tyler, grandson of President John Tyler who lived there. Contact: *info@sherwoodforest.org.*; *www.fortpocahontas.org.*

21. May 19-20: Annual Battle of New Market, Virginia.

On expanded site at original battlefield. All proceeds go for preservation projects at New Market Battlefield. Sponsored by New Market State Historical Park and the Great American Civil War Society. G.A.C.W.S., 2449 Heidlersburg Rd., Gettysburg, PA 17325.

22. May 25-27: Battle of Port Jefferson Civil War Reenactment in Jefferson, Texas.

Hosted by the 18th Texas Volunteer Infantry Regiment. Contact: Marion County Chamber of Commerce; *www.battleofportjefferson.com.*

23. May 31-June 3: Anniversary of first land battle of the Civil War, Philippi, West Virginia.

Contact: Blue & Gray Reunion, P.O. Box 911, Philippi, WV 26416.

24. July 6-8: Battle of Rich Mountain, West Virginia.

Primary fundraising event for Rich Mountain. Hosted by West Virginia Reenactors Association. Sponsored by Rich Mountain Battlefield Foundation. RMBF, P.O. Box 227, Beverly, WV 26253; *www.richmountain.org*

25. July 6-8: Gettysburg battle reenactment at the Yingling Farm, Gettysburg, Pennsylvania.

Sponsored by The Gettysburg Anniversary Committee. For more information, contact: Gettysburg Anniversary Committee, P.O. Box 3482, Gettysburg, PA 17325-3482.

26. July 7-8: Battle of Monocacy, Maryland, commemoration.

For more information, contact: Lake County Discovery Museum, c/o Civil Monocacy National Battlefield; *ww.nps.gov/mono.*

27. July 14-15: The Battle of Corydon during Morgan's Raid, Corydon. Indiana.

Contact: Harrison County, Indiana Parks and Recreation Department, 124 South Mulberry Street, Corydon, IN 47112.

28. July 20-22: Anniversary of the Battle of Buffington Island in Portland, Ohio.

All actions are fought on part of the original battlefield. Hosted by the 91st Ohio Volunteer Infantry, Co. B, sponsored by The Meigs County Historical Society and Harris Farms.

29. August 3-5: Anniversary Reenactment of the First Battle of Manassas/Bull Run in Leesburg, Virginia.

In association with Civil War Preservation Trust. A donation will be made toward battlefield preservation. Sponsored by Civil War Times Illustrated and America's Civil War magazines; *www.firstmanassas.com.*

30. September 15-16: Old Town Helena, Alabama Civil War Battle.

Sponsored by Alabama State Militia Artillery.

31. October 6-7: Battle of Perryville, Kentucky.

Commemoration and reenactment. Contact: The Kentucky Civil War Sites Preservation Program, KY Heritage Council.

32. October 13-14: Battle of Columbus-Belmont. General Grant's first battle.

For more information, contact: The Kentucky Civil War Sites Preservation Program, KY Heritage Council.

33. October 20-21: Battle at Cedar Creek Middletown, VA.

Proceeds to benefit the Cedar Creek Battlefield Foundation, P.O. Box 229 Middletown, VA 22645; *cedarcrk@visuallink.com.*

34. November 2-4: The Atlanta Campaign with Battle of Peachtree Creek & Battle of Pickett's Mill at Georgia International Horse Park, Conyers, Georgia.

Sponsored by Civil War Times Illustrated and America's Civil War magazines.

35. December 8-9: Anniversary of the Battle of Fredericksburg, Virginia.

Sponsored by the City of Fredericksburg, Historic Fredericksburg Foundation, Ferry Farm, and others. Contact: The Fredericksburg Visitor Center, Fredericksburg Reenactment, 706 Caroline St., Fredericksburg, VA 22401; *fburgreenactment@aol.com.*

CHAPTER 32

The Civil War in Print and on the Web

THE CIVIL WAR HAS inspired more than 70,000 books, along with countless articles and other works. For someone interested in the war, this blizzard of information can seem daunting. However, almost all scholarly works include citations for the same standard set of reference works. The first and most important is the 128-volume *Official Records of the War.* Originally published in the late 1880s, the *Official Records* form the backbone for almost every book written about a military campaign or battle. In addition, two books by Ezra Warner, *Generals in Gray* and *Generals in Blue,* give thorough biographies on every general who participated in the war. A reference library that includes the following 12 titles will provide a vast array of information to anyone interested in learning more about the war.

12 Standard Reference Titles

1. *The Civil War Dictionary* by Mark Boatner.
2. *The Confederate Generals* by William C. Davis.
3. *Bibliography of the Civil War* by Charles Dornbusch.
4. *A Compendium of the War of the Rebellion* by Frederick Dyer.
5. *Historical Times Illustrated Encyclopedia of the Civil War* edited by Patricia Faust.

Confederate General JEB Stuart, selected as the 33rd most influential figure of the war. (*Battles and Leaders*)

6. *The Southern Historical Society Papers* by William J. Jones.
7. *Lee's Lieutenants: A Study in Command* by Douglas Southall Freeman.
8. *The Civil War Day by Day* by E. B. Long.
9. *The War of the Rebellion: Official Records* by the U.S. War Department.
10. *The Photographic History of the Civil War* edited by William C. Davis.
11. *Generals in Blue* by Ezra Warner.
12. *Generals in Gray* by Ezra Warner.

☆☆☆

Two trilogies, *The Centennial History of the Civil War* by Bruce Catton and *The Civil War: A Narrative* by Shelby Foote, provide vivid writing and fine historical work about the war; while Catton's book leans slightly toward the Union side, Foote counters with a slight Southern bent. Taken together, they provide a wonderful overview of the military campaigns of the war and of the commanders who masterminded them. The four-volume set, *Battles and Leaders of the Civil War*, includes hundreds of articles written for *Century Magazine* by leading Civil War participants in the 1880s. These and the other works on the following list provide a wide variety of perspectives about the war and the way it was fought.

12 General Military Works

1. *The Centennial History of the Civil War* by Bruce Catton.
2. *The Civil War: A Narrative* by Shelby Foote.
3. *Army of the Heartland: The Army of Tennessee, 1861-1862* by Thomas Connelly.
4. *Autumn of Glory: The Army of Tennessee, 1862-1865* by Thomas Connelly.
5. *Lee's Lieutenants: A Study in Command* by Douglas S. Freeman.
6. *How the North Won: A Military History of the Civil War* by Herman Hathaway.
7. *Battles and Leaders of the Civil War* edited by Robert Johnson.
8. *The Annals of the War, Written by Leading Participants* by A. K. McClure, ed.
9. *Attack and Die: Civil War Military Tactics* by Grady McWhitney.
10. *The Union Cavalry in the Civil War* by Stephen Starr.
11. *Lincoln Finds a General* by Kenneth Williams.
12. *The Long Arm of Lee* by Jennings Wise.

After his hopes for a third presidential term were dashed in 1880, Ulysses S. Grant focused his energy on the business of making money. As he had throughout his life, Grant failed in this endeavor and turned to writing his memoirs. With the help of Mark Twain, he signed a contract that would provide him with 70 percent of any profits made from the publication of his memoirs. When he was diagnosed with throat cancer several months later, Grant accepted the invitation of Joseph Drexel to spend the summer at his country estate in Mount McGregor. While he was there, many of his old wartime friends and adversaries came to pay their respects to the dying general, including William Tecumseh Sherman, Phil Sheridan, Simon Bolivar Buckner, James Longstreet, and Winfield Hancock, but Grant kept doggedly to his work. Shortly before he died on July 23, 1885, Grant finished what proved to be a huge literary and financial success. The two-volume set, all sold by subscription, sold more than 300,000 copies and earned his wife Julia Dent Grant a royalty check for $200,000, the largest ever written at the time. However, Grant had plenty of company when it came to writing his memoirs about the war. The following list includes just a few of the major military figures of the war who penned their wartime recollections for money and posterity:

12 Military Autobiographies

1. *Personal Memoirs of U.S. Grant* by Ulysses S. Grant.
2. *The Life and Letters of George Gordon Meade* by George Meade.
3. *Narrative of Military Operations* by Joseph E. Johnston.
4. *The Military Operations of General Beauregard* by P. G. T. Beauregard.
5. *The Civil War Papers of George B. McClellan* by George McClellan.
6. *Memoirs of W. T. Sherman* by William T. Sherman.
7. *Lieutenant General Jubal Anderson Early C. S. A.* by Jubal Early.
8. *Advance and Retreat* by John Bell Hood.
9. *Personal Memoirs of Philip Henry Sheridan* by Philip Sheridan.
10. *From Manassas to Appomattox* by James Longstreet.
11. *Destruction and Reconstruction* by Richard Taylor.
12. *The Passing of the Armies* by Joshua L. Chamberlain.

Led by the *Scribner's* and *Century* magazines, which focused on the experiences of Northern generals, and the Southern Historical Society, which published a magazine featuring articles written primarily by Southern officers and generals, the circulation of periodicals that catered to Civil War veterans thrived during the 1880s. When interest in the war waned with the eventual passing of all the old veterans, these magazines died off as well. It wasn't until the centennial celebration of the war that renewed interest brought the Civil War back to life in the pages of popular magazines. In 1959, the *Civil War Times* began publishing a small black-and-white magazine in Gettysburg that featured the motto: "A non-partisian, illustrated magazine devoted to America's most exciting and crucial period." The *Civil War Times* soon changed its name to the *Civil War Times Illustrated* and enjoyed a monopoly in the Civil War market until several other Civil War-related magazines joined the fray in the 1970s and 80s. Perhaps the most interesting of these is *Blue*

and Gray, which eschewed the traditional format established by the *Civil War Times Illustrated* of four or five heavily illustrated articles, in favor of featuring tours and in-depth information on a particular historical site or area. An enthusiast armed with a few back issues of *Blue and Gray* can visit many little known or poorly marked Civil War sites, as well as gain additional insight about the larger Civil War battlefields.

7 Popular Civil War Periodicals

1. *America's Civil War*

741 Miller Dr. SE, D-2, Leesburg, VA 20175; *www.thehistorynet.com/AmericasCivilWar*

Popular general interest magazine featuring numerous pictures and illustrations and articles (one year/7 issues - US: $17.95 Canada: $24.95).

2. *Blue & Gray Magazine*

522 Norton Rd. Columbus, OH 43228; *www.bluegraymagazine.com*

Features guided tours of interesting Civil War historical sites along with articles and more (one year/7 issues - US: $19.95).

3. *Civil War Book Review*

2143 Belcourt Avenue Nashville, TN 37212; *www.civilwarbookreview.com*

Features reviews of all major works about the Civil War (one year/4 issues - US: $16.00).

4. *Civil War Times Illustrated*

6405 Flank Drive, Harrisburg, PA 17112; *www.thehistorynet.com/CivilWarTimesIllustrated*

Very similar to America's Civil War (one year/7 issues - US: $17.95 Canada: $24.95).

5. *Civil War Journal*

P.O. Box 510 Acworth, GA. 30101; *www.go-star.com/cwj*

Includes information for reenactors, relic hunters, collectors, and Civil War buffs (one year/6 issues - US: $12.00).

6. *The Civil War News*

Monarch Hill Rd. Tunbridge VT 05077; *www.civilwarnews.com*

Includes information for reenactors, living history, and coming events (one year/11 issues - US and Canada $24.00).

7. *North and South*

P.O. Box 1027, Escondido, CA 92033-1027; *www.northandsouthmagazine.com*

Official magazine of the Civil War Society with articles, pictures, and illustrations (one year/7 issues - US and Canada $29.95).

☆☆☆

Since the development of software that displayed the World Wide Web in a format that used text and graphics, and especially after the appearance of Netscape in 1994, the Civil War has also been enthusiastically embraced on the Internet, and there are now literally hundreds of thousands of Web sites devoted to the war. While many of these sites are of limited value due to their lack of verifiable references, institutions like the Library of Congress and the National Park Service have made available important primary documents, official accounts of the battles, overviews of the strategies and tactics used by Civil War commanders, and reliable maps to thousands of online users. In addition, thousands of amateur Civil War historians how have a forum for their interest in the war, and they have produced a wide array of interesting and informative Web sites. While it would be impossible to select the best or most engaging of these sites without spending countless hours researching all the available Web sites, the following list includes a number of interesting Web sites on a variety of Civil War-related topics:

36 Interesting Civil War Web Sites

1. Antietam—a photographic tour: *www.enteract.com/~westwood*
2. Antietam National Battlefield: *www.nps.gov/anti/home.htm*
3. Appomattox C.H. National Park: *www.nps.gov/apco*
4. Assassination of Lincoln: *www.tiac.net/users/ime/famtree/burnett/lincoln.htm*
5. Battle of Fredericksburg: *members.aol.com/lmjarl/civwar/frdrksburg.html*
6. Battle of Gettysburg: *www.geocities.com/Athens/Delphi/4633*
7. Battle of Mill Springs: *www.geocities.com/Pentagon/Quarters/1864/Default.htm*
8. Battle of New Market: *www.vmi.edu/~archtml/cwnm.html*
9. Battle of the Wilderness: *home.att.net/~hallowed-ground/wilderness_tour.html*
10. The Civil War Artillery Page: *www.cwartillery.org*
11. Civil War Battle Summaries: *www2.cr.nps.gov/abpp/battles/tvii.htm*
12. Civil War in Charleston: *www.awod.com/gallery/probono/cwchas/cwlayout.html*
13. Civil War Traveler: *www.civilwartraveler.com*
14. Clara Barton N.H.S.: *www.nps.gov/clba*
15. Fredericksburg and Spotsylvania: *www.nps.gov/frsp/vc.htm*
16. Ford's Theatre N.H.S.: *ww.nps.gov/foth/index2.htm*
17. Gettysburg: *www.militaryhistoryonline.com/gettysburg*
18. Gettysburg Address: *lcweb.loc.gov/exhibits/gadd*
19. Gettysburg N.M.P.: *www.nps.gov/gett/home.htm*
20. Harper's Ferry National Park: *www.nps.gov/hafe/home.htm*
21. Longstreet Chronicles: *tennessee-scv.org/longstreet*
22. Manassas N.B.P.: *www.nps.gov/mana/home.htm*

23. Monitor and Merrimack: *www.ironclads.com*
24. Monocacy National Battlefield: *www.nps.gov/mono/home.htm*
25. Official site of the *HL Hunley*: *www.hunley.org*
26. Petersburg National Battlefield: *www.nps.gov/pete/mahan/PNBhome.html*
27. Richmond National Battlefield: *www.nps.gov/rich/home.htm*
28. Robert E. Lee Memorial: *www.nps.gov/gwmp/arl_hse.html*
29. Selected Civil War Photographs: *memory.loc.gov/ammen/cwphome/html*
30. Siege of Petersburg: *members.aol.com/siege1864*
31. Stonewall Jackson: *www.vmi.edu/~archtml/jackson.html*
32. This Week in the Civil War: *www.civilweek.com*
33. US Civil War Center: *www.cwc.lsu.edu/cwc/index.htm*
34. Vicksburg N.M..P.: *www.nps.gov/vick/home.htm*
35. Wars of the US Navy: *www.history.navy.mil/wars/index.html*
36. Wilson's Creek N.M.P.: *www.nps.gov/wicr/*

CHAPTER 33

Outside the War

IT IS EASY TO forget that while the Civil War was raging, many other important events were occurring in America. The growth of the Federal government was probably the most significant of these changes, because legislators in Washington, D.C., enacted laws establishing the first income tax, the first inheritance tax, and a national banking system. All these forever changed the political, social, and economic landscape in the United States.

In addition, such events as the first oil-well fire and the first divided highway presaged the changes that would occur in the transportation system during the next century. Brooklyn built the first enclosed baseball park, the Oneida Football Club was organized in Boston, and the first peep show was constructed. These events foreshadowed the growth of the American entertainment culture that would follow in the wake of the war. The following is a list of some of the things going on in America during the 1860s:

Austrian Archduke Maximilian, named Emperor of Mexico by Napoleon III. (Library of Congress)

41 Non-War Firsts in America

1861

1. First creamery established in Walkill, New York.
2. First fly-casting tournament in Utica, New York.
3. First peep show machine patented in Cincinnati, Ohio.
4. First oil-well fire near Oil Creek, Pennsylvania.
5. First divided highway built in Carver, Massachusetts.
6. First transcontinental telegram sent across Atlantic Ocean.
7. First passport system established in the United States.

1862

8. First enclosed baseball park built in Brooklyn, New York.
9. First football club, Oneida Football Club, established in Boston, Massachusetts.
10. First orthopedic hospital for the ruptured and crippled established in New York City.
11. First Federal polygamy legislation authorized.
12. First Federal income tax law enacted.
13. First Federal inheritance tax law established.

1863

14. First national banking system established in United States.
15. First Turkish bathhouse opened in New York City.
16. First fire extinguisher patent granted.
17. First thanksgiving holiday celebrated by national proclamation.
18. First accident insurance company, Travelers Insurance Co., established in Hartford, Connecticut.
19. First newspaper printed on wood pulp paper in Boston, Massachusetts.
20. First woman surgeon graduated from New England Medical College in Boston, Massachusetts.
21. First pill manufactured and sold commercially in Philadelphia, Pennsylvania.
22. First water conduit built to supply the city of Chicago, Illinois, with drinking water.
23. First four-wheeled roller skate was invented by James L. Plimpton.

1864

24. First Pullman car built in Chicago, Illinois.
25. First women army officer appointed as an assistant army surgeon.
26. First state boiler inspection law passed in Connecticut.
27. First commercial production of Borax from Borax Lake, California.
28. First salmon cannery went into production in Washington, California.
29. First hunting license fee charged in state of New York.

30. First Federal cigarette tax established.

31. First institution of the higher education for the deaf opened in Washington, D.C.

32. First coin to use "In God We Trust" minted.

33. First railroad tracks made of steel produced in Alatoona, Pennsylvania.

34. First Travers Stakes race held in Saratoga Springs, New York.

1865

35. First patent issued for a coffee percolator.

36. First cracker manufactured in Albany, New York.

37. First potato chip introduced for commercial consumption.

38. First national bank failure occurred in Attica, New York.

39. First oil well drilled by torpedoes in Titusville, Pennsylvania.

40. First soap in liquid form patented in New York City.

41. First non-ivory billiard ball mass produced.

☆☆☆

The people of the United and Confederate States of America might have been too distracted to notice it, but important events were also occurring in other countries around the globe. The three major events that would come to have the most impact were the emancipation of the serfs of Russia in 1861, the end of the bloody Taiping Rebellion in China, and the establishment of a French protectorate over Cambodia.

Tsar Alexander II decided in 1856 that it was "better to abolish serfdom from above than to wait until serfs begin to liberate themselves from below." However, it wasn't until 1861 that the peasants were freed from servile status and a procedure was established by which they became landowners. In China, the Taiping Rebellion, which had raged for 14 years and claimed more than 20

18 NOTABLE PAINTINGS OF THE CIVIL WAR ERA

1. *The Consecration* by George Cochrane Lambdin

2. *Reveille on a Winter Morning* by Henry Bacon

3. *Death of Ellsworth* by Alonzo Chappel

4. *Recognition* by Constant Mayer

5. *Departure of the Seventh Regiment* by George Hayard

6. *Writing to Father* by Eastman Johnson

7. *Wagons in the Shenandoah Valley* by Johannes A. Oertel

8. *Fight for the Standard* by an unknown artist

9. *Artillery on the Potomac* by A. Wordsworth Thompson

10. *A Fire Barge in New Orleans Harbor, April 24, 1862* by Xanthus B. Smith

11. *Cheering Stonewall Jackson* by Charles Hoffbaur

12. *First Reading of the Emancipation Proclamation of President Lincoln* by Francis Bicknell Carpenter

13. *The Last Meeting of Lee and Jackson* by Everett B.D. Julio

14. *The Sunset Gun, Fort Sumter* by John Gadsby Chapman

15. *Farragut's Fleet, April 24, 1862* by J. Joffray

16. *Reception at the White House* by Peter F. Rothermel

17. *Alabama and Kearsage* by Edouard Manet

18. *Refugees from Fredericksburg* by D.E. Henderson

million lives, finally ended in 1864 when the city of Nanking fell to government forces and the leader of the rebellion, Hung Hsiu-ch'üan, committed suicide. The impact of the rebellion was especially significant, as the Ch'ing dynasty was never again able to establish an effective hold over the country. The modern-day Chinese Communists still trace their origin back to the days of this rebellion.

The international event that would come to have significant consequences for the United States was the emergence of France as a power in Southeast Asia. Along with its forays into Mexico and Italy, French Emperor Napoleon III, fearing British and Siamese expansion into the Mekong River delta, established a protectorate in Cambodia. In 1863, French naval officers persuaded King Norodom to sign a treaty that gave France control of Cambodia's foreign affairs, and a French admiral participated in Norodom's coronation. It wouldn't be until after World War II that France would make Cambodia an autonomous state within the French Union. After events in the region spun out of control, and the United States stepped in for a weakening France in the 1960s, America became embroiled in an unwinnable guerrilla conflict in the region known as the Vietnam Conflict.

29 International Events During the Civil War Years

1861

1. King of Naples surrendered to Garibaldi; Italy proclaimed a kingdom by its Parliament.
2. Warsaw massacre; troops fired on Polish demonstrators against Russian rule.
3. Czar Alexander II emancipated the Russian serfs.
4. Archaeopteryx fossil discovered at Solnhofen, Germany.
5. Danubian Principalities of Moldavia and Wallachia united to form Romania.

1862

6. Bismarck became Prussian Prime Minister and advocated unification of Germany.
7. French physicist Jean Foucault successfully measured the speed of light.
8. Taiping rebels were suppressed near Shanghai and Ningpo, China.
9. Italy annexed Venetia (held by Austria), Rome, and parts of the Papal States (occupied by French troops).

1863

10. Poles in Russian-occupied Poland rebelled in the January Revolution.
11. Civil war broke out in Afghanistan and Uruguay.
12. Saxon and Hanoverian troops entered the province of Holstein.
13. Construction of London underground railroad begun.
14. French established a protectorate over Cambodia.

15. French troops captured Mexico City; Austrian Archduke Maximilian proclaimed Emperor.

1864

16. Denmark was invaded by Austria and Prussia.
17. Italy renounced its claim on Rome; Florence made the capital city.
18. Louis Pasteur invented pasteurization of wine.
19. Geneva Convention established neutrality of battlefield medical facilities.
20. Cyclone destroyed Calcutta, India; 70,000 people killed.
21. Lake Albert, source of the Nile River, was discovered by Samuel White Baker.
22. Chinese provincial armies suppressed the Taiping Rebellion and recaptured Nanking.

1865

23. Bismark and Napoleon III met in Biarritz, France.
24. English Lord Palmerston died and was succeeded by Lord John Russell.
25. King Leopold I of Belgium was succeeded by his son, Leopold II.
26. Crete revolted against Turkish rule.
27. Alfred Nobel invented dynamite.
28. Black Friday hit London's Stock Exchange.
29. Paraguay waged war against Brazil, Argentina, and Uruguay.

The international world of art and literature also did not stand still during the conflict going on in America. Among the world's greatest authors hard at work during this time were Fydor Dostoyevsky, Charles Dickens, and Victor Hugo. While Dostoyevsky published three of his most famous and influential works during this time, Victor Hugo's novel *Les Miserables* was more widely read in America and had a direct impact on the war. While imprisoned in the Ohio State Penitentiary in Columbus, Ohio, Thomas Hines, an officer captured and imprisoned with General John Hunt Morgan, read Hugo's novel and was inspired by the wonderful escapes described in the book. In an article for *Century Magazine* in 1891, Hines explained that the book "led me to the line of thought that terminated in the plan of escape adopted." Inspired by this book, Hines, Morgan, and several other of Morgan's officers were able to successfully escape from the prison.

Hugo's book was also translated and published in Richmond, Virginia, and was gobbled up by many soldiers in Robert E. Lee's army desperate for something to read during the terrible campaign in 1864-65. Many of the soldiers, unfamiliar with the Gallic pronunciation, called the book "Lee's Miserables," and soon came to refer themselves in the same manner. Battered, outnumbered, and outgunned by General Grant's army, the name fit, and according to historian J. Tracy Power, "the sobriquet was gloomy, and there was something tragic in the employment of it; but it was applicable."

19 Masterpieces of the Art World

1861

1. Russian author Fyodor Dostoyevsky published *The House of the Dead.*
2. Charles Dickens finished *Great Expectations.*
3. The Royal Academy of Music was founded in London, England.

1862

4. Russian Ivan Turgenev published *Fathers and Sons.*
5. Victor Hugo released *Les Misérables.*
6. Verdi composed the grand opera *La Forza del Destino.*
7. Actress Sarah Bernhardt made her debut at Comedie Francaise.

1863

8. Edward Everett Hale wrote *Man without a Country.*
9. Henry Longfellow published *Tales of a Wayside Inn*, featuring "Paul Revere's Ride."
10. Jules Vern wrote his first novel, *Five Weeks in a Balloon.*
11. Philosopher John Stuart Mill published *Utilitarianism.*

1864

12. Henrik Ibson wrote *The Crown Pretenders.*
13. Leo Tolstoy published *War and Peace.*
14. John Quincy Adams Ward completed his sculpture, *Indian Hunter.*
15. Fyodor Dostoyevsky released *Notes from the Underground.*
16. Jules Verne published *A Journey to the Center of the Earth.*
17. Anton Bruckner composed his *Symphony in D Minor* and *Mass No. 1 in D Minor.*

1865

18. Fyodor Dostoyevsky released *Crime and Punishment.*
19. Anglican clergyman Charles Kingsley published *Hereward the Wake.*

APPENDIX

Battles of the Civil War

Battle	Date	Union Cmdr.	Conf. Cmdr.	Union Cas.*	Conf. Cas.*
1861					
Philippi, W. Va.	6/3	Morris	Porterfield	<1%	1%
Big Bethel, Va.	6/10	Pierce	D.H. Hill	2%	1%
Booneville, Mo.	6/17	Lyon	Marmaduke	<1%	2%
Rich Mountain, W. Va.	7/11	Rosecrans	Pegram	4%	23%
Carrick's Ford, W. Va.	7/13	Morris	Garnet	2%	3%
Bull Run, Va. (1st)	7/31	McDowell	Beauregard	9%	6%
Wilson's Creek, Mo.	8/10	Lyon	McColloch	22%	10%
Carnifax Ferry, W. Va.	9/10	Rosecrans	Floyd	2%	<1%
Lexington, Mo.	9/12-9/20	Mulligan	Price	100%	<1%
Santa Rosa, Fla.	10/9	H. Brown	Anderson	3%	1%
Ball's Bluff, Va.	10/21	Baker	Evans	49%	5%
Belmont, Mo.	11/7	Grant	Polk	20%	13%
1862					
Mill Springs, Ky.	1/19	Thomas	Crittenden	7%	13%
Fort Henry, Tenn.	2/6	Grant	Tilghman	<1%	96%
Roanoke Island, N.C.	2/8	Burnside	Wise	2%	86%
Fort Donelson, Tenn.	2/12-2/16	Grant	Buckner	10%	79%
Valverde, N. Mex.	2/21	Canby	Sibley	7%	8%
Pea Ridge, Ark.	3/7-3/8	Curtis	Van Dorn	10%	4%

Casualties = Wounded, captured, or killed soldiers.

Battle	Date	Union Cmdr.	Conf. Cmdr.	Union Cas.*	Conf. Cas.*
1862 (cont.)					
New Bern, N.C.	3/14	Burnside	O'B. Branch	4%	12%
Lee's Mill	3/16	McClellan	Magruder	17%	6%
Valley Campaign	3/23-6/9	Various	Jackson	10%	19%
Kernstown, Va.	3/23	Shields	Jackson	7%	17%
Glorietta, N. Mex.	3/26-3/28	Chivington	Scurry	12%	36%
Island #10, Tenn.	4/7-4/8	Pope	MacKall	<1%	100%
Fort Macon, N.C.	4/11-4/25	Parke	White	<1%	100%
New Orleans, La.	4/18-5/1	Butler	Lovell	2%	17%
Williamsburg, Va.	5/5	Sumner	Longstreet	6%	5%
West Point, Va.	5/7	Franklin	G.W. Smith	2%	<1%
McDowell, Va.	5/8	Schenck	Jackson	5%	6%
Princeton, W. Va.	5/15-5/18	Cox	Marshall	6%	<1%
Front Royal, Va.	5/23	Kenly	Jackson	9%	<1%
Winchester, Va.	5/25	Banks	Jackson	16%	3%
Fair Oaks, Va.	5/31-6/1	McClellan	J. Johnston	12%	15%
Shiloh, Tenn.	6/6-6/7	Grant	A. Johnston	16%	24%
Cross Keys, Va.	6/8	Fremont	Jackson	6%	4%
Port Republic, Va.	6/9	Tyler	Jackson	21%	13%
Seven Days Campaign	6/25-7/1	McClellan	Lee	16%	21%
Oak Grove, Va.	6/25	McClellan	Lee	4%	4%
Mechanicsville, Va.	6/26	Porter	Lee	2%	9%
Gaines' Mill, Va.	6/27	McClellan	Lee	20%	15%
Malvern Hill, Va.	6/29-7/1	McClellan	Lee	10%	11%
Booneville, Miss.	7/1	Sheridan	Chalmers	5%	6%
Jackson, Miss.	7/9-7/16	Sherman	J. Johnston	2%	4%
Murfreesboro, Tenn.	7/13	T. Crittenden	Forrest	9%	15%
Baton Rouge, La.	8/5	T. Williams	Breckinridge	15%	18%
Cedar Mountain, Va.	8/9	Banks	Jackson	30%	8%
Kettle Run, Va.	8/27	Hooker	Ewell	8%	5%
Bull Run, Va. (2nd)	8/29-8/30	Pope	Lee	13%	19%
Richmond, Ky.	8/29-8/30	Manson	K. Smith	82%	7%
Chantilly, Va.	9/1	Kearny	Jackson	13%	8%
Harper's Ferry, W. Va.	9/12-9/15	Miles	Jackson	91%	2%
South Mountain, Md.	9/14	McClellan	Lee	6%	14%
Antietam, Md.	9/17	McClellan	Lee	16%	23%
Iuka, Miss.	9/19	Rosecrans	Price	5%	9%
Blackford's Ford.Va.	9/20	Porter	A.P. Hill	12%	11%
Corinth, Miss.	10/3	Rosecrans	Van Dorn	10%	11%
Perryville, Ky.	10/8	Buell	Bragg	10%	19%
Prairie Grove, Ark.	12/7	Blunt	Hindman	13%	14%
Fredericksburg, Va.	12/13	Burnside	Lee	11%	6%
Chickasaw Bayou, Miss.	12/29	Sherman	Pemberton	4%	1%
Stones River, Tenn.	12/29-1/2/63	Rosecrans	Bragg	22%	27%

Battle	Date	Union Cmdr.	Conf. Cmdr.	Union Cas.*	Conf. Cas.*
1863					
Arkansas Post, Ark.	1/11	McClernand	Churchill	4%	98%
Suffolk, Va. (siege)	4/11-5/4	Peck	Longstreet	1%	5%
Bayou Teche, La.	4/12-4/14	Banks	Taylor	2%	4%
Port Gibson, Miss.	5/1	Grant	Bowen	4%	14%
Chancellorsville, Va.	5/2-5/4	Hooker	Lee	11%	19%
Vicksburg Siege	5/15-7/14	Grant	Pemberton	7%	100%
Champion's Hill, Miss.	5/16	Grant	Pemberton	7%	11%
Port Hudson, La. (siege)	5/27-7/9	Banks	Gardner	15%	100%
Brandy Station, Va.	6/9	Pleasonton	JEB Stuart	8%	5%
Winchester, Va.	6/13-6/15	Milroy	Ewell	38%	1%
Gettysburg, Pa.	7/1-7/3	Meade	Lee	21%	30%
Helena, Ark.	7/4	Prentiss	Holmes	6%	21%
Battery Wagner, S.C.	7/18	Gillmore	Taliaferro	29%	10%
Chickamauga, Ga.	9/18-9/20	Rosecrans	Bragg	29%	17%
Kelly's Ford, Va.	10/7	French	Rodes	<1%	9%
Rappahannock Station, Va.	10/7	Sedgwick	Early	3%	73%
Bristoe Station, Va.	10/14	Warren	A.P. Hill	4%	9%
Chattanooga, Tenn.	11/23-11/25	Grant	Bragg	10%	10%
Mine Run, Va.	11/27-12/1	Meade	Lee	2%	2%
1864					
Olustee, Fla.	2/20	Seymour	Finegan	4%	18%
Pleasant Hill, La.	4/9	Banks	Taylor	11%	13%
Plymouth, N.C.	4/17-4/20	Wessells	Hoke	95%	10%
Atlanta Campaign (I)	5/4-6/17	Sherman	J. Johnston	10%	14%
Wilderness, Va.	5/5-5/7	Grant	Lee	17%	13%
Port Walthal Junction, Va.	5/6-5/7	Brooks	B.R. Johnson	8%	7%
Todd's Tavern, Va.	5/8	Sheridan	J.E.B. Stuart	2%	3%
Spotsylvania, Va.	5/8-5/19	Grant	Lee	22%	18%
Drewry's Bluff, Va.	5/12-5/16	Butler	Beauregard	26%	14%
New Market, Va.	5/15	Sigel	Breckinridge	16%	11%
Bermuda Hundred, Va.	5/20	Butler	Beauregard	6%	5%
North Anna, Va.	5/21-526	Grant	Lee	3%	4%
Hawes' Shop, Va.	5/27-5/28	Gregg	Hampton	9%	14%
Cold Harbor, Va.	6/2	Grant	Lee	12%	3%
Piedmont, Va.	6/5	Hunter	Jones	10%	32%
Brice's Cross-Roads, Miss.	6/10	Sturgis	Forrest	29%	14%
Trevilian Station, Va.	6/11-6/12	Sheridan	Hampton	13%	14%
Tupelo, Miss.	6/13-6/15	A.J. Smith	S.D. Lee	5%	20%
Petersburg, Va.	6/15-6/18	Grant	Lee	18%	Unk
Atlanta Campaign (II)	6/18-9/2	Sherman	Hood	8%	27%
Petersburg Siege	6/19-4/65	Grant	Lee	38%	43%
Kennesaw Mtn., Ga.	6/27	Sherman	J. Johnston	13%	3%

Battle	Date	Union Cmdr.	Conf. Cmdr.	Union Cas.*	Conf. Cas.*
1864 (cont.)					
Atlanta, Ga.	6/22	Sherman	Hood	12%	22%
Ezra Church, Ga.	6/28	Howard	S.D.Lee	5%	25%
Monocacy, Md.	7/9	Wallace	Early	31%	5%
Peach Tree Creek, Ga.	7/20	Sherman	Hood	8%	14%
Petersburg Mine, Va.	7/30	Grant	Lee	18%	13%
Deep Bottom, Va.	8/14-8/19	Hancock	Lee	10%	5%
Weldon Railroad, Va.	8/18-8/21	Warren	A.P. Hill	22%	11%
Ream's Station, Va.	8/25	Hancock	A.P. Hill	19%	5%
Jonesboro, Ga.	8/31	Howard	French	1%	7%
Winchester, Va.	9/19	Sheridan	Early	12%	12%
Fisher's Hill, Va.	9/22	Sheridan	Early	2%	14%
Pilot Knob, Mo.	9/27	Ewing	Price	18%	13%
New Market Hts., Va.	9/28-9/30	Grant	Lee	17%	19%
Poplar Springs Church, Va.	9/30-10/1	Warren	A.P. Hill	12%	5%
Allatoona, Ga.	10/5	Corse	French	36%	32%
Cedar Creek, Va.	10/19	Sheridan	Early	13%	10%
Decatur, AL.	10/26-10/29	Granger	Hood	2%	1%
Boydton Plank Road, Va.	10/27-10/28	Grant	Lee	4%	9%
Fair Oaks, Va.	10/27-10/28	Weitzel	Longstreet	6%	2%
Franklin, Tenn.	11/30	Schofield	Hood	4%	21%
Honey Hill, S.C.	11/30	Hatch	G.W. Smith	14%	4%
Savannah, GA. (siege)	12/10-12/21	Sherman	Hardee	<1%	8%
Nashville, Tenn.	12/15-12/16	Thomas	Hood	6%	26%
1865					
Wilmington, N.C.	1/18-1/22	Schofield	Bragg	<1%	14%
Fort. Fisher, N.C.	2/12-2/16	Terry	Bragg	16%	32%
Kinston, NC	3/8-3/10	Cox	Bragg	9%	10%
Averasboro, N.C.	3/16	Sherman	J. Johnston	4%	10%
Mobile, Al. (siege)	3/17-4/12	Canby	Maury	4%	55%
Bentonville, N.C.	3/19-3/21	Sherman	J. Johnston	7%	13%
Fort Stedman, Va.	3/25	Grant	Lee	5%	20%
Dinwiddie C.H., Va.	3/29-3/31	Grant	Lee	6%	11%
Five Forks, Va.	4/1	Sheridan	Pickett	3%	29%
Petersburg, VA.	4/2	Grant	Lee	7%	13%
Selma, AL.	4/2	Wilson	Forrest	4%	91%
Sailor's Creek, Va.	4/6	Grant	Gordon	3%	44%
Appomattox, Va.	4/9	Grant	Lee	10%	46%

Sources

Introduction

American Heritage. *Civil War Chronicles*, 1993.

Catton, Bruce. *American Goes to War: The Civil War and Its Meaning in American Culture*. Hanover, New Hampshire: Wesleyan University Press, 1958.

Connelly, Thomas and Barbara Bellows. *God and General Longstreet*. Baton Rouge: Louisiana State University Press, 1982.

Hartwig, D. Scott. *A Killer Angels Companion*. Gettysburg, Pennsylvania: Thomas Publications, 1996.

Toplin, Robert Brent (ed.). *Ken Burns's The Civil War: Historians Respond*. New York: Oxford University Press, 1996.

Chapter 1: Looking Back, Looking Forward

Blumenson, Martin. *Patton: The Man Behind the Legend, 1885-1945*. New York: William Morrow, 1985.

Davis, Burke. *Our Incredible Civil War*. New York: Holt, Rinehart and Winston, 1960.

DeGregorio, William. *The Complete Book of U.S. Presidents*. New York: Wings Books, 1997.

Foner, Eric. *A Short History of Reconstruction, 1863-1877*. New York: Harper & Row, 1990.

Kallman, Publishers, 1996. Originally published in New York, 1883.

Manchester, William. *American Caesar: Douglas MacArthur 1880-1964*. Boston, Massachusetts: Little, Brown and Company, 1978.

McCulloch, David. *Truman*. New York: Simon & Schuster, 1992.

McPherson, James M. *Battle Cry of Freedom: The Civil War Era*. New York: Ballantine Books, 1989.

Phisterer, Frederick. *Statistical Record: A Treasury of Information about the U.S. Civil War*. Carlisle, Pennsylvania: John Kallman, Publishers, 1996. Originally published in New York, 1883.

U.S. War Department. *The War of the Rebellion: A Compilation of the Official Records of the Union and Confederate Armies. 128 volumes*. Washington, D.C.: Government Printing Office, 1880-1901.

Chapter 2: Timeline to Secession

Abrahamson, James L. *The Men of Secession and Civil War, 1859-1861*. Wilmington, Delaware: SR Books, 2000.

Berky, Andrew S. and James P. Shenton (eds.). *The Historian's History of the United States, Vol. 1*. New York: G.P. Putman's Sons, 1966.

Blum, John M., Bruce Catton, Edmund S.Morgan, Arthur M. Schlesinger, Kenneth M. Stampp, and C. Vann Woodward. *The National Experience: A History of the United States to 1877*. New York: Harcourt, Brace & World, 1968.

Harley, Sharon. *The Timetables of African-American History: A Chronology of the Most Important People and Events in African-American History*. New York: Touchstone, 1995.

Miller, William Lee. *Arguing about Slavery*. New York: Vintage Books, 1995.

Chapter 3: Dividing the Union

Boatner, Mark M. *The Civil War Dictionary*. New York: David McKay Company, 1959.

McPherson, James M. *Battle Cry of Freedom: The Civil War Era*.

Chapter 4: Family Ties

Morris, Richard B. (ed.). *Encyclopedia of American History*, Sixth Edition. New York: Harper and Row, 1982.

Boatner, Mark M. *The Civil War Dictionary*.

Garrison, Webb. *The Amazing Civil War*. Nashville, Tennessee: Rutledge Hill Press, 1998.

Waugh, John C. *The Class of 1846: From West Point to Appomattox, Stonewall Jackson, George McClellan and Their Brothers*. New York: Ballantine Books, 1994.

Chapter 5: This Month in 1861

Denney, Robert E. *Civil War Years: A Day-by-Day Chronicle of the Life of a Nation*. Falls Church, Virginia: Sterling Publishing Company, 1994.

Mosocco, Ronald. *The Chronological Tracking of the Civil War per the Official Records of the War of the Rebellion*. Wingate, North Carolina, 1995.

Chapter 6: You're in the Army Now

Davis, Burke. *Our Incredible Civil War*.

McPherson, James M. *Battle Cry of Freedom: The Civil War Era*.

Wiley, Bell Irvin. *Embattled Confederates: An Illustrated History of Southerners at War*. New York: Bonanza Books, 1964.

Chapter 7: A Soldier's Daily Life

Davis, William C. *The Civil War Cookbook*. Philadelphia, Pennsylvania: CLB Publishing, 1993.

Erdosh, George. *Food and Recipes of the Civil War*. Baltimore, Maryland: Rosen Publishing, 1997.

Haythornthwaite, Philip. *Uniforms of the Civil War: In Color*. New York; Sterling Publishing Company, 1990.

Madden, David (ed.). *Beyond the Battlefield: The Ordinary Life and Extraordinary Times of the Civil War Soldier.* New York: A Touchstone Book, 1999.

Chapter 8: This Month in 1862

Denney, Robert E. *Civil War Years: A Day-by-Day Chronicle of the Life of a Nation.*

Mosocco, Ronald. *The Chronological Tracking of the Civil War per the Official Records of the War of the Rebellion.*

Chapter 9: The Battles

Daniel, Larry J. *Shiloh: The Battle That Changed the Civil War.* New York: Simon and Schuster, 1997.

Dyer, Frederick H. *A Compendium of the War of the Rebellion.* Des Moines, Iowa: The Dyer Publishing Company, 1908.

Livermore, Thomas L. *Numbers and Losses in the Civil War in America: 1861-1865.* Bloomington, Indiana: Indiana University Press, 1957.

Sears, Stephen W. *Landscape Turned Red: The Battle of Antietam.* New York: Houghton Mifflin, 1983.

Wright, John W. (ed.). *The New York Times 1999 Almanac.* New York: Penguin Reference, 1998.

Chapter 10: The Leaders

Armstrong, Richard L. *11th Virginia Cavalry.* Lynchburg, Virginia: H.E. Howard, Inc., 1989.

Garrison, Webb. *The Amazing Civil War.*

Brown, Russell K. *Fallen in Battle: American General Officer Combat Fatalities from 1775.* New York: Greenwood Press, 1988.

Freeman, Douglas Southall. *Lee's Lieutenants, Volume 3: Gettysburg to Appomattox.* New York: Charles Scribners Sons, 1944.

Fox, William F. *Regimental Losses in the American Civil War 1861-1865.* Albany, New York: Rainbow Printing Company, 1889.

Garrison, Webb. *Friendly Fire in the Civil War: More than 100 True Stories of Comrade Killing Comrade.* Nashville, Tennessee: Rutledge Hill Press, 1999.

Chapter 11: Death: The Currency of War

Trotter, William R. *Silk Flags and Cold Steel.* Winston-Salem, North Carolina: John F. Blair Publisher, 1988.

U.S. War Department. *The War of the Rebellion: A Compilation of the Official Records of the Union and Confederate Armies.*

Chapter 12: Outlaws and Raiders

Brownlee, Richard S. *Gray Ghosts of the Confederacy: Guerrilla Warfare in the West 1861-1865.* Baton Rouge, Louisiana: L.S.U. Press, 1958, 1986.

Schultz, Duane. *Quantrill's War: The Life and Times of William Clarke Quantrill.* New York: St. Martin's, 1996.

Sensing, Thurman. *Champ Ferguson: Confederate Guerrilla*. Nashville, Tennessee: Vanderbilt University Press, 1942.

Stern, Philip. *Secret Missions of the Civil War.* New York: Wings Books, 1959, 1987.

Chapter 13: Winning and Losing on the Battlefield

U.S. War Department. *The War of the Rebellion: A Compilation of the Official Records of the Union and Confederate Armies.*

Chapter 14: This Month in 1863

Denney, Robert E. *Civil War Years: A Day-by-Day Chronicle of the Life of a Nation.*

Mosocco, Ronald. *The Chronological Tracking of the Civil War per the Official Records of the War of the Rebellion.*

Chapter 15: This Day in the Civil War: April 10, 1863

Jones, Archer. *Confederate Strategy from Shiloh to Vicksburg*. Baton Rouge, Louisiana: Louisiana State University Press.

Willett, Robert L. *America in Conflict: April 10, 1863*. New York: Plume Books, 1997.

Chapter 16: Women and the War

Burgess, Laura, ed. *The Civil War Letters of Sarah Rosetta Wakeman, alias Pvt. Lyons Wakeman, 153rd Regiment, New York State Volunteers 1862-1864*. New York: Oxford University Press, 1996.

Leonard, Elizabeth D. *All the Daring of the Soldier: Women of the Civil War Armies*. New York: W. W. Norton, 1999.

Chapter 17: Black Soldiers

Quarles, Benjamin. *The Negro in the Civil War*. New York: Da Capo Press, 1989.

Trudeau, Noah Andre. *Like Men of War: Black Troops in the Civil War, 1862-1865*. New York: Little, Brown and Company, 1998.

Wise, Stephen. *Gate of Hell: Campaign for Charleston Harbor, 1863*. Columbia, South Carolina: University of South Carolina Press, 1994.

Chapter 18: This Month in 1864

Denney, Robert E. *Civil War Years: A Day-by-Day Chronicle of the Life of a Nation.*

Mosocco, Ronald. *The Chronological Tracking of the Civil War per the Official Records of the War of the Rebellion.*

Chapter 19: By the Numbers

Davis, Burke. *Our Incredible Civil War.*

Garrison, Webb. *The Amazing Civil War.*

Wright, Mike. *What They Didn't Teach You About the Civil War*. Novato, California: Presidio, 1996.

Chapter 20: Notable and Quotable

Bartlell, John, Kaplan, Justin, eds. *Bartlett's Familiar Quotations: A Collection of Passages, Phrases, and Proverbs Traced to Their Sources in Ancient and Modern Literature*, 16th edition. Boston, Massachusetts: Little, Brown and Company, 1992.

Bedwell, Randall, ed. *May I Quote You General Longstreet? Observations and Utterances from the South's Great Generals*. Nashville, Tennessee: Cumberland House Publishing, 1997.

Bierce, Ambrose. *The Devil's Dictionary*. Cleveland, Ohio: The World Press, 1911.

McPherson, James M. *Battle Cry of Freedom: The Civil War Era*.

Morris, Ray Jr. *Ambrose Bierce: Alone in Bad Company*. New York: Crown Publishers, 1995.

Underwood, Lamar, ed. *The Quotable Soldier*. New York: The Lyons Press, 2000.

Chapter 21: Stories from the Telegraph Office

Bates, Davis Homer. *Lincoln in the Telegraph Office: Recollections of the United States Military Telegraph Corps during the Civil War*. Lincoln, Nebraska: University of Nebraska Press, 1995.

Swank, Walbrook. *Humorous Stories Told of and by Abraham Lincoln*. Shippensburg, Pennsylvania: White Mane Publishing, 1996.

Chapter 22: On and Under the Water

Anderson, Bern. *By Sea and by River: The Naval History of the Civil War.* New York: De Capo Press, 1962.

Department of the Navy. *Civil War Naval Chronology*. Washington D.C., 1971.

U.S. War Department. *Official Records of the Union and Confederate Navies in the War of the Rebellion*, 30 volumes. Washington DC, 1894-1922.

Chapter 23: Accidental Deaths

U.S. War Department. *The War of the Rebellion: A Compilation of the Official Records of the Union and Confederate Armies*.

Chapter 24: The Legend of Stonewall

Boatner, Mark M. *The Civil War Dictionary*.

Civil War: The Magazine of the Civil War Society, April 1996.

Vandiver, Frank. *Mighty Stonewall*. College Station, Texas: Texas A&M University Press, 1992.

Chapter 25: The Cult of Robert E. Lee

Connelly, Thomas. *Marble Man: Robert E. Lee and His Image in American Society*. Baton Rouge, Louisiana: L.S.U. Press, 1978.

Freeman, Douglas S. *Robert E. Lee, 4 Volumes.* New York: Simon and Schuster, 1977.

Piston, William. *Lee's Tarnished Lieutenant: James Longstreet and His Place in American History.* Athens, Georgia: University of Georgia Press, 1990.

Chapter 26: The Strange Journey of Sam Grant

Buell, Thomas B. *The Warrior Generals: Combat Leadership in the Civil War.* Crown Publishers, Inc, 1996.

Simpson, Brooks, D. *Ulysses S. Grant: Triumph over Adversity, 1822-1865.* Houghton Mifflin Company, 2000.

Smith, Jean Edward. *Grant.* Simon and Schuster, 2001

O'Brien, Steven. *Ulysses S. Grant.* Chelsea House Publishers, 1990.

Chapter 27: Court-Martials

Lowry, Thomas. *Tarnished Eagles: The Court-martials of Fifty Union Colonels and Lieutenant-Colonels.* Mechanicsburg, Pennsylvania: Stackpole Books, 1997.

Chapter 28: This Month in 1865

Denney, Robert E. *Civil War Years: A Day-by-Day Chronicle of the Life of a Nation.*

Mosocco, Ronald. *The Chronological Tracking of the Civil War per the Official Records of the War of the Rebellion.*

Chapter 29: The Death of Abraham Lincoln

Bishop, Jim. *The Day Lincoln Was Shot.* New York: Bantam Books, 1955.

Garrison, Web. *The Lincoln No One Knows: 38 Mysteries of One of America's Most Admired Presidents.* Nashville, Tennessee: Rutledge Hill Press, 1993.

Kundardt, Jr., Philip B., Philip B.Kundardt III, and Peter W. Kundardt. *Lincoln: An Illustrated Biography.* New York: Alfred A. Knopf, 1992.

Morris, Jan. *Lincoln: A Foreigner's Quest.* New York: Simon and Schuster, 2000.

Randall, J.G. *Lincoln the President: Midstream.* New York: Dodd, Meade & Company, 1952.

Tidwell, William A. *Come Retribution: The Confederate Secret Service and the Assassination of Lincoln.* New York: Barnes and Noble Books and the University of Mississippi Press, 1988.

Chapter 30: The Top 50 Influential Figures of the War

Wooster, Robert. *Civil War 100: A Ranking of the Most Influential People in the War Between the States.* Secaucus, New Jersey: Citadel Press, 1998.

Chapter 31: Reenacting: The Spice of Life

Hadden, R. Lee. *Reliving the Civil War: A Reenactors Handbook.* Mechanicsburg, Pennsylvania: Stackpole Books, 1996.

Chapter 32: The Civil War in Print and on the Web

Civil War: The Magazine of the Civil War Society, February 1995.

Thomas, William G. and Alice E. Carter. *The Civil War on the Web: A Guide to the Very Best Sites.* Wilmington, Delaware: SR Books, 2001.

Chapter 33: Outside the War

Grun, Bernard. *The Timetables of History: A Horizontal Linkage of People and Events.* New York: Simon and Schuster, 1946.

Kane, Joseph Nathan. *Famous First Facts: A Record of First Happenings, Discoveries, and Inventions in American History.* New York: H.W. Wilson Company, 1981.

Powers, J. Tracy. *Lee's Miserables: Life in the Army of Northern Virginia from the Wilderness to Appomattox.* Chapel Hill, North Carolina: The University of North Carolina Press, 1997.

Appendix: Battles in the Civil War

Livermore, Thomas L. *Numbers and Losses in the Civil War in America.*

Sidebars

Bowman, John. *Who Was Who in the Civil War.* New York: Random House, 1994.

Carson, Clayborne. *Guide to American History.* New York: Viking, 1999.

Jacobson, Dorranne. *Civil War in Art.* Edison, New Jersey: Smithmark Publishing, 1996.

Smith, Page. *Trial by Fire: A People's History of the Civil War and Reconstruction.* New York: Viking, 1990.

U.S. War Department. *The War of the Rebellion: A Compilation of the Official Records of the Union and Confederate Armies.*

Warner, Ezra. *Generals in Blue: Lives of the Union Commanders.* Baton Rouge, Louisiana: L.S.U. Press, 1964.

Wear, Terry. *And the Horse's Name Was: A Dictionary of Famous Horses from History.* Metuchan, New Jersey: Scarecrow Press, 1993.

Wooster, Robert. *Civil War 100: A Ranking of the Most Influential People in the War Between the States.*

Indexes

Subject Index

Names Index

About the Author

Donald Cartmell is the senior writer/researcher for the acclaimed Civil War Web page, *This Week in the Civil War* (*www.civilweek.com*). The Web site chronicles the Civil War on a daily basis, utilizing primary source material such as the *Official Records of the War of the Rebellion*. The site has received numerous awards in its four-year existence, was recommended by *The History Channel*, and was favorably reviewed in *The Civil War on the Web: A Guide to the Very Best Sites*. Don lives and works as a librarian in Lake George, New York.